RUNNING
INJURY-FREE

RUNNING
INJURY-FREE

How to Prevent, Treat
and Recover from Dozens
of Painful Problems

By Joe Ellis, D.P.M., Adviser, **RUNNER'S** WORLD

with Joe Henderson, Columnist, **RUNNER'S** WORLD

Rodale Press, Emmaus, Pennsylvania

Runner's World is a registered trademark of Rodale Inc.

Printed in the United States of America
Rodale Inc. makes every effort to use acid-free, ∞ recycled ♺ paper

Cover and Book Designer: Charles Beasley
Cover Photographer: John Kelly
Illustrator: Susan Rosenberger

Library of Congress Cataloging-in-Publication Data

Ellis, Joe.
    Running injury-free : how to prevent, treat and recover from dozens of painful problems / by Joe Ellis, with Joe Henderson.
        p.   cm.
    Includes index.
    ISBN 0–87596–221–1 paperback
    1. Running—Accidents and injuries. 2. Leg—Wounds and injuries.
3. Foot—Wounds and injuries.   I. Henderson, Joe, 1943–   . II. Title.
RC1220.R8E44 1994
617.1'027—dc20   93–46231
                                                                CIP

Distributed in the book trade by St. Martin's Press

            16   18   20   19   17   paperback

RODALE

WE **INSPIRE** AND **ENABLE** PEOPLE TO IMPROVE
THEIR LIVES AND THE WORLD AROUND THEM

This book is dedicated to my wife, Deborah, and my children, Tiffany and Nicholas, for their constant inspiration and motivation.

—Joe Ellis

CONTENTS

ACKNOWLEDGMENTS

Completing this book was a team effort: Two authors' names appear on the cover, but many other teammates helped carry this project between its start and finish lines.

We thank our editors at Rodale Press—Debora Tkac, Sharon Faelten and Sara Henry—who acted as "coaches," giving us pats on the back or kicks in the pants when needed. And we thank our *Runner's World* editors, Amby Burfoot, Bob Wischnia and Cristina Negron, who gave us training in writing articles that was invaluable in tackling a project of this length.

Joe Ellis also thanks his professional colleagues for their support. They include outstanding physical therapist Patricia S. Yavorsky, director of Progressive Sports Therapy; H. Peter Goehrig of Asics; Marty Lillis of the Lillis Group; orthopedic surgeon Dr. Jeff Bronson; and Dr. Paul Scherer, who first showed him how to present scientific papers.

Joe Henderson thanks Steve Subotnick, D.P.M., Steven Roy, M.D., and the late George Sheehan, M.D., the physicians and podiatrists who taught him about sports medicine while working their magic on his own feet.

Finally, we both express appreciation to our families and co-workers, who graciously tolerate calls at all hours of the day and night from runners with injury and training questions.

INTRODUCTION

Back in the hazy pre-history of modern distance running, some 20-odd years ago, I ran as most other runners did then—which is to say unwisely. We ran too many miles and too many races without much cushioning or support in our shoes and without cross-training or other ways of supplementing our training.

We ran until we faltered. Then we ran some more, surrendering only when our feet and legs refused to take another step. By 1972 I'd run myself into a seemingly dead-end injury. I finally went to a doctor for this heel problem.

Like most physicians at the time, he had little training or experience in treating otherwise healthy people who refused to stop the activity that gave them pain. Most physicians advised: If it hurts to run, then don't run until it stops hurting. Which is basically the advice my doctor gave me.

Resting an injury is half the solution, at best. Rest can be essential in certain stages of some injuries, but it rarely gives lasting relief because it addresses only symptoms, not causes.

Most running injuries result from overuse—the cumulative stresses of the activity itself—rather than a traumatic accident. We usually get hurt from running farther, faster or more often than our body can tolerate.

As luck would have it, a podiatrist sought me out to discuss a story he wanted to write for *Runner's World* magazine, which I edited at the time. He wanted to talk about new ways of dealing with running injuries—and of course I wanted to talk about my injury.

Podiatry was a little-known profession then, at least among runners. If we were aware of podiatrists at all, we thought they only trimmed away corns and removed ingrown toenails.

My first podiatrist evaluated how I moved, then prescribed corrective exercises for tight leg muscles, special shoe inserts, known as orthotics, for foot irregularities and a change in shoes to better match my foot type. This podiatrist never told me to stop running. He said, "Run within the limits of pain."

Even after treatment, the pain seriously limited my running. I'd left the injury untreated for too long. So I had minor surgery to remove a bony growth that sawed constantly on my Achilles tendon. With this irritant gone, the other prescribed changes could do their job. The prescription of stretching exercises, orthotics and proper shoes still serves me well more than 20 years later.

Podiatrists were the leaders of the sports-medicine revolution, but now they have lots of company. Their determination to root out the causes of injuries instead of merely treating symptoms and their concentration on long-term prevention rather than temporary cures have spread to many other specialties.

The primary author of this book, Joe Ellis, D.P.M., is one of those podiatrists who helped usher in the modern era of sports medicine. Dr. Ellis became part of the first generation of sports-medicine specialists when he graduated from the California College of Podiatric Medicine in 1976. At about that same time, he also joined the first great wave of runners as they flooded first the roads—and then doctors' offices.

Dr. Ellis now mingles his work and hobby in his podiatric practice at La Jolla, California. He has worked with thousands of runners and has almost as many stories to tell, some of which you'll read in this book. They brim with the helpful, hopeful advice that just might save your running career.

—Joe Henderson

Chapter 1

WHY RUNNERS GET HURT

I'm often asked, "What separates world-class runners from the rest of the pack?" My first answer is "freedom from injury."

Very few runners can tolerate high levels of training for many years. Many runners have the talent to rank among the best, but injuries slow them down or force them into an early retirement.

Injuries are, unfortunately, a fact of the runner's life. While running is an excellent way to improve the cardiovascular system, it puts tremendous strains on the musculoskeletal system. Runners' feet and legs take more pounding than they are made to handle, making runners the most frequent visitors to sports-medicine specialists with problems ranging from minor aches and strains to torn Achilles tendons and damaged knees.

Runner's World surveys conducted since the 1970s have shown that in any given year about half the magazine's readers have their running program interrupted by injury. According to a survey of 10,754 runners I helped conduct, 75 percent of male runners and 80 percent of female runners have suffered at least one injury serious enough to halt their running at least temporarily. More than half of them sought professional treatment.

Note: *Throughout the book, use of the first person "I" refers to Joe Ellis.*

The Perils of Overuse

The number-one reason for injuries is overuse—running too much, too fast, too soon or too often. We term all of these overuse problems "training errors." This is a polite way of saying that your body cannot handle the stresses that you have placed on it.

Nevertheless, runners are frequently tempted to overdo. Bob Babbitt of *The Competitor* magazine once asked finishers of the Long Beach Marathon, "What would you do differently in preparing for your next endurance event?" The unanimous answer: Train more.

Runners forget that there is a limit to how much training the body can absorb and that rest and recovery are as vital to improvement as hard work. Training too much and not listening to the signals that your body gives when it needs rest are the main reasons that injury rates are so high among runners.

That's the bad news about running injuries. But there's good news, too:

■ Most of these injuries result from training mistakes that can be prevented or corrected without elaborate or expensive medical care.

■ Other problems, such as misalignment, can be accommodated with proper shoes and special shoe inserts.

■ Few running injuries are serious enough to disrupt your everyday life or end your running career.

No doubt about it: Runners who ward off injuries by listening to their bodies—and adjusting their training programs in response—stand the best chance of reaching their potential.

If you heed your body's signs of fatigue and overuse and react accordingly, you will outrun and outlast the runners who try to go all-out all the time.

Who You Are and How You Run

There's one sure way to beat running injuries: *Don't get them in the first place.* That may sound ridiculously obvious, but it's

RUNNING INJURIES: THE DIRTY DOZEN

Much of this chapter explains *why* runners get hurt. This table tells you *where* they get hurt. In the survey of 10,754 runners mentioned on page 1, these were the most common sites of injury—conditions I term the "dirty dozen" running injuries. The figures given are the percentages of runners who reported ever having suffered that particular injury. Seventy percent of the runners were male; 30 percent were female. This survey was conducted with James R. White, Ph.D., an exercise physiologist at the University of California, San Diego, and a research team that included athletic trainers, coaches, sports-medicine specialists and world-class runners.

In chapters 10 through 21, I'll tell you how these injuries can be treated and—in many cases—avoided.

The 12 Most Common Injuries for Runners

Injury Type	Incidence (%)	
	Men	Women
Knee	23.0	21.3
Achilles tendon/calf	16.2	4.3
Metatarsal	10.5	9.5
Toenails/blisters	9.3	1.7
Hip/groin	8.5	14.7
Plantar fascia/heel	8.2	4.0
Ankle sprain	6.5	13.3
Shin splints	6.0	20.0
Nerve injuries	2.3	1.3
Quadriceps	2.2	0.9
Hamstrings	1.8	5.1
Back	1.8	2.0

easier said than done. Most runners don't realize they're headed for a problem until the injury actually occurs.

That's where the Injury Predictor Quiz at the end of this chapter comes in. This quiz helps you take a detailed, discerning look at your potential for different running injuries. It asks about your physical makeup and your running habits and tells you what you can do to help avoid injury.

To take this quiz, all you need is a tractograph, which you can purchase for less than $10 at a stationery store, and, in some cases, a friend to help. The only test you can't administer yourself is the body-fat test; you can get this done at a medical clinic, at a health fair or by your physician. Here's how to administer the simple self-tests required for this quiz.

1. Are You Male or Female?

Unfortunately, gender does make a difference when it comes to running—and women come up short. Women's hips are, on average, wider than men's. Therefore, a woman's foot strikes the ground at a greater angle than a man's. This promotes overpronation, an excessive inward rolling of the foot, which can lead to a variety of injuries.

What's more, women's tissues are more elastic than men's. This makes women more liable to ligament and joint damage.

Injury statistics also indicate that women are more susceptible to stress fractures than men. Women's bones tend to be smaller and, consequently, less able to absorb the shocks of running.

To counteract these gender-based tendencies, women may need to do specific exercises designed to strengthen leg muscles and promote flexibility. (See chapter 23 for specific exercises.) It's also especially important that women find shoes that meet their biomechanical needs. (See chapters 4 and 5.)

2. What Is Your Body-Fat Percentage?

The more you weigh, the greater the shock and stress your body sustains with each step you run. The more pounds you're carrying over your appropriate body weight, the more likely it is that those shocks and stresses will translate into running injuries.

If you're overweight, you may tend to develop a wider running stance, hitting the ground with your feet farther apart than they'd be if you weighed less. That wider stance puts stress on your medial tendons—the ones along the insides of your legs—and may cause you to overpronate (roll inward excessively). Overweight runners are at high risk for injuries related to the shock of running impact, as well as those caused by lack of foot stability, such as muscle strains and tendinitis.

The best measure of ideal weight is *not* the scales or a chart that lists how many pounds you should weigh. A much more reliable figure is percentage of body fat. There are several ways to check your body-fat percentage. Underwater weighing is probably the most accurate, but it's also the most involved and expensive.

Having skinfold measurements taken with calipers is a reliable alternative. Bioelectrical impedance analysis (BIA) is another economical possibility, although some experts think BIA tends to overestimate the body fat of lean people—including most runners. Both tests can be performed for around $50 by an exercise physiologist, cardiologist, internist or other professional trained in the technique.

Average body-fat percentages for runners are about 12 percent for men and 18 percent for women; more than 15 percent for men or 20 percent for women will result in negative points on the Injury Predictor Quiz.

To reduce your chances of weight-related injuries, take a slow, easy approach to your running program. Alternating running with walking while you cut back on fatty and sugary foods will help take off a few unwanted, unneeded pounds.

3. Do You Have One Leg Shorter Than the Other?

Although no one's body is *exactly* symmetrical, pronounced differences in leg length can cause problems for runners. There are two kinds of discrepancies: structural and functional.

In structural discrepancies there is a real, measurable difference in length of the bones. In functional discrepancies the bones may be the same length, but because of biomechanical problems the legs look and work as if one is shorter than the other. This could happen in a person if the pelvis is tilted, for example.

A difference greater than a quarter-inch between the right and left legs usually causes lateral-hip pelvic pain (on the outside of the longer leg) or low-back strains. Such injuries occur when the upper body tries to compensate for the lower body's imbalance by twisting or bending.

How do you know if you have a leg length difference? Take a look at your running shoes: The shoe on a longer leg will wear down more quickly than the other. Or stand in front of a mirror with your hands resting on top of your hips: If one hand appears higher, that leg is probably longer than the other.

A lift in the shoe of the shorter leg should solve the problem. Start with a ⅛-inch lift. If that's not enough, try a higher one.

4. How High Are Your Arches?

In general, the arch of your foot determines how your feet and legs will function when you run. Flat feet, with little or no arch, can cause problems, as can feet with very high arches.

To check your arches, take what's called the "wet test." When you step out of the shower, step on a brown paper grocery bag. Put your full body weight on the foot that you are checking.

Now step away and check your footprint. If you can see the full outline (or almost a full outline) of your foot, you have a flat foot. An ant would not have a chance to escape underneath this foot type.

The high-arched foot type produces a completely different tracing. The heel and the ball of the foot yield the greatest

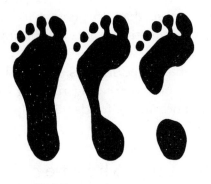

WET TEST

Check your foot type by stepping into water, then onto a dry surface or a piece of absorbent paper (such as a brown paper bag). The outline at left indicates a flat foot, the middle outline is normal and the right outline indicates a high-arched foot.

impressions, while you will usually see only a very faint line along the outside portion of the foot.

Sometimes that line disappears. This indicates the pressure points are strictly at the heel and the ball of the foot and the entire arch is well above the supporting surface. A rigid, high arch is very stiff and doesn't give much when you run.

A runner with a normal arch will see an imprint of the heel, about half of the arch and the ball of the foot. The arch will actually collapse a little bit as you run and walk, allowing a normal amount of pronation or rolling in.

Both flat feet and high-arched feet tend to be prone to injury, but you can compensate somewhat with the right shoes and orthotics, which I discuss in chapters 4 and 5.

5. Do You Overpronate?

Pronation is natural—it's the rolling-in motion that occurs after the outside heel of your shoe strikes the ground. A little bit of pronation (four to six degrees) is good, but either too much or too little can make you highly susceptible to a host of running injuries.

Finding out whether you have flat arches via the wet test is one of the best ways to diagnose pronation problems. The flatter your arch, the more support is needed in the shoe. But the condition of your running shoes' heel counters—the firm cups that hold your heels in place—can also be a tipoff.

A SIGN OF OVERPRONATION

Heel counter
support

Internal heel
counter

Have a friend watch you standing or running. If the heels tilt inward, you probably suffer from at least mild overpronation. If your shoes appear distorted *after* you take them off, with the heels tilted inward, you're a moderate overpronator. Heel counters broken down toward the inside are a sign of severe overpronation.

The heel counters of underpronators generally tip outward. The more excess wear in that direction, the bigger your underpronation problem. This problem can be dealt with by buying the right kind of shoe.

6. What's Your Q-Angle?

The Q-angle is the angle of intersection of your tibia (shinbone) and your quadriceps muscle. To measure your Q-angle, you'll need a tractograph.

Use the tractograph as shown below to measure the angle of intersection of two imaginary lines: one that bisects your thigh and kneecap, and one that passes from the kneecap through the tibial tubercle, the bony protuberance directly below your knee near the top of your shinbone. A normal angle is 8 to 10 degrees for men and 15 degrees for women.

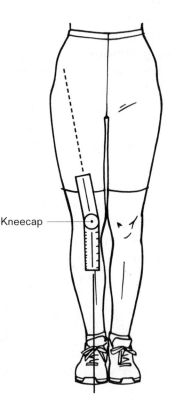

Q-ANGLE

This test requires a tractograph, a simple device for measuring angles. Stand with your feet together and place the tractograph on your kneecap. Line up one arm of it with the bony protrusion at the top of the pelvis, and the other on the prominence of the upper shinbone. (To help line it up, you can align a yardstick with the upper arm of the tractograph.)

Kneecap

Overpronation can make an excessive Q-angle worse. Shoes with good motion control can help check overpronation, reduce the Q-angle and cut down your chances of knee injuries.

If your Q-angle is particularly high, you may need orthotics. Strengthening your quadriceps, which is detailed in chapter 17, can help minimize the symptoms of knee pain that may come with a high Q-angle.

7. Are You Bowlegged?

Bowleggedness can mean trouble for both overpronators and underpronators. For overpronators, and most bowlegged runners fall into this category, it may contribute to excessive foot motion. For underpronators, it may create ankle instability.

Most people's legs bow slightly. To check yours, stand with your feet together and note the distance between your knees. If they almost touch, you're only mildly bowlegged. But if you look more like you just dismounted a horse, your problem is more severe.

There's not much you can do about being bowlegged, so you must take great care in selecting your running shoes. Again, most bowlegged runners are prone to overpronation and should consider buying very stable shoes. (See chapter 5.)

8. Are Your Calves Flexible?

Flexibility is one of the most important indicators in the prediction and prevention of running injuries. Good flexibility lets your joints and muscles move as they are supposed to when you run.

In contrast, if your muscles are tight and your joints stiff, your body will be less able to resist abnormal biomechanical forces such as excessive pronation. Running, unfortunately, creates muscle imbalances and increases inflexibility in the muscles running down the back of your legs.

The calf muscles (gastrocnemius and soleus) are attached to the Achilles tendon, and work to lift up the heel and flex the foot downward when you run. When calf muscles are too tight, the heel of the foot that's supporting your body's weight will get pulled off the ground prematurely. This in turn yanks hard on the Achilles tendon and may cause it to become inflamed. This injury is almost always the direct result of too-tight calf muscles.

Inflexible calf muscles can also lead to what people refer to as shin splints, pain caused by a variety of different afflictions of the lower leg. Plantar fascia pain (under the arch or heel) can also be caused by tight calf muscles. (When a muscle is tight, it also pulls hard at its attachments.)

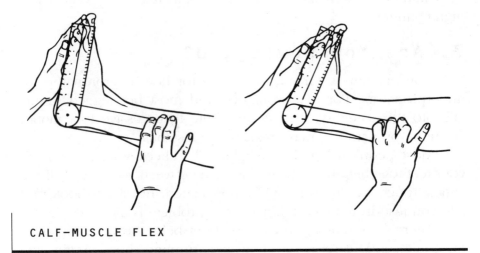

CALF—MUSCLE FLEX

Test calf flexibility by lying on your back and locking your knee. Have a companion place your foot in its normal, relaxed position. Then bend the foot as far toward the knee as possible, checking the angle with a tractograph.

To test your calf-muscle flexibility, lock your knee and bend your foot up as far toward your knee as you can. Have a friend use a tractograph to measure the angle formed by your foot and leg as shown above. Your foot should be able to flex up at least 15 degrees from its perpendicular position. That amount of flexibility will give you a normal range of motion.

If you come up short on this test, you should immediately begin a stretching program designed to lengthen your calf muscles. (See chapter 23 for flexibility exercises.)

9. Do Your Hamstrings Flex?

The hamstrings are the muscles and tendons behind your knees and thighs. Your hamstrings need to be long enough to allow your knees and hips to move freely through their proper range of motion. Hip pains and injuries to the knee and thigh occur when the hamstrings are too inflexible.

To test your hamstring flexibility, lie on your back and lift your leg as far as you can while keeping your knee locked. You should be able to form at least a 90-degree angle with your other leg. If you can't, you'll have to start stretching. Chances are that if your calf muscles are too tight, your hamstring muscles will be as well. (You'll find a stretching program in chapter 23.)

10. Check Your Iliotibial Band

One of the most common knee injuries is an inflammation of the iliotibial band (ITB) where it joins the tibia just below the kneecap. This problem usually has a double cause: excessive pronation and a tight ITB.

When the band is too tight, it tends to rub against the lateral femoral condyle (a bony structure on the outside of your knee) and

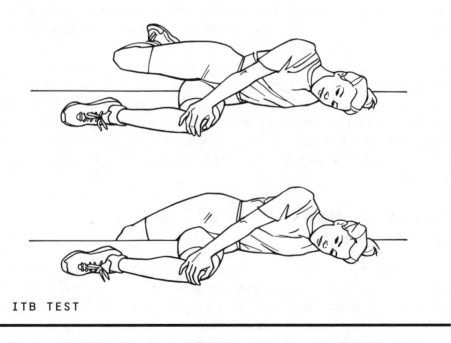

ITB TEST

To measure the flexibility of your iliotibial band, lie on the edge of a table with your knees bent. Allow the top leg to drop backward behind you. It should fall to at least table level.

become inflamed. To check whether your ITB is too tight, give yourself the ITB or Ober test, as shown on page 11.

If your ITB is tight, the solution is simple: Stretch the ITB. (See chapter 18.) In addition, you might need to take steps to minimize your overpronation with shoes, orthotics or both, which are covered in chapters 4 and 5.

11. How Long Have You Been Running?

Many studies cite training errors as the most common cause of running injuries. Remember the curse of the injured runner: Too much, too fast, too soon or too often.

Beginning runners are more likely to get injured than those who have been at it a while. The muscles, joints, tendons, ligaments and bones of a beginner aren't used to the rigors of running's repetitive stresses. The first four months of running are the most critical. For beginners, shin splints are a common problem and stress fractures can occur because leg muscles develop quickly and may actually overpower the bones.

If you're just starting to run, begin slowly and gradually with a combination of slow jogging and walking. A related warning to runners who cut way back on their training during the winter: A high number of injuries occur in March and April, foiling runners who rush back into full-scale training too quickly. (A good general rule of thumb is to increase your mileage no more than 10 percent each week.)

12. How Many Miles a Week Do You Run?

Assuming that you've been consistently running a certain number of miles for at least three months, you can use your weekly total to predict the likelihood of an injury. The rule is simple: The more miles you cover, the more likely you are to get injured.

Kenneth Cooper, M.D., president and founder of the Cooper Aerobics Center in Dallas and author of best-selling books on aerobic exercise, concluded after extensive research that 12 to 15 miles per week is the optimum amount. Dr. Cooper says running two to three miles a day, three to five days a week, is enough to be aerobically fit while minimizing the chances of getting hurt.

But many fitness devotees assume that more is better. They think that if 12 to 15 miles per week is good for their health, twice as much must be twice as beneficial. In fact, Dr. Cooper has found that after 15 miles fitness returns diminish and injury rates climb.

Many runners exceed that figure, of course, and do so without getting hurt. But if you're injury-prone or discover from this quiz that you're at high risk for injury, cutting back your mileage may be one easy way to beat the odds.

13. Do You Progress Too Quickly?

You shouldn't increase your mileage by more than 10 percent per week, as mentioned previously. So if you ran 25 miles last week, don't add more than 2½ miles to your total this week.

That 10 percent is the amount your body can tolerate without increasing your chances of injury. Anything more puts you at significant risk.

14. Do You Take Time to Fully Recover?

If an injury has caused you to miss more than two weeks of running, you must return slowly and easily. Most runners are champing at the bit after that kind of layoff, but the first few weeks back are crucial in preventing future injury.

Unfortunately, an injury doesn't make you stronger; it makes you susceptible to a recurrence. To keep that from happening, make yours a careful comeback. If your injury is three months old or less, a good rule is to start back at 50 percent or less than what you were previously doing. (See chapter 22 for more details.)

15. When Do You Run?

Statistics show that if you run in the afternoon or evening, you'll have fewer injuries than if you run the first thing in the morning. The soft tissues (muscles, tendons and ligaments) are tighter and less forgiving in the morning, before your normal daily activity has warmed them up. Muscle strains and various tendinitis complaints are also more likely to crop up during morning runs.

Morning runners do have one advantage, however. Statistics show that they're more likely than afternoon or evening runners to stick with a running program.

16. What about Speedwork?

Doing speed training on the track, or time trials on the road, is a great way to improve your racing performances. It's also a great way to get hurt. The risks of speedwork are highest when you're taking your first fast steps and when you really pick up the pace.

Once you're used to a reasonable amount of fast running, your body ought to be able to handle the stress. But always be sure to warm up before a speed session and to cool down afterward. Follow a sane speedwork program that tailors your training pace to your race pace.

17. Do You Race?

Runners who race have a 10 percent greater likelihood of injury than runners who don't. And the more often you compete, the bigger the risk.

To improve your chances of staying healthy, race only when you're certain your training is adequate for both the distance of the race and the pace you're planning to maintain. And accept the fact that there are some days when you're just not up to par or when the weather conditions are bound to slow you down. Know your limitations, and adjust your pace accordingly.

THE INJURY PREDICTOR QUIZ

Choose the most appropriate response for each question below and then add up your points. For more information about how to answer the questions and interpret your responses, refer to the numbered sections in the text.

1. Your sex? _____

male 0
female 1

2. Your body-fat percentage? _____

Men:
below 15% 0
15 to 20% 1
21 to 25% 2
26% and above...............3

Women:
below 20% 0
20 to 25% 1
26 to 30% 2
31% and above...............3

3. Your leg-length discrepancy? _____

$\frac{1}{8}$ inch or less 0
$\frac{1}{8}$ to $\frac{3}{16}$ inch 1
$\frac{3}{16}$ to $\frac{1}{4}$ inch 2
$\frac{1}{4}$ to $\frac{3}{8}$ inch 3
over $\frac{3}{8}$ inch......................4

(continued)

4. How high are your arches?　　　　_____

```
completely flat ..................4
moderately flat..................2
normal arch.........................0
moderately high
    (little flattening).................1
very high (little
    flattening) ........................4
```

5. How much do you pronate?　　　_____

```
severe overpronation..........5
moderate overpronation......3
mild overpronation ..............1
normal pronation.................0
mild underpronation ............1
moderate underpronation....2
severe underpronation........5
```

6. What's your Q-angle?　　　　_____

Men:

```
less than 11 degrees ..........0
11 to 15 degrees................2
16 to 20 degrees................4
21 degrees and over...........5
```

Women:

```
less than 16 degrees ..........0
16 to 19 degrees................2
20 to 23 degrees................4
24 degrees and over...........5
```

7. Are you bowlegged? _____

    normal to mild...................0
    moderate 1
    severe 3

8. Your calf-muscle flexibility? _____

    more than 15 degrees 0
    11 to 15 degrees..............2
    6 to 10 degrees...............3
    0 to 5 degrees.................4
    less than 0 degrees 5

9. Your hamstring flexibility? _____

    more than 90 degrees 0
    85 to 90 degrees..............2
    75 to 84 degrees..............3
    60 to 74 degrees..............4
    less than 60 degrees 5

10. Your iliotibial band flexibility? _____

    reasonably flexible 0
    very tight 3

11. How long have you been running? _____

    four months or more.........0
    two to four months 1
    one month or less.............3

(continued)

THE INJURY PREDICTOR QUIZ—CONTINUED

12. What's your weekly mileage? _____

15 miles or less 0
16 to 25 miles 2
26 to 45 miles 6
46 miles or more 10

13. Are you increasing your mileage? _____

less than 10% a week 0
10 to 15% a week 4
more than 15% a week...10

14. Are you coming off an injury? _____

no recent injury................0
after 2 to 3 week layoff.....2
after 3 weeks or more 4

15. When do you usually run? _____

noon, evening, night 0
morning 1

16. Do you practice speedwork? _____

no speedwork...................0
continuing regular speed
    workouts 2
just beginning speed
    workouts 4
markedly increasing pace
    of speedwork 8

17. How often do you race? _____

    never................................0
    2 times a year or less........2
    3 to 6 times a year............4
    7 or more times a year......6

Your Total Score: _____

INTERPRETING YOUR SCORE

10–15 Congratulations! You're not likely to get a running injury.

16–26 You have a slightly better than average chance of sustaining an injury. To lessen your chances even further, concentrate on one or two of the areas in which you scored poorly.

27–37 You have a 50-50 chance of becoming injured. To bring the odds more into your favor, work on those areas in which you scored poorly.

38–49 You are almost certainly going to sustain an injury, if you aren't already injured. You know what you are doing wrong, and you owe it to yourself to correct the mistakes. Make sure you know the names of good sports-medicine specialists in your area.

50+ You have a lot of work ahead. Make sure your health insurance is paid up.

Chapter 2

READING AND HEEDING YOUR PAINS

Like all athletes, runners are used to pain. In fact, they often distinguish between "good pains" and "bad pains." They consider some pains a natural part of hard effort. Actually, from a medical viewpoint there are no good pains: Some pains are just not as bad as others. All pains are warning signs and, like traffic signals, need to be recognized and heeded.

Pain means that pain fibers are being stimulated somewhere in your body. Only the degree of stimulation and individual reaction to it differ. How you react to pain is determined by many factors, including the thickness of the nerves, their distribution and location relative to the injured area, and the protective lining that surrounds the nerves. To further complicate your body's ability to interpret messages from the nervous system, the brain can manufacture chemicals such as endorphins that block or distort that information.

This was brought home to me when I first treated an athlete, while I was still a student at the California College of Podiatric Medicine. Mark had just completed the rigorous Dipsea Run, a grueling race up and down Mount Tamalpais just north of San Francisco.

Mark came to the clinic complaining of pain on the outside of his leg. Like many runners, he'd waited a week after the pain occurred before scheduling his appointment—and even then did so only at the insistence of his wife.

He told me that the pain had begun about three miles into the race, but his wife and friends were waiting for him at the finish line and he didn't want to disappoint them by dropping out. X-rays confirmed that he had suffered a fracture of his fibula, a bone in his lower leg. His case illustrates the tremendous ability of the brain to control pain. At any other time a fracture of the fibula would have resulted in sharp, debilitating pain rather than the mere annoyance it was during the race.

Such reports of fractures, tears, sprains and strains happening to runners who go on to complete their runs are common. I'm reminded of the famous X-rays taken of a runner immediately after the Boston Marathon, showing a displaced fracture of his tibia—not a little crack, but a fairly major separation of the large bone in the leg. The runner admitted he thought he felt "a little snap somewhere around the six-mile mark." Yet he ran another 20 miles on the fractured leg to finish this grueling race.

I also remember reading the amazing story of another runner who was shot in the head while training to qualify for the Boston Marathon. Only after finishing his run did he realize he'd been struck by a bullet.

Other runners deny pain completely: Many of the runners who visit my office talk about "discomfort" rather than pain. When I try to pin them down as to exactly where the pain is, they say, "Oh, I'm not in pain. It's just *uncomfortable.*" I have seen patients with fractures who called their problem "discomfort."

Pain can also be masked by various mechanisms in the body. A good example is a running patient of mine who had a horse fall on his leg. This accident occurred on a Saturday and he immediately went to a hospital emergency room because of severe, sharp pain in his knee. The knee was thoroughly checked and found to be only slightly bruised.

It wasn't until two days later that this man noticed a throbbing pain in his lower leg. X-rays of the leg showed two fractures around the ankle. By then, his knee was no longer painful, but he could barely walk due to the ankle pain.

What happened? His knee pain "overrode" the other pains to the point where he didn't even know his leg was injured, much less broken.

Pay Attention to Those Pains

Discomfort or pain is always a strong signal that something is wrong. Whether it's a sore toenail or a pain in a muscle, tendon or joint, pay attention to it. It will only get worse if you keep running. Even something as minor as a hot spot on the bottom of your foot can lead to serious consequences.

Consider what happened to Doug, who felt a blister forming under his heel halfway through a 10-K race. He ignored the signs and went on to finish the event. When I saw Doug two days later, his heel looked like raw meat and infectious red streaks extended up his leg. Doug was allergic to many antibiotics and the infection was resistant to those he could tolerate.

By the time his problem was solved, four weeks had passed with no running. Was running those extra three miles worth the medical bills, the discomfort and the month off from running—not to mention the potential loss of his limb?

In hindsight, Doug admits that no, it wasn't.

Each pain has something important to tell you. Far too often I have patients come to see me with long-term injuries, some after fighting to run through pain for years. By the time I see them, it may take a great deal of time and effort to repair the injury—and sometimes permanent damage has been done. In most cases, earlier treatment would have resolved the problem quickly and these runners could have avoided needless suffering.

Serious overuse injuries don't happen overnight. Any overuse injury involves a buildup of stresses and trauma to your bones, joints, muscles and tendons—or even nerves. Your body always tries to adapt and relieve the stresses. If you put even more stress on the sore area while it is going through these adaptive changes, you will likely develop a full-blown injury.

Whenever you have an injury or long-term inflammation, scar tissue forms. This tissue is inelastic, adheres to anything surrounding it and is usually weaker than the tissue it replaces. It leaves the surrounding tissue more susceptible to chronic injury. So running through pain only sets you up for more serious, more frequent and more lasting injuries.

Pain tells you that you have already crossed the line past sensible training and that your excessive training is actually working against you. *Never* try to run through pain. For that matter, never bike or swim, stretch or lift through pain. Pain isn't a necessary part of training: Top coaches and athletes, sports-medicine professionals and exercise physiologists have long since shown that you do not need to subject yourself to great pain to build strength or endurance.

Pain is a sign that your body cannot accept the stress you have placed upon it and is begging for some rest. Heed the warnings.

When Your Body Says STOP, Listen!

Sharp pains are always a major warning sign of trouble. Whether they occur while you are running or after you run, something major is going wrong.

You must stop whatever what you're doing and have your injury evaluated promptly: You may have a stress fracture, muscle injury, tendon tear or one of many other abnormalities. Your body has few better mechanisms than presenting a sharp pain to your brain that says "Stop!" It is a major red light with a traffic cop sitting at the intersection.

If you keep training through sharp pains, I can almost guarantee that you are on a collision course with trouble. Basically, the sharp-pain sensation is fair warning that you are headed for a great deal of time off, diagnostic testing, possible casting or surgery—*if* you don't take immediate corrective action. Unless you are running away from a mugger or are on your way to an Olympic gold medal, *stop*.

I know one fellow who was running a marathon when he felt a sharp pain in his leg. Because he was leading the race at the time, he kept going. Finally, at around mile 22, the pain became so severe that he was forced to drop out.

He found out later he was suffering from compartment syndrome, which shuts off most of the blood supply to the lower leg and foot. His injury was so severe that he was hospitalized and had surgery to return normal blood supply to his foot.

SOUNDS OF INJURY

Pain is not your only clue to an injury. Many runners have *heard* their injury before they've felt it. A "snap," "crackle," "pop" or grinding sound can indicate an injury before the site becomes painful. Achilles tendon ruptures sometimes occur this way.

Dave, a 2:30 marathoner, was playing in a pick-up basketball game when he felt snapping in his lower leg and fell down. He experienced little pain or swelling, but he'd lost some control in his foot. Because the same thing had happened in another basketball game five years earlier, Dave knew almost immediately what had happened: a complete rupture of an Achilles tendon.

You may think this type of injury would be excruciatingly painful, but the sound and subsequent lack of function are often your first clues—and not only for Achilles injuries.

Another runner I treated was running when he felt a slight "pop" in his calf. Startled, he turned around, thinking he'd been stung by a bee or that a kid with a BB gun had shot him.

In fact, this runner had ruptured a calf tendon, the plantaris. He finished his run without a lot of pain, then noticed that the back of his leg had turned black and blue.

Ankle sprains tend to occur loudly, with snapping and crackling sounds that may indicate tears to ligaments or tendons. But you can't tell how bad the injury is by the amount of swelling that

Had he stopped when he first felt the sharp pain, chances are no serious damage would have occurred. This runner wound up missing about six months of running—all for ignoring that one sharp pain.

How do you know when a pain is severe enough to warrant stopping your activity? As a general rule, if what you feel is just a little annoying, you can continue to run—and make a note of it in your training log. But if this sensation causes you significant discomfort or makes you change your gait, that's a different matter.

follows the sprain. A soccer player, Dan, came to see me after tripping in a sprinkler hole on the playing field. His ankle looked like it had a softball imbedded in it, and casting or surgery appeared likely. Yet the X-rays and MRI tests on his ankle showed no tears or breaks. He was playing soccer again within three weeks.

On the other hand, I've seen runners whose ankle sprains had made an unpleasant sound when the injury occurred, but produced little pain or swelling. These runners at first thought their injuries were relatively minor—only to find out later that they'd suffered complete tears of the lateral ligaments that required surgical repair.

A persistent grinding sound around the joint, even in the absence of pain, also indicates an injury that needs attention. This is especially true around the big toe, ankle and knee. Generally, this grinding means the joint is not tracking or gliding normally and that there has been erosion of the cartilage which normally separates the bones from each other and allows the joint to function smoothly.

When cartilage wears away, bone rubs against bone and the joint itself is eventually damaged. By having any grinding, crunching or clicking sensation evaluated early, you can minimize the loss of cartilage and perhaps avoid permanent damage.

Twinges before and after Runs Are Significant, Too

You may be harboring an injury even though you feel little if any pain during the run. Soreness *before* the run that disappears as you warm up—only to reappear after you've cooled off—is a strong indicator that something is amiss.

Soft-tissue injuries (primarily those to the muscles but also involving tendons and ligaments) almost always cause more pain and loss of function before and after the run than while you are running. This is because soft tissues become very tight when cold. As you warm them up they stretch out, resist injury better and give off fewer pain signals.

Then, after you've stressed these tissues and rested for a while, they cool and tighten again. Lactic acid and other by-products of muscular work build up also, contributing to discomfort and pain.

The symptom may be as mild as the muscles cramping up or becoming uncomfortable from the accumulation of lactic acid. Many runners ignore this—and do so at their peril. The pain is your body's way of telling you that you've exceeded its ability to perform the amount of work that you asked it to.

Let's say that you just finished a five-mile training run. You get in your car and drive home. When you step out of the car your calf muscle cramps up, and it remains sore the next day.

This is a clear signal to take it easy. Reduce your distance by at least 30 percent until your pain goes away. Forget about trying to adhere to a rigid training schedule when your body isn't up to it.

A sore calf muscle that seems minor one day can develop into an Achilles tendon tear if you continue your workouts. If you don't ease off, this mild pain can cost you weeks or months of time to recover from a serious injury.

Deb, an exercise physiologist and fitness instructor at a college in my area, is a good example. Deb was teaching two marathon classes while training for the marathon herself; she ran with her classes and then sometimes did additional workouts. Her groin area became so sore that she could hardly walk. Anyone watching her walking across campus might think she needed crutches. She shuffled and limped, moaned and groaned. She had a hard time even getting up after sitting.

But Deb's pains would go away when she got into her run. Because she could run relatively pain-free, she figured she was okay—that this was only a muscle problem. She continued training and ran the marathon she'd trained for.

When she was finally evaluated for her pain (after the race, naturally), it turned out that Deb had a three-month-old pelvic fracture. The end result: four months of no running and continued pain in that area for more than a year.

The lesson here: Just because the injured area feels better after it warms up, don't think everything is okay. This is just another way that running tricks you into thinking you're hurting less than you really are.

Every pain means something. Note each and every ache or pain in your training diary—looking for patterns of cause, duration and cure.

Soreness You Can Live With

Now that I've scared you with all of the bad things that can happen when pain is ignored, let's talk about inconveniences that you *can* work through. After all, you can't go running to a doctor every time something feels a little weird. If you rested every time you had the slightest ache or pain, you might spend more time reading running-injury books than you do running.

In your quest for better performance, you will sometimes feel pain that appears first as muscle soreness after an extra-long or extra-fast workout. Instead of either ignoring this soreness or fighting it, accept it as an invitation to ease off until the discomfort subsides. Hard training is essential if you are to improve, but equally critical is the recovery period between these bouts of work. Without the rebuilding phase, temporary pains can grow into full-fledged

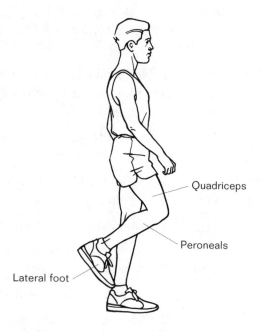

Quadriceps

Peroneals

Lateral foot

WHERE SORENESS HITS

Hard workouts and races often leave soreness in their wake. This most commonly strikes the quadriceps muscles of the upper leg, the peroneals of the lower leg and the outside (lateral) edge of the foot. These pains usually disappear after a few days of rest or light training.

PAIN CHECKLIST

Whenever you feel pain, no matter how slight, you should try to figure out what it means. Ask yourself the following questions about your pain or pains. For every Yes, refer to the possible solution given. The pains are listed roughly in order of seriousness, from least to most severe.

_____1. Did your pain begin after an extra-hard effort (such as a race) and last less than three days?

_____2. Did your pain result from a sudden increase in training (from slow to fast, for instance), a change in surface or terrain (flats to hills) or a switch in shoes (training to racing model)?

_____3. Does one type of running (such as speedwork) cause your pain while another type (say slow distance) causes no problem?

_____4. Do you feel pain before running which then eases or even disappears as you warm up?

_____5. Did your pain first appear only after you'd cooled off from the injuring run?

_____6. Does your pain increase during the run?

_____7. Does your pain cause a change in your running form (such as favoring one leg)?

_____8. Did your pain occur sharply in mid-run?

_____9. Did your pain recur at an old injury site?

_____10. Do you "hear" the source of your pain?

injuries. (I define "normal" pain as mild discomfort that disappears within a few days; pain that lasts longer I call an injury.)

It isn't uncommon to experience soreness in certain muscle groups after a particularly hard or fast run. Generally, this occurs in

What the pain means:

1. It probably was normal post-effort soreness requiring no treatment other than reduced training or rest.

2. Back away from this experiment until the pain subsides, then make change more gradually and carefully the next time.

3. Obviously, avoid the aggravating runs. But at the same time, try to correct your sensitivity toward them: Seek professional advice to find out if you need different shoes, an orthotic or other treatment.

4. Don't brush off this discomfort as unimportant because it doesn't interfere with running. It signals an unresolved problem which could escalate.

5. Recognize that the working body has ingenious ways of masking pain until it has completed its work. You may not feel it until the next time you run.

6. Treat this symptom as more serious than pains that decrease or ones that remain constant. Increasing pain means you're clearly making the condition worse with each step you take.

7. Pay attention to even the most subtle changes. These are a tipoff to the injury's severity and can trigger secondary injuries in other areas now under unusual stresses.

8. Stop immediately! Anything traumatic enough to override the body's pain-masking mechanism must be taken quite seriously.

9. Accept the fact that there probably is scarring in that area and you have a permanent weakness for that sort of injury.

10. Be aware of grinding, creaking, cracking, snapping or popping sounds. They warn of possibly permanent damage being done to tendons, ligaments, cartilages or bones.

one of three areas: the quadriceps muscles in the front of your thigh, the peroneal muscles and tendons on the lateral (outside) part of your lower leg, and your foot. There are specific reasons for these areas becoming sore.

Quadriceps. As a group, the quadriceps are a team of work-horses—the largest muscle group in your body and the one you call upon most to propel you forward. Despite their large size, the quadriceps can be overused just like any other muscles.

At one time, the San Diego Marathon had its finish line in the huge stadium where the Chargers football team and the Padres baseball team play. Race organizers put all the T-shirts and souvenirs in the upper rows of the stadium. After the race, the marathoners had to walk up the numerous flights of stairs in the stadium to get their finishers' T-shirts. It was a tough climb after a 26.2-mile race, but walking back down was the real problem.

As the runners started down, they placed a tremendous strain on their quadriceps, which were already crying for relief. I wondered what uninformed observers might have thought if they'd seen these normally healthy people being led, carried or otherwise helped downstairs.

Time—and little or no additional training—heals this problem rather quickly. Within a few days, these same people were walking—and running—normally again.

Peroneals. The peroneal muscles and tendons run down the lateral side (outside) of your leg, attach to your foot and work to keep it firmly on the ground. This muscle group helps stabilize your foot. As soon as your foot strikes the ground, your peroneal muscles contract so that your foot will pronate (roll inward) and stay flat on the ground. The peroneals protect against your foot turning outward, which can cause an ankle sprain.

The faster or longer you run, the more these muscles have to work. That is why soreness of the peroneals is a common complaint after races. Again, time and little or no training are the cures for this complaint.

Feet. Most runners initially strike the ground on the outside of the foot. When you stand, you can see that the distance between your feet on the ground (called your base of gait) is narrower than the width of your hips. That is why your leg and foot make contact with the ground at an angle. This means the initial force of impact is on the outside of your foot. Repetitive impact can cause bruising and pain along the outer edge of the foot, especially as you start to run longer distances or increase your speed.

Abrupt changes in running surface can overwhelm your ability to absorb shock, as shown by one runner who trained exclusively on grass and soft dirt trails. He told me, "I ran on these surfaces in order to avoid injuries, especially stress fractures." But when he entered a half-marathon that was run entirely on asphalt and concrete, he experienced so much post-race pain on the outside of his foot that I suspected a stress fracture.

Fortunately, this wasn't the case. But it struck home the lesson that you have to prepare your foot and leg muscles to take the pounding of a 13.1-mile race.

What Can Cause Muscle Aches

Short-term muscle soreness is a normal part of most runners' lives as they push their limits of distance or speed. They must do this from time to time or they never improve—*but* they shouldn't ignore what the soreness is telling them.

I knew a physical education instructor, Diane, who complained to me, "Whether the race distance is a 5-K or a marathon, I always run an eight-minute-per-mile pace." I asked her what her training pace was. "Around eight minutes per mile," she answered, which didn't surprise me.

When Diane started doing speed workouts to decrease her pace, she made the mistake of keeping her mileage high at the same time. She soon developed her first injury, a pain on the outside of her foot. She eased back her training until that cleared up, then resumed with a combination of lower mileage and some speedwork. The injury never returned and her racing pace improved.

The lesson here is that both speed training and distance running are stressful. Never increase both at the same time. In fact, if you *increase* one factor, *decrease* the other—at least temporarily. And don't run extra-long distances or perform speedwork while you're experiencing this normal soreness. Wait it out for a day or so to avoid triggering a serious injury.

Chapter 3

IT STARTS IN YOUR FEET

Why do so many runners get injured? The answer begins at footfall. The foot is most often ground zero for a running injury. Even problems as far removed as the knee, hip or lower back usually originate with a foot irregularity.

When you walk you always have one foot in contact with the ground. Running is different. Running can be viewed as a series of "crashes." Your entire body leaves the ground and then crashes back to the earth. When you propel yourself forward on a run, you also propel yourself *upward* and your leading foot hits the ground with a force equal to five times or more your body weight. This means that a 160-pound person's impact with the ground may equal 800 pounds with each step. Multiply this by hundreds of steps per mile and you realize how much repetitive stress a runner is subjected to.

Not only do you absorb tremendous impact forces, but the muscles of your feet and legs also work hard to stabilize your feet on the ground.

To understand why runners get injured, you need an introduction to anatomy and biomechanics: You have to know how the foot works with the leg to understand what can go wrong and what can be done to correct problems.

Anatomy of a Foot

One of my classmates in medical school, David, was a former Army medical corpsman who had served in Vietnam. After our first semester of anatomy, he recalled treating a soldier with a foot wound.

"Don't worry," he had told the soldier. "You're lucky it's only your foot."

But after learning that there are 28 bones in each human foot, 33 complex joints, more than 40 muscles and tendons and some 100 ligaments, David realized he may have underestimated the amount of damage that bullet could have caused. And so it is with running injuries: A "small" foot problem can spell big trouble.

One-quarter of all of the bones in the body are in the feet. There are three groups: tarsals, metatarsals and phalanges.

Tarsals. Of the seven tarsal bones, perhaps the most important is the talus, the foot's connection to the lower leg.

This relatively small bone fits into the opening between your two leg bones (the tibia and fibula) and with them makes up the ankle joint. This means that not only does it take your body's

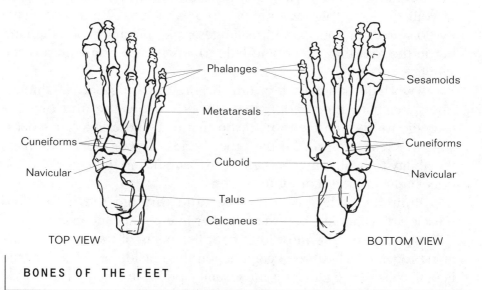

TOP VIEW

Phalanges

Sesamoids

Metatarsals

Cuneiforms

Cuneiforms

Navicular

Cuboid

Navicular

Talus

Calcaneus

BOTTOM VIEW

BONES OF THE FEET

Twenty-eight bones support and, working with muscles and tendons, propel each foot as you run, repeatedly absorbing impact.

weight, but it's also instrumental in flexing your foot up and down—a necessary motion for running and walking.

Along with the heel bone (calcaneus) below it, the talus forms the subtalar joint—the most important one in a runner's foot. It allows your foot to pronate (roll inward) and supinate (roll outward).

Directly in front of the talus and calcaneus are two more tarsal bones, the navicular and the cuboid. These four bones together form another important joint called the midtarsal. It controls your arch, allowing it to lock and keep the foot rigid, or unlock to loosen up the foot. The three remaining tarsal bones are the wedge-shaped bones that help connect the rearfoot to the metatarsals.

Metatarsals. These long, thin bones make up most of the foot's length and fracture easily. This is where stress fractures almost always occur in your foot.

The front ends of these five bones are called the metatarsal heads and form the metatarsal arch. This arch makes up the ball of your foot and can occasionally collapse. When this happens, you tend to get pain and calluses under the ball of your foot.

Phalanges. Generally, three phalanges together make up each of your toes—the big toe only has two, while the fifth toe can have two or three. In your hand, phalanges make up much of its length, but in the foot they contribute little to length and primarily provide stability.

Two little bones underneath the big toe are called sesamoids. They attach to the tendon that flexes the big toe and provide leverage for the muscle to work on that toe. These little guys occasionally break and, unlike the other bones in your feet, don't have the ability to heal. Once broken, scar tissue fills in the crack and the bones remain in two or more pieces.

Running under, around, over and through the bones and muscle are ligaments, nerves and other interconnecting tissue.

Ligaments. The most important ligaments of the foot hold the ankle together. The three ligaments on the outside of the ankle (the lateral collateral ligaments) are usually pulled or torn in an ankle sprain.

On the inside of the ankle the deltoid ligament attaches from the tibia to the talus, calcaneus and other foot bones and ties those bones together. This ligament is difficult to tear—to do so, your foot has to land with a twist inward instead of outward.

Along the bottom of your foot is the plantar fascia, also known as the long plantar ligament. Like all ligaments, the plantar fascia does not have a good blood flow nor any true ability to stretch. An injury to this area of the foot usually involves small or large tears in the fascia. These tears heal with scar tissue that easily becomes painful and inflamed.

Nerves. The main nerve that runs into your foot is the tibial nerve. It travels from the back of your leg, down around the inside ankle bone and along the bottom of your foot. Along the way, it splits off into several branches.

There are a few places along its travels where the tibial nerve can cause you problems, particularly where it runs down the inside of your ankle and passes through a tunnel with your tarsal bones on one side and the flexor retinaculum on the other. This makes the nerve susceptible to compression injuries known as tarsal tunnel syndrome.

The nerve that ends in a branch between the third and fourth toes can also become irritated. This leads to a condition called Morton's neuroma.

So much for *what* can go wrong. Now I'll explain why the simple act of putting one foot in front of the other can sometimes present problems.

Biomechanics: The Way You Move

Don't let the word biomechanics intimidate you. It simply means the study of human motion—the mechanics of getting from one place to another.

The bones and joints work together as a unit with the muscles and other connective tissue to propel you forward. If everything operates perfectly, your feet and legs function at their best. But if there is one slight abnormality or malfunction the whole network can fall apart and an injury can occur.

It may seem to you that your injury occurred suddenly. But the problem may have been in the making for years of wear and tear before serious pain finally occurred.

Look at my friend and patient Craig, who came into the office one day and declared that a big bump had *suddenly* formed on the top of his foot. "It wasn't there last week," he stated. "I'm sure it was caused by that tight pair of shoes I wore to my brother's wedding this past weekend."

An X-ray showed that the bump was in fact a large bone spur that couldn't have popped up overnight. It had been slowly growing over the first metatarsal cuneiform joint for a long time.

I had a hard time convincing Craig that this spur had been years in the making. Then his wife produced a picture taken five years before on the beach at Maui. The bone prominence was visible even then, although only about half of its current size.

Craig was partially right, however. That tight pair of dress shoes he'd worn a few days earlier was the final instigator of his pain. But even if he hadn't worn the snug shoes, at some point—maybe the next week, maybe the next year—he would have felt symptoms. It was inevitable—he had an abnormal growth in a place that his running shoe put pressure on.

The real reason behind the bone growth was that, in Craig, that particular joint moved when it should have been stable. The culprit: inherently faulty mechanics combined with the stresses of long-term running.

Basics of Biomechanics

The purpose of your feet and legs is really to get your head from Point A to Point B with as little shock, jarring or trauma as possible. Your brain is susceptible to bruising when it is shaken around too much, so the gentler the ride the better. Every joint between your feet and your head is a shock absorber. Not only do joints allow motion by bending, but they also help absorb impact. When the joints are working properly, you can enjoy a relatively smooth ride.

The forward and back motion of your feet and legs as you walk or run may seem simple, but it is actually an extraordinarily complex series of motions involving all the muscles, tendons, bones, joints, ligaments and nerves working in harmony.

No two steps are exactly alike. The angle of your foot, the wear of your shoe, the slant of the running surface or even a tiny pebble under your foot cause you to strike the ground differently. So your brain has to digest and feed back all of that information. This process is so sophisticated that it has been impossible to devise a completely accurate mathematical or computer model of your foot. Yet your brain provides both motion and feedback, in milliseconds, thousands of times daily.

But just as you don't need to know how rubber is manufactured in order to change a flat tire, you don't need a graduate course in biomechanics to figure out why your feet and legs fail. All you need to learn are a few simple principles.

When You Hit the Ground

The feet and legs undergo the stress during the weight-bearing portion of the running gait, which causes most of the problems. The weight-bearing action occurs in three phases: heel strike, midstance and propulsion.

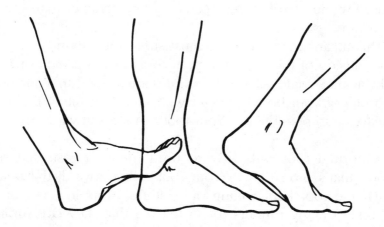

GAIT CYCLE

While in contact with the ground only briefly, the runner's foot makes a complex series of adaptations to the surface. The three phases of this process are heel strike, when the foot takes the impact of landing; midstance, when the foot is in maximum contact with the ground; and propulsion, when the foot pushes off for another stride.

Heel strike. Every year, several runners come to me for help because their heel strike is abnormal. When a gait analysis of one such runner, Mark, showed nothing wrong, I asked Mark why he thought there was a problem. He pointed to his shoes and said, "Look at the bottom of the heels. They wear out on the outside, instead of evenly in the middle."

What Mark didn't realize was that almost *all* runners strike the ground on the outside, rear portion of the heel. This is called the "supinated" position and is the *normal* way to land.

You're meant to land this way—for many reasons. The basic reason is anatomical: Your hips are wider than the distance between your feet as you run. You can see this base of gait clearly if you run on the beach: Just look at your footprints in the sand and notice how far each one is from a line between your prints. (You can also check your base of gait by standing naturally and measuring the distance between your feet.)

Runners whose feet fall almost directly in line with each other as they run have a very narrow base of gait. Yours might not be that narrow, but it will almost certainly be narrower than the width of your hips.

This means that your foot must strike the ground at an angle, on the outside of the heel. But your foot can't support your body's weight at that angle—it's just too unstable. Nor can your muscles support all of your body's weight with your foot tilting like that. So that leaves two possibilities: Your foot can roll outward or it can roll inward.

A normal foot rolls inward until the foot rests flat on the ground—that's pronation. If your foot rolls outward, that's supination. (If the foot kept rolling out without stopping, you'd sprain your ankle.) Many runners try to tell me that they oversupinate—but that's very rare.

Lowell Weil, D.P.M., a sports podiatrist from Des Plaines, Illinois, has seen more than his share of abnormal gait types while treating both professional and recreational athletes. And the only runners who oversupinate, says Dr. Weil, are some sprinters and people whose toes point inward.

I'd guess that, at most, 2 percent of the population over-

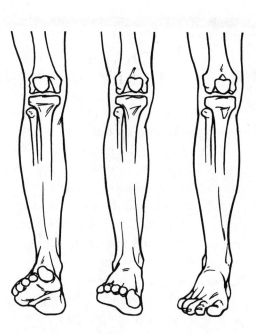

PRONATING FOOT

As the foot makes contact with the ground (*left*), the foot rolls inward or pronates (*center*), which causes the lower leg to twist inward (*right*).

supinates. Very few of them are distance runners, because their feet probably won't allow this type of activity.

Midstance (flat-foot). After you strike the ground, your foot should roll inward four or five degrees. This pronation allows your foot to be flat on the ground and support your body's entire weight. Some runners don't have enough motion to allow their feet to reach a flat position—not surprisingly, these people often suffer chronic ankle sprains.

Rolling in also loosens up the bones and joints in your foot. Just as the grinders in the America's Cup sailing races change the tension and position of the sails, so too does pronation alter the foot's alignment from tighter to looser and back again. The pronating foot becomes nice and loose so that it can adapt to a rough or uneven ground surface. Remember, you never know exactly what type of surface you are stepping on—your body must adapt constantly.

The pronation mechanism lets your foot adapt instantly and helps you maintain your balance. Along with the loose bone structure of your foot, pronation also allows increased shock absorption.

CHANGES OF STYLE:
EARLY WARNING SIGNS

Has your stride suddenly lengthened or shortened? Are you more sure-footed on one side than the other?

Be alert for such warnings. Since your body tends to substitute other muscles for those that are injured, any alteration in your gait or running style may signal a problem.

It will probably be difficult to identify exactly what the abnormality is, but you'll know that something is wrong. One leg might feel stronger than the other. Or you might notice that one of your shoes feels "funny" during your run or your running form doesn't flow as freely as it once did.

You may notice the change in your upper body, rather than your legs, as it attempts to balance out an abnormality below. A change in the swing of your arms, for instance, might mean they are working harder to compensate for a leg problem.

Conversely, a change in gait may reflect an upper-body injury. A runner once came to me complaining that he took two steps with his right foot for every step he took with his left. This young man obviously was exaggerating, but he did recognize that his gait had changed dramatically.

An orthopedic surgeon, Jeff Bronson, M.D., discovered that this runner had fractured his collarbone without realizing it while skiing. He thought that he'd just bruised his shoulder and never considered that this injury would affect his running. But his upper-body muscles were guarding the injured area, causing his sudden change in style.

Your body will *always* attempt to compensate for injuries. If one leg hurts, you will subconsciously put more force on the op-

As your foot rolls inward, it disperses the tremendous forces that occur as your heel hits the ground.

The more you pronate, the longer this dispersion takes because more of your foot is involved and your shock absorption abil-

posite leg. If one set of muscles is injured, your body will substitute other muscles to do the same job.

While this might provide temporary relief, your body might not resume its normal—and more functional—gait even after the original problem is resolved.

For instance, I recall one runner whom I treated for a hip problem. Her right hip hurt whenever she ran more than a mile or two. Pelvic pain of that sort is often due to one leg being longer than the other, but her legs were the same length and we couldn't find anything wrong with her bones or joints.

Then we analyzed her gait and could see that she was quite obviously favoring her left leg and putting most of the force on her right leg, the injured one. We couldn't figure out why—until! we happened to look inside an old pair of her running shoes.

A nail had poked out of the heel area and had been slightly jabbing her in the bottom of her heel. She didn't sense any pain from the nail, but her body reacted by favoring that side and placing the force on the other leg. As a result, her opposite hip started hurting.

Even more interesting was the fact that she hadn't worn those shoes for a month. However, her nervous system still remembered the problem and attempted to rectify it.

The instigating force (the nail) was removed when she got a new pair of shoes, but her body continued to favor the leg. All we had to do was send an "all-clear" message to her brain via brief physical therapy. She concentrated on returning to her former style of running, and the pelvic pain disappeared.

ities are greater. If you pronate only slightly, you don't absorb shock well because your foot doesn't loosen up and the risk of jarring injuries multiplies.

So you might think, "The more pronation I have, the safer I'll be. If a little shock absorption and foot adaptation are good, more must be better, right?"

Wrong. Excessive pronation has a negative influence on the third phase of the gait cycle, propulsion.

Propulsion (toe-off). Near the end of your gait cycle, your foot must act as a rigid lever to propel you forward during the push-off phase. You no longer want or need your foot to absorb shock. You're now asking this relatively small structure to take your entire body weight and push you either upward or forward—or both.

Your foot does this by rolling back toward the outside, which causes the joints and bones to lock up. That motion is called re-supination. Since you first made contact with the ground in a supinated position, you are essentially moving your foot back toward that position. Resupination has exactly the opposite effect of pronation—it makes the foot rigid and ready for propulson.

Mechanical Irregularities

This all seems like a fairly simple system and it would work pretty well if not for all the variations in gaits and foot types.

Most of us have some type of alignment problem in the feet and legs—bowlegs, knock knees, overpronation or underpronation, for example. We just aren't perfectly designed. These problems usually don't show up in walking, but they surface during a run because the forces are so much greater.

It's like the tires of your car being out of alignment. If you just drive to the store and back at 30 miles an hour a few times a week, no problem. But if you start taking that same car out on the freeway every day, look out.

When you train long, fast and often, you enter the "freeway" of running. When you combine excessive distance, speed or frequency with inherent misalignments, the end result—sooner or later—will be an injury.

Alignment problems are the rule rather than the exception. Approximately 50 percent of runners overpronate (six degrees or more) after heel strike; another 25 percent underpronate (less than four degrees of pronation). This means there's only one chance in four that you have an ideal gait.

Let's use the most common problem of overpronation to illustrate mechanical irregularities. Shoe manufacturers call this "excess motion."

When a runner pronates excessively, the foot strikes the ground normally (that is, on the outside of heel) and begins to roll inward. It rolls in that normal four to five degrees and then, uh-oh, it rolls in even more.

Too much motion. Too much pronation. Too loose a foot. When your foot overpronates, your muscles really get into the act. They try to stabilize the foot and keep it from becoming too mobile.

As the muscles struggle to compensate for too much motion, they fatigue and become stretched or stressed; a host of problems ensue.

When the foot overpronates, it doesn't have time to resupinate (or roll back out) properly. So when the time comes to push off with that foot, it isn't prepared.

But your brain still commands, "Push off!" You do as told but with a foot that is still loose at a time when it should be stable. We call this a "hypermobile" foot. Its bones take quite a jostling and this is a major cause of forefoot stress fractures.

All of your muscles, fighting to hold everything together tightly, undergo great strain. As if that were not enough, your whole leg rotates inward when you pronate.

This means that your knee rotates in about the same number of degrees as you pronate. Too much pronation of your foot equals too much torque of your knee. Your knee was designed to flex and extend all day long, but it wasn't meant to absorb more than a few degrees of torsion.

Excess torque not only causes problems in the knee, but it also sends the stresses up the thigh and into the hip and lower back. Your upper body also has to counterbalance every movement your lower body makes. When your right leg goes forward, your left arm compensates so you can keep your balance. Otherwise you'll lose your center of gravity and fall over.

One runner who sought my advice, Sue, overpronated severely after heel strike. As a result, her feet rolled in when she ran, her knees turned inward, and when her leg kicked back it moved to the outside.

Her arms also swung awkwardly and her upper body twisted wildly as she ran. Believing this was inefficient, she tried to control this motion. But her upper body was working this way to *compensate* for the motion of her feet and legs.

I told her, "Forget all about your arms and instead concentrate on your feet." When we controlled her excessive pronation with orthotics, her arm action naturally smoothed out. Her body realized that it didn't have to keep up the wild movement because there was no longer any excessive motion in her lower body to counterbalance.

Later, Sue told me, "I used to run only at night because I was embarrassed over having such a funny running style. Now I'm actually running races—during the day."

In summary, when you overpronate, you absorb a great deal of shock. But the downside is that your foot has too much motion and you are prone to motion- or instability-type ailments such as tendinitis, plantar fasciitis and knee strain. Underpronation has the opposite effect. This foot type is very stable but absorbs shock poorly.

Analyzing Your Foot Type

The best way to determine whether you underpronate or overpronate is to have someone follow you as you run and look at the back of your heel immediately after you make contact with the ground. The more the heel rolls inward, the more pronation occurs. As long as you aren't running too fast, your friend should be able to spot your motions easily.

If that doesn't work, there are a number of ways to tell where you fit into the biomechanical scheme—whether you overpronate, underpronate or have a normal gait. Start by taking a look at your basic foot type.

In chapter 1 you determined whether you have flat feet, higharched feet or normal feet. This information can give you a fairly good idea of how your foot functions and how much it pronates. In normal feet the arch collapses a bit as you run, allowing just enough pronation to plant your foot correctly and absorb shock. If everyone had perfect feet the number of injuries to runners would decline phenomenally. But the odds are three in four that you weren't born with perfect feet. So let's look at what it means to be flat-footed or high-arched.

Flat feet. Runners with flat feet tend to be overpronators: The arch is meant to hold up your foot and prevent abnormal motion. If it collapses too much more pronation occurs.

Everyone is born without an arch. Most children develop arches as they grow older. Some never do; they grow up to have completely flat feet.

Other people develop an arch and then over the years start to lose that arch, for reasons not entirely known. Arches don't collapse overnight—they almost always fall gradually. As with most other foot conditions, you generally don't notice that your arch has fallen until symptoms develop.

Several times a year, a middle-aged patient will come into the office and tell me that his feet are still growing. He'll say something like, "It's the weirdest thing, Doc. I've been a size 10½ most of my life and over the last few years I've grown a full shoe size."

This change in size is the giveaway. As the arch falls, the foot gets longer. There isn't any true growth, but the flattening of the arch lengthens the foot.

High-arched feet. People who look as if they could put a golf ball under their arch and still not feel it tend to underpronate. Their feet are like bricks, with a very small amount of motion. They hit the ground and the shock radiates straight up the leg to the shin, knee and hip.

This is the toughest of all foot types to deal with because the problem is lack of motion. Sports medicine has found a number of ways to control excessive motion, but it is very difficult to create motion when none is present.

Several years ago, orthopedic surgeon John Beck, M.D., and I were speaking to a group of physical education instructors. We were answering questions from the audience, fielding the questions according to our respective areas of expertise. Then a young woman asked, "I have a knee problem and a very high-arched foot type. What do you doctors suggest?"

I looked at Dr. Beck and said, "Well, it's a knee problem. You should answer it."

He turned back to me and said, "No, I think the question is more pertinent to the high arch. That's up your alley."

Neither of us is normally shy about expressing our opinions. But because the problem of knee injuries due to a high-arched, rigid foot is so difficult to address, it took us several minutes to decide who should answer this woman's question.

The bad news is that, like flat-footedness, high arches can actually grow worse through the years. With age, the arch can become higher and the shoe size smaller. I've had patients tell me, "I think my feet are shrinking."

Their feet aren't getting smaller, but they do need my help, just as other runners with obvious biomechanical irregularities do.

The help that we sports-medicine professionals give them can range from simply suggesting a change in shoes, to prescribing strengthening and stretching exercises, to fitting them for orthotics that compensate for problems in structure and motion that may be causing injuries.

Chapter **4**

RUNNING SHOES:
WHERE FORM MEETS FUNCTION

No running shoe is designed to last forever. Some runners, however, persist in using their favorite shoes long after they've outlived their usefulness—with sometimes painful results.

Like Rick, who came to my office one day with a painful foot ailment—peroneal tendinitis in one of the tendons along the outside of his ankle.

Following routine procedure, we had asked Rick to bring in his running shoes as possible clues to his problem. When I opened the treatment room door, I first thought an angry skunk had taken up residence.

Then I saw where the odor came from. These worn pieces of leather and foam had once been running shoes, but now they bore little resemblance to their original condition. The soles had been patched with so much glue from a glue gun that no rubber was visible. Part of the back of the shoe had come completely unglued and had actually lifted away from the sole. The uppers had worn through and were held together by duct tape. No brand or model identification could be seen.

I asked Rick why he brought those particular shoes. He looked at me with surprise and said, "Your staff told me to bring in my current running shoes, and I run in these."

When I suggested that it might be time to get a new pair, he said, "Why? These shoes have served me perfectly well. Until they completely rot out, I plan to keep using them."

I politely pointed out that he was, after all, in my office for a foot injury. And his shoes already met my definition of "rotted out." Rick got the message: He bought a new pair of shoes and his pains quickly resolved.

The shoe is your most important piece of equipment. A properly selected athletic shoe, accurately matched with your specific needs, can lessen the impact of mistakes such as running too many miles before you're ready or trying to do speedwork before you have a proper mileage base. Proper shoes can also reduce the chance of injury by helping compensate for any biomechanical problems, such as high-arched and rigid feet or bowlegs.

Wending Your Way through Shoe Terminology

Selecting a shoe is no easy task. It's not uncommon for a runner to come into my office with a completely bewildered look that says: How do I know which shoes to choose?

Dorothea is typical of the runners I see. "There are so many different shoes and features out there that I don't know where to begin," she complains. "There's gel, air, encap, EVA, torsion bars, cantilevers and some terms I can't even pronounce, much less figure out what they do."

Running shoes *have* become high-tech—and the terminology so complex that you may think you need a Ph.D. in biomechanics to discuss your needs with a store clerk. You can find shoes designed for motion control, stability, flexibility, racing, use with orthotics, use on various surfaces and just about every other factor that manufacturers can address. There are even shoes with lights on their heels!

Advertising from shoe companies isn't much help. It seems, for instance, that most manufacturers' shoes offer "maximum" shock absorption and "maximum" stability or motion control. It's hard to

SHOE TERMS YOU SHOULD KNOW

Achilles notch: A depression cut into the back of the heel collar to provide a secure fit and prevent irritation of the Achilles tendon.

Anatomical last: A footbed contoured in such a way that the midsole material wraps around the heel counter. So, instead of a flat platform, the midsole takes a concave shape that accommodates your heel for greater stability.

Blown rubber: The lightest, most cushioned type of rubber outsole material. Air is injected into the rubber compound to lighten and soften it. Few outsoles today are made entirely of blown rubber because it lacks durability, but many outsoles have blown rubber in the forefoot and midfoot for lightness and cushioning, with a harder carbon rubber in the high-wear area of the heel.

Board last: One of three ways shoes are constructed. A fully board-lasted shoe is made by gluing the upper to fiberboard before it's attached to the midsole. Board-lasting promotes stability and provides a good platform for orthotics, but it lacks flexibility.

Cantilever: A concave outsole design in which the outer edges flare out on impact to dissipate shock.

Carbon rubber: The most durable kind of rubber outsole material. It's a solid rubber with a carbon additive that improves durability.

Combination last: A shoe that is board-lasted in the rearfoot for stability but slip-lasted in the forefoot to promote flexibility. (To find out if a shoe is combination-lasted, remove the sockliner; if you find a fiberboard in the rearfoot and stitching in the front, it is.)

Curved: Curve-lasted shoes are banana-shaped and provide less medial support than a straighter shoe but allow greater foot motion. Generally, curve-lasted shoes are for biomechanically efficient, fast runners who want a more responsive, flexible shoe.

(continued)

Cushioning: Since a runner generates force of about three times his or her body weight with each footstrike, the cushioning properties of a shoe are designed to absorb the shock. Cushioning is primarily a function of the midsole.

EVA: Ethylene vinyl acetate is the most commonly used midsole foam in running shoes. Compression-molded EVA is heated and compressed into the shape of the midsole. It's light, resilient and has good cushioning properties. Every running shoe company uses EVA in at least some of its midsoles.

External heel counter: A rigid plastic collar that wraps around the shoe heel for support and to control excess pronation.

Flex grooves: Placed in the midsole of the forefoot, flex grooves make a shoe more flexible at toe-off.

Foot frame: A wrapping on top of the midsole or an additional piece that cradles the foot for added support. The foot frame prevents the foot from rolling over.

Forefoot stability strap: A leather or plastic overlay on both sides of the midfoot area that reinforces the upper and provides stability and support.

Heel counter: A firm, usually plastic cup that is encased in the upper and surrounds the heel. It controls excessive rearfoot motion.

Heel plug: In multidensity outsoles, the most durable rubber, which is placed in the high-wear area of the heel.

Last: A foot-shaped piece of wood, plastic or metal on which a shoe is built. The shape of the last determines the shape of the shoe. The straighter the last, the straighter the shoe and the greater the medial support. Generally, runners who need maximum

see how *every* athletic shoe company could have the best shock absorption and best motion control.

While new technology does allow shoe companies to incorporate more and better innovations into running footwear, it also com-

support and/or who overpronate opt for straight or slightly curved shoes; faster, lighter runners who need less support prefer curve-lasted or semicurved shoes.

Lateral: The outer edge of the shoe.

Medial: The inside edge (or arch side) of the shoe.

Metatarsal pad: A soft wedge of EVA placed under the ball of the foot to add shock absorption and comfort for forefoot strikers.

Midsole: The layer of cushioning material located between the upper and outsole. The most important component of the shoe, it's usually made of EVA, polyurethane or some combination of the two.

Motion-control: Designs or devices that control the inward rolling (pronation) of the foot.

Outsole: The material on the bottom of the shoe that comes in direct contact with the ground.

Polyurethane (PU): A synthetic rubber common in midsoles. It's firmer and more durable than EVA but has a less cushioned feel. Polyurethane is used in combination with EVA in many models, with the polyurethane in the rearfoot for firmness and durability and EVA in the forefoot for flexibility and lightness.

Slip last: The most flexible type of shoe construction. In a slip-lasted shoe, the upper is stitched together like a moccasin and then glued to the midsole. This allows for a better fit.

Straight last: The shape of the shoe is relatively straight on the medial side, which adds stability. The straighter the last, the greater the medial support.

Upper: The part of the shoe above the midsole.

plicates the task of selecting the features that fit your specific needs. But this is exactly what you must do: Arm yourself with the facts needed to pick the shoe ideal for you. But first you need to understand the individual components of the shoe itself.

Take a Look at Outsoles

A good running shoe is built from the bottom up; a poor one is designed from the top down.

In other words, the designers of a quality shoe are first concerned with the technical features of the sole—and aesthetics come last. The designers of a poor shoe, however, put looks first with functional properties as an afterthought.

Your shoe-anatomy lesson begins where the rubber meets the road—this part of your shoe is called the outsole. The material in direct contact with the ground is primarily designed for traction and durability, and helps absorb some shock as well. Hard, solid rubber serves well in those ways but is quite heavy.

In an attempt to lighten the shoes, most manufacturers use a combination of carbon rubber and "blown" rubber on the outsoles. Carbon rubber is rubber with carbon added for increased durability; blown rubber is rubber that has been expanded by heating, so it's lighter and better at absorbing shock but also less durable than

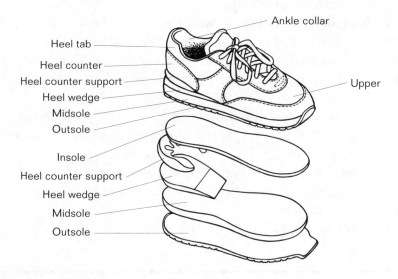

SHOE ANATOMY

Several key elements make up the modern running shoe, designed to give support and flexibility where needed.

solid rubber. The carbon rubber goes only on the areas of extreme wear such as the heel, while blown rubber covers the rest of the sole's outer surface.

When outsoles wear down, they can create biomechanical imbalances and cause injuries, as they did for Doug, a runner I treated. Doug discovered after consulting his training log that he developed shin splints after about 100 miles of wear on his shoes. He assumed the shoes had lost shock absorption at that point, so this 25-mile-per-week runner faithfully purchased a new pair every month. This got old after a while—not to mention expensive.

"A shoe should last more than 100 miles," he complained to me. I agreed. After studying his gait and shoes, I realized that he tended to drag his foot forward immediately after his heel hit the ground, causing the outside of his soles to wear out rapidly. Doug overpronates, and that little extra wearing of the shoe increased the angle at which his foot hit the ground, causing more motion—and his shin splints.

Once he started applying hot glue to keep the outside of his heel from prematurely wearing down, his problems ended. (Commercial preparations like Shoe Goo would have served the same purpose.) Doug could run in a pair of shoes six months or so—a much more acceptable time period for the mileage he was doing.

The Midsoles: The Heart of the Matter

In general, the midsole of the shoe provides most of the shock absorption and stability to keep your foot in proper contact with the ground. This is where you'll see the greatest quality differences between various brands and models—as well as the greatest innovations.

It's tough to provide both shock absorption and stability at the same time: Cushioning and motion control are generally inversely related. The more you have of one, the less you usually have of the other.

Shock absorption depends largely on how compressible the midsole material is: The more it compresses, the more movement the shoe allows. The less the midsole compresses, the better the shoe controls motion. But it also gives you a harder ride.

Most running shoes have foam materials in the midsole, either ethylene vinyl acetate (EVA), polyurethane (PU) or a combination of both.

EVA—the old standby. EVA foam has long been a popular material—it is relatively light and provides acceptable shock absorption and stability. But because EVA foam consists of air cells that are not sealed, it wears down rather quickly. The constant compression and decompression that occur during running eventually cause the midsole to lose much of its shock-absorption capabilities—the air cells within the foam become distorted, compressed or broken down.

Most researchers believe that EVA loses 40 percent of its ability to absorb shock within 500 miles of running. Also, excessive abnormal foot motion such as overpronation can cause EVA to break down unevenly, thereby exaggerating the biomechanical imbalance and possibly causing injury. Finally, EVA doesn't hold up well to heat and moisture.

To overcome these problems, some shoe companies use dual-density midsoles, with a softer EVA on the outside of the midsole where the most shock is likely to occur from footstrike and a harder EVA toward the inside of the midsole for stability as the foot rolls inward. Using two types of material allows better shock absorption yet reduces motion. When you hit the ground on the outside of the shoe, the outer portion absorbs more shock because it is softer. Then as your foot rolls in, the firmer material on the inner side of the midsole keeps you from rolling too far.

The pros and cons of polyurethane. Polyurethane (PU), long used for both the midsoles and outsoles of court shoes, is also used in running shoes. It's a sealed foam that holds up significantly longer than EVA. PU returns to its original shape after being compressed better and more quickly than EVA, and heat and moisture won't affect it as much.

So why don't all the shoe companies use PU?

Because it is heavier than EVA. Besides giving a greater load to carry, a heavier shoe places more strain on the muscles of the foot and leg, increasing the chances of an injury.

Several shoe companies have tried to offset the weaknesses of the two midsole materials by combining them. Some use a basic

EVA midsole surrounded by PU to try to protect the EVA from breakdown. Unfortunately, this approach appears to have little if any effect on the rate of breakdown.

Technology moves in. Two other innovations have enjoyed much greater success: the additions of air and gel to the midsoles. Air canals, one of the first major developments in midsole technology, were pioneered by Nike. The air, which provides excellent shock absorption, is encapsulated in PU. Since the air canals are completely sealed, they basically last forever.

The disadvantage of air lies in the extreme amount of motion that it allows. It's like standing on an air mattress. It's very soft but allows you to move a lot, giving no stability and, if your feet are too loose to start with, possibly increasing the risk of injury from excessive motion.

Gel shoes, developed by Asics, incorporate a silicone-based gel compound into a compression-molded EVA midsole. This manufacturing method involves sealing the gel for better shock absorption. The EVA supplies the stability, while the gel gives extra shock absorption. Like air canals, the gel won't break down with use.

The Lowdown on Uppers

Despite the flashy colors and eye-catching designs, the upper part of the shoe *isn't* just for looks—it also provides valuable support.

The way the upper attaches to the midsole has traditionally been a problem for the runner with an excessive amount of motion. Too much pronation (inward rolling of the foot) causes the area around the inside ankle bone to push inward against the upper of the shoe. This additional force can cause the rear part of the upper, the heel counter, to pull away from the midsole or to bend inward.

To counteract this, many shoes have heel-counter reinforcements to protect that area from breakdown. These supports range from thin plastic external half circles just above the midsole to vertical midsole extension collars.

The plastic half circle is primarily aesthetic and gives little functional support. The extension collar, however, is actually the EVA or polyurethane midsole molded as a unit to support the heel counter.

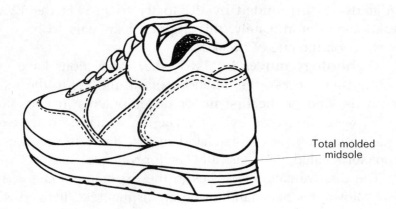

Total molded
midsole

TOTAL MOLDED MIDSOLE

Various types of reinforcement are built into shoes at the back. The total molded midsole is designed to control excessive pronation and to keep the shoe's heel area from breaking down with prolonged use.

This collar prevents the counter from being pushed inward or outward as the foot rolls, and limits the breakdown of the counter.

Except for the rigid heel counter, the upper is designed of soft materials for comfort. Variable lacing systems improve the fit of the shoe since they allow adjustment for different foot widths.

If the upper of your shoe doesn't fit well, excessive motion may result and injuries may occur. In particular, calluses, blisters and damaged toenails result from poorly fitting shoes.

To ensure that you get shoes that fit properly, shop near the end of the day when your feet are slightly swollen. The heel should fit snugly, but your toes should not touch the ends of the shoe. Always try on shoes, as sizes vary between brands and sometimes even in different models of the same brand. Most men's shoes are in a D width and women's in a B width, but some brands offer width choices. Also, some brands run narrower or wider than others.

Shoes with full-grain or suede leather uppers tend to be more supportive than those made largely of nylon. But leather is also heavier, warmer and less resistant to moisture and heat changes, which can break it down. Synthetic leathers, which look and feel like leather but are actually made of plastic, are usually preferable to the natural variety because they share its support characteristics but are stronger and more durable.

Nylon and mesh uppers give a little less support than leather, but are usually lighter, "breathe" better and are more adaptable to changing weather and surface conditions. This material allows moisture to escape from the shoe, which keeps the shoe drier and helps cool your feet through evaporation. Most shoes combine nylon or mesh for coolness and lightness and leather for support.

Last but Not Least

The word "last" carries two important meanings in the shoe world: It describes both a method of construction *and* the shape of the shoe.

How your shoes are made. The upper part of the shoe is manufactured separately from the lower part (midsole and outsole) and then the parts are joined. The traditional method for wedding them is to glue the upper to a thin fiberboard and then cement it to the midsole and outsole. This is called "board lasting."

A second method called "slip lasting" eliminates the fiberboard. The upper, made like a moccasin, is sewn into one piece that encircles the foot. This is glued directly to the sole unit.

A combination last combines the two methods. The most popular of these comes with the rearfoot board-lasted and the forefoot slip-lasted. To figure out what kind of last is used in a shoe, pull out the innersole. In a board-lasted shoe you can see the smooth board, while in a slip-lasted shoe you'll see a line of stitching running up the middle. In a combination shoe you'll see a board in the back of the shoe and stitching near the front.

The advantage of board lasting is that it gives the foot more stability: It rests on a flat, firm surface. The disadvantage is that you sacrifice some cushioning.

The opposite is true of slip lasting. The foot rides directly on the midsole, which is always being compressed and is moving around. You get the maximum amount of shock absorption this

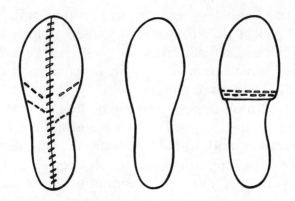

SHOE CONSTRUCTION

If you pull the insole out of running shoes, you can see how they're made. In slip-lasted shoes (*left*) you can see the stitching that sews the shoe together in a "moccasin" style; in board-lasted shoes (*middle*) you can see a firm, smooth fiberboard; in combination-lasted shoes (*right*) you'll see a board in the back of the shoe and stitching in the toe area. Slip-lasted shoes are for runners who need a flexible shoe with added cushioning; board-lasted shoes provide maximum stability and motion control; combination-lasted shoes provide a compromise.

way but also maximum motion. If you have excessive pronation to begin with, this type of lasting will only add to your woes.

Find the optimum shape. The other use of the term "last" has to do with the form on which the shoe was made. All shoe companies use a model of the foot called a last; these vary according to size and width. They also vary from company to company and sometimes even from model to model.

So while you might get a comfortable fit in one model of Brand Z, another model from the same company might fit differently. To make matters even more complicated, how the upper is stretched over the last can make the shoe tighter or narrower.

Some companies use painstaking research to find correct size and length ratios, while others just use the last that their factory recommends. Shoes made in the United States will differ greatly in width and length from those made in Asia, where most shoes are made.

At one time women's shoes were just smaller models of men's, but now most major athletic shoe manufacturers realize that the proportions of a woman's feet differ from a man's. They sell women's running shoes made on lasts specifically designed for women's feet, and usually advertise that fact. Unfortunately, unless the shoe company tells you in its ads, it's difficult to know how their lasts are designed.

Another difference in lasts is the curve, or the angle from the heel to the toe area. A so-called straight-lasted shoe has very little angle from the rearfoot to the forefoot. Theoretically, it could be worn on either foot without a difference being noticed.

But since most feet have some degree of curve, most running shoes, even those called straight-lasted, have some curve to the last. No company makes a completely straight shoe now, although several models still carry that designation. Those shoes usually have about three degrees of curvature, while the average curve for running shoes is five to seven degrees. In chapter 5 I'll tell you how to determine which type of last you require.

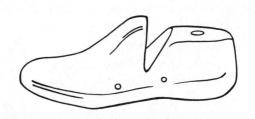

SHOEMAKER'S LAST

Shoes are built on a model called a last. The shapes and sizes of lasts vary markedly among manufacturers.

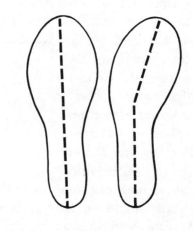

LAST SHAPES

You can get shoes that are built on a straight last or a curved last. Shoes with a straighter construction generally restrict motion, while curved ones allow more.

WHEN YOUR SHOES' TIME HAS COME

So how long can you run in your shoes? There's no hard and fast rule, but a normal running shoe will last between 300 and 500 miles. You can also tell if your shoes are nearing the end of their useful life by eyeballing them. The outersole of the shoe should still have plenty of tread on it, *never* worn into the midsole. The upper material should be intact, without holes or tears. When you set your shoes on a level surface, the back of the heel counter should be sitting straight up and down, not listing off to one side.

I once read an advertisement featuring a runner who had logged more than 2,000 miles in one pair of shoes. That's more than four times the suggested life of the shoe. This runner's shoes looked like rejects from a thrift shop.

Pushing your shoes this far is like driving your car without changing the oil. It will work sometimes, but sooner or later an expensive problem will certainly pop up.

You can help avoid trouble by *never* running in a shoe to the point that it's worn out or even close to it. You can wear them around the house or garden, as long as you don't walk or stand too long in them.

TIME TO SAY GOODBYE

Running shoes have a finite life span—and these have passed it. Severely worn soles, compressed soles and distorted heel counters mean you're overdue for a new pair.

Innersoles: Built for Comfort

The innersole, also called the "sock liner," is usually highly touted by shoe companies. Its function, however, is minimal.

The innersole is designed to create a comfortable surface for your foot. Most of the time, the top cover is nylon or terry cloth. The remainder of the innersole is usually a foam material.

Arch supports are often incorporated into the innersoles or added to the bottom of the shoe. They *look* as if they have some function—but they don't. If you have a high-arched foot, the support in the shoe doesn't come into contact with the arch. But if you have a flat foot, your arch will rub against the so-called arch support in the innersole. That ends up being highly uncomfortable, so you have to trim it or pull it out.

Many runners think an arch support is an important part of a shoe, which is why the manufacturers put these soft foam objects into shoes but design them to stay out of your way. Most innersoles are removable so you can take them out to dry and air out. You can also wash them by hand, but not in a machine. The entire innersole can also be replaced with a new one—or, if necessary, an orthotic support that really does something. If you're having arch or heel pain, think about seeking even more support than your innersole provides.

If you have orthotics, custom-made inserts that help stabilize the foot, you can remove the shoes' innersoles and replace them with your custom-made devices. This alleviates the top complaint against orthotics: that they make the shoes fit too tightly.

Chapter 5

MATCHING THE SHOE
TO YOUR NEEDS

So your shoes are worn out—or you're just taking up the sport—and it's time to lay out some cash for a new pair. After reading the last chapter, you're well up on shoe terminology. What's next?

One of my patients, Milt, has two criteria for shoe selection: He buys either the most expensive shoes he can find or those with the fanciest colors. Then, after he runs in them for a week or two, he comes into my office to ask where he went wrong in his selection. I've told him this is a backward and expensive way to go about picking shoes. Milt, however, doesn't seem to care.

More commonly, runners make the mistake of looking for "bargains." They don't see past the price tag. A running buddy of mine used to brag about how much money he saved by buying discount, off-brand shoes. These gems cost him as little as $10 or $15. He would show off a new pair every three or four weeks. "After all," he pointed out, "I can buy four pairs of new shoes for every pair you buy and still have money left over."

That worked fine for about nine months, until he developed a stress fracture that ended up costing him quite a bit more than the price of a pair of top-quality shoes. He stopped his bragging after that.

Bargain Shoes Are No Bargain

Soon after I started running, in 1974, I saw a name brand of athletic shoes and the house brand side by side on a shelf at a department store. At a glance the shoes seemed identical, except for different stripes.

In fact, the salesclerk told me, "Both were made by the same company and will perform exactly the same." But on closer examination I could see that the name brand was lighter, more cushioned, more flexible and generally better constructed than the other brand. The house brand was stiff, heavy, and the stitching was already coming apart. (I generously choose to believe that the salesman was misinformed, not intentionally misleading.)

The simple fact is that reputable manufacturers only sell shoes under their own label and don't make them for anyone else. They also don't sell defective products. The same, unfortunately, cannot be said of the cheap impostors. The buyer must truly beware of these shoes.

How do you know if the shoe you pick up is really the brand it says it is? There's always the chance that you're buying an illegal knockoff, a shoe that *looks* like the real thing but isn't. Unfortunately it's tough to tell, although it can help to look the shoe over to check the quality of the construction.

What to Look For

Almost all running shoes are specifically designed for certain foot types and vulnerabilities. You need to know how to match those features up with your particular requirements. If you can do that, you can significantly reduce your chances of injury—and add to your comfort and performance. The reverse, of course, is also true. Choose your running shoes passively, sloppily or cheaply and you'll suffer for it.

Most of the major athletic shoe manufacturers know the different foot types and design specific shoes for specific biomechanical needs. But they sometimes have a hard time communicating with the runners who purchase these shoes.

I remember a shoe ad that boldly stated that one of its models had an "anti-pronation system"—which implies that you want to eliminate pronation. This is the *last* thing you want to do, because pronation is a natural and necessary part of running. (I suspect the advertisers intended these shoes to limit pronation for those people who overpronate.)

Another company used to advertise shoes for "supinators," while failing to explain that only a tiny percentage of the population supinates excessively (roll their feet outward too much). Many of the runners who purchased these shoes ended up exaggerating their biomechanical abnormalities—and creating the injury they thought the shoes would prevent.

Learn to select shoes based upon your foot type, biomechanical considerations and injury history. You learned in chapter 1 how to tell if you pronate excessively (a sports-medicine specialist can also tell you). Once you know this, you're well on your way to getting the right shoe.

Overpronators Have Specific Needs

The excessively pronated foot usually has all the shock absorption it needs but lacks stability. When you overpronate, your feet roll inward too much, then loosen up and provide a great deal of shock absorption.

Look for a firm shoe with lots of support. The more motion-control devices such as multidensity midsoles and reinforced heel counters you can find on the shoe the better. You'll sacrifice a little bit of shock absorption, but don't worry about that because your feet already do a pretty good job in that regard.

The outsole for the overpronator should be firm carbon rubber to give a stable base. The rear-heel area should be made of solid rubber to provide extra protection against wear and to maintain the flat platform of the sole. You don't want biomechanical problems to be exacerbated by an outsole that quickly wears down on the outside portion of the heel. To find out what rubber was used in a particular shoe, read the hang-tag that accompanies most running shoes and describes their features. If you can't find a description on

TAKE CARE OF YOUR SHOES
AND THEY'LL TAKE CARE OF YOU

You polish your car. You keep your bicycle clean and lubricated. You paint your house and wash the windows.

But your running shoes often get kicked into a corner of a room—wet, dirty and neglected. The elements can be tough on running shoes. Hot, humid or wet runs accelerate the breakdown of the material in the shoe, especially at the midsole.

It's best to have at least two pairs of running shoes. They need not be the exact same brand or model, but they do need to be similar in lasting and functional features. This way you can alternate shoes for your runs, allowing each pair time to dry from your perspiration or from rainy workouts. (Shoes should dry at least 24 hours; 48 hours is ideal.) Alternating shoes will also extend the life of each pair.

Many runners aren't aware that most athletic shoes can be washed—which will make them not only *look* better but, in some cases, smell better. Wash them by hand, with a soft brush, mild soap and cold water and then let them air-dry.

Don't try what my friend Maurice did. He placed his shoes in the oven to dry after a run. Unfortunately, his wife came home and turned on the oven to preheat it without checking inside. Maurice soon faced two problems: eliminating the aroma of melted shoe from his house *and* figuring out what new shoes to buy.

Store your shoes in a cool, dry area. One patient came to my office with a pair of shoes with the outersole significantly bigger than the midsole. It turned out that she had left the shoes on the back seat of her car with the sun beaming down on them. Even though it wasn't a particularly hot day, the heat still became so intense that the midsole shrunk.

Whenever you're in doubt about the condition of your shoes, either ask the opinion of someone who specializes in shoes or play it safe and get a new pair. Shoes are your most important investment in running. If you take good care of them, they will take care of you.

the shoe or in the box, ask the salesclerk. The store will normally have tech sheets which fully describe the characteristics of the shoe, including sole type and material.

Avoid extra-soft or cantilevered soles. These look like a sideways C with the open end of the C on the ground; when your foot hits the ground the outsole compresses and absorbs shock. The additional shock absorption these shoes provide will create even more motion.

Likewise, you will want a fairly firm midsole. Look for a dual-density midsole with the firmer material on the inside edge to help control the overpronation. This construction is fairly easy to spot, since the midsole will usually come in different colors. The midsole might be white and the firmer material gray, for instance.

A totally board-lasted shoe (or, if you can't find one, a rear board-lasted shoe) provides stability. The straightest-lasted shoe that is comfortable gives extra protection against overpronation.

The firmest possible heel counter further minimizes excessive motion. Squeeze the back of the heel counter to determine its firmness; the firmer the better. The upper of the shoe should also have a variable lacing system for better fit and function. Variable lacing has two sets of eyelets placed alternately: Runners with narrow feet can use the eyelets farther from the tongue and those with wide feet can use the closer eyelets. Leather reinforcements in the saddle and forefoot area are preferable. This helps resist sideways motion and reinforces the shoe's upper.

Stability in a shoe is extremely important for the overpronator. Avoid highly cushioned soles, very soft or air midsoles, slip-lasted shoes, flimsy heel counters, weak upper support or those shoes curve-lasted nine degrees or more. (To determine the curve, ask the store clerk to locate the tech sheets.)

The Underpronators

Essentially, you can simply reverse everything I've just said for this type of foot, which hardly rolls inward at all once it strikes the ground and usually has a high arch. If you underpronate—or are one of the very rare people who supinate too much—you will respond best to the shoes that supply the greatest amount of cushioning. The softer, the better—as long as it won't wear out in a week or two. Because this foot type doesn't roll in and out very much, motion is limited, so it does a poor job of absorbing shock.

Shock-absorbing characteristics in a shoe help to compensate for your foot type and a flexible shoe gives your foot a little more freedom to move. With this foot type, forget about motion-control devices such as dual-density midsoles—you don't need them and they might do more harm than good by preventing motion that your foot might need. More motion, not less, is required of runners with this foot type. Shoes designed to prevent motion will also usually be firmer, which is not what you want for a high-arched foot.

The midsole should be soft or made of gel or air canals. A slip-lasted shoe is preferable, as is a last with a curve of seven degrees or greater. (See the tech sheets to determine the curve.)

"Corrective" Shoes for Common Running Injuries

Using your newly found knowledge of biomechanics, you can find the shoes most likely to alleviate your particular problem.

Hip pains. This pain usually occurs on the outside of the hip area. Mechanically, the symptoms can be reduced through better shock absorption. Look for soft midsoles and slip lasting. Forget pronation control.

Knee pains. If the pain is on the outside of the knee, look for a shoe with a dual-density midsole, rear-board lasting and the firmest possible heel counter to control the motion. If the pain is on the inner side of the knee, it's probably related to excessive shock and you need a shoe with soft midsoles, no motion control and cushioned innersoles.

Shin splints. These most commonly plague new runners and female runners. Women tend to have wider hips than men, so their feet strike the ground at a slightly greater angle than men's feet. Because after footstrike the foot then pronates so it will be flat on the ground, women need more motion than men to reach that position. This makes the muscles work harder and increases the likelihood of shin splints.

New runners of either sex often develop this injury because

WHICH SHOE FOR YOU?

When searching for your ideal shoe, start by determining your foot, gait, leg type and degree of motion at the top of this chart. (Refer back to chapter 1.) Then match "yes" responses to the shoe characteristics listed down the left side.

	Arch			Pronation		
Shoe Features	Flat feet	High arch	Normal arch	Over-pronation	Under-pronation	Normal-pronation
Soft midsole	no	yes	yes	no	yes	yes
Firm midsole	yes	no	yes	yes	no	yes
Motion control	yes	no	no	yes	no	no
Orthotic insole	yes	no	no	yes	no	no
Slip-lasted	no	yes	yes	no	yes	yes
Combination lasted	yes	no	yes	yes	no	yes
Flatter outsole	yes	no	yes	yes	no	yes
Waffle outsole	no	yes	yes	no	yes	yes
External heel counter	yes	yes	no	yes	yes	no

the muscles on the front and insides of their legs are weak. This muscle problem usually solves itself as runners become more fit.

When the shin pain is caused by a muscular or tendon strain—

Leg Structure			Motion		
Bow legs	Knock knees	Normal	Excess	Little	Normal
no	yes	yes	no	yes	yes
yes	no	yes	yes	no	yes
yes	no	no	yes	no	no
yes	no	no	yes	no	no
no	yes	yes	no	yes	yes
yes	no	yes	yes	no	yes
yes	no	yes	yes	no	yes
no	yes	yes	no	yes	yes
yes	yes	no	yes	yes	no

which only a doctor can diagnose—the likely cause is usually too much pronation. Choose a combination-lasted shoe rather than one with a full-board last. The combination lasting allows more flexibility in the forefoot, which reduces strain on the inflamed tissue.

However, shin splints can also result from irritation to the lining of the leg bones. With this type of injury, pain radiates up and down most of the leg's length. This comes from too much jarring; you need shock-absorbing shoes with good flexibility, soft midsoles and a lot of cushioning.

Achilles tendinitis. This is pain and inflammation in the large tendon that connects the heel and the calf muscles. It has two main causes: too much work by your calf muscle and tightness in the posterior muscle groups. Go with a shoe designed for the overpronator, with a thick, very firm rearfoot midsole and a plastic internal heel cup that supports your heel and keeps your tendon from stretching excessively.

Also look for a shoe with a flexible forefoot that further lessens the work that the Achilles tendon must do. Your calf muscle and Achilles tendon flex your foot downward and help you push off in running. Your forefoot bends so that your heel can lift off the ground but your toes remain on the ground for stability. If your shoe doesn't flex well at the forefoot, your calf muscles will have to work harder to lift your heel—creating an overuse situation.

To test a shoe's flexibility, simply bend it with your hands. The easier it flexes, the less your Achilles tendon will be stretched.

Chronic ankle sprains. These usually result from too much motion at the joint or previous injuries that have stretched out the ligaments that help stabilize your ankle, especially those on the outside. Look for stability and a firm midsole. Shoes with firm and relatively flat soles and midsoles, board-lasting and straight-lasting give the best support.

Plantar fasciitis and heel-spur syndrome. The plantar fascia is a long, supportive band of tissue that runs along the bottom of your foot from your heel, through the arch and into the ball of the foot. When strained, you normally feel pain under your heel or in your arch. Sometimes the pull becomes so great that it causes a bone spur to form under your heel. Plantar fasciitis and heel-spur syndrome are generally caused by a collapsing arch and a tendency toward overpronation. Shoes for overpronators with built-in arch support, dual-density midsoles and firm heel counters offer a partial solution because they give your foot more support, but you also

FOREFOOT FLEXIBILITY

One of the simplest tests you can perform while shopping for a shoe is to bend it at the point where the ball of your foot would rest. The sole should bend easily. Otherwise, your foot and leg muscles must work overtime just to flex the shoe.

need more support under the arch. You can get this from over-the-counter supports or custom-made orthotics. These inserts work best with board-lasted shoes with removable innersoles.

Metatarsal pains. Excessive impact usually causes metatarsal stress fractures and other symptoms beneath the ball of your foot. A forefoot slip-lasted shoe gives the greatest amount of cushioning in this area. This should also be the most flexible shoe you can find. Look for the softest midsole available, such as those with gel or air.

Chapter 6

FIRST AID FOR RUNNERS

Dave is one of my favorite patients. Over the past 15 years he has probably suffered at least a dozen injuries—almost all due to errors in his training.

What makes Dave so interesting is his innovative but often ill-designed methods of self-treatment. He always attempts to treat his problem with the worst possible method.

He sits in a Jacuzzi when he should be applying ice. He lifts weights when he has an injury that should be immobilized. If he needs to rest to recuperate, you just know he's going to go out and try to finish a 20-miler.

By the time Dave comes into the office, besides the original injury, we have to treat the additional damage Dave has inflicted upon himself *plus* other injuries caused by his body trying to compensate for the original injury. (When you have an injury, you favor the injured area by placing more force on another part.) I try to schedule Dave as my last patient of the day because it usually takes quite a while to run through his list of problems—most of them occurring *after* he tried treating his initial injury.

The sad part is that the original injury usually wasn't too big of a deal.

You don't want to end up like Dave. Once you recognize that an injury has occurred or is about to happen, you can act quickly to minimize the damage and speed the recovery. You just need to know the methods at your disposal and how they work—as well as the possible side-effects of your actions once you start playing doctor.

Proceed Cautiously with Self-Treatment

The laws of averages still say that you will sustain at least one serious injury in your career. In fact, the average is four or five injuries per running career.

Like most runners, you'll probably attempt to treat the injury yourself before seeking professional medical treatment. There's nothing wrong with that, *provided* you have a reasonable idea of what you're doing. Trying to self-administer the incorrect treatment is worse than just leaving your injury alone. You might compound the problem and slow down the healing. And the longer an injury goes without proper treatment, the harder it is to correct.

Look at one runner I treated, who had what he thought were shin splints. He decided that he could overcome his problem with stretching and massage therapy.

But after a month of this—and his continued attempts to run— he finally came to my office. I discovered a stress fracture of his lower leg. All of his massage treatments and running had irritated the injury to the point that it was so inflamed he couldn't even walk normally.

I placed a cast on his leg—in part to help the fracture heal, but also to keep him from monkeying around with it. A condition that normally would have allowed him to run within six weeks sidelined this poor fellow for twice that long.

So consider yourself warned. While there are various ways to treat yourself, you must also know the limitations of self-treatment—as well as your own limitations.

RICE Is a Nice Start

With few exceptions—nerve injuries, for instance—your first-aid treatment begins with "RICE"—which stands for Rest, Ice, Compression and Elevation.

Whenever you're injured, inflammation occurs and this inflammation is what causes much of your pain. This inflammation is your body's natural response to an injury. It comes with five signs and symptoms: redness, swelling, warmth, pain and diminished function of the inflamed area.

As soon as the injury occurs, the small blood vessels around the injured area dilate, becoming larger and allowing more blood into the area. The increased blood flow causes the redness and increases the temperature around the injury site.

RICE FOR RELIEF

Injuries invariably involve inflammation, which, if left unchecked, will delay healing. You need to rest the injury, as well as ice, compress and elevate it, to help halt inflammation. An excellent way to do this is with an ice bag strapped in place with an elastic bandage.

The dilated blood vessels also allow certain proteins to filter into the surrounding tissues, and some of these proteins irritate the tissues, causing swelling. This swelling and irritation cause the pain and diminished function.

You may not see or *feel* all five of these signs and symptoms, but they're always present. An injured ankle, for instance, may not look swollen, but if it hurts there's swelling someplace—maybe at the cellular level or between spaces in the tissues. The same is true with the redness, warmth and loss of function. If the injury hurts (and what injury doesn't?), you're experiencing the signs and symptoms of inflammation at some level whether you know it or not.

Even though inflammation is inevitable, how much swelling you get depends on the extent of the injury and your actions immediately afterward. RICE is your first line of defense for injuries.

The Value of Rest

This is the most important treatment of an injury. But it also has the dubious distinction of being the most ignored.

Many runners believe they'll turn into a blob of fat if they miss any running. They think that five years of training will go down the drain if they're out for a week.

Fear not. "Rest" doesn't necessarily mean that you must cease all activity. You may have to take a day or two off to keep inflammation down in the injured part, but often you can either temporarily take up another activity or begin running again soon thereafter.

In some cases, rest just means finding an appropriate treatment to take stress away from the injured area. Carl, another runner I treated, hurt his big toe joint by stubbing it on a coffee table in the dark. It swelled badly but only hurt when he pushed off during running.

We fashioned a simple splint for the toe that wouldn't allow it to bend as much as normal. This was all the "rest" Carl needed and he was able to keep running.

The point here is that you have to take stress off the injury. When an area becomes injured, you have exceeded its ability to perform the work you're asking it to do. So medical experience and common sense tell you to decrease the activity.

Sometimes "rest" does mean cutting back on or temporarily quitting running, but it seldom means that you must cease *all* activity. In most cases you can substitute another activity. (Various cross-training options are detailed in chapter 22.)

But before you jump into another sport, evaluate your injury and pinpoint its location. Don't settle for generalities; find the *exact* location as well as the motions that cause it to hurt you.

For instance, an ankle sprain might hurt when you bend your ankle inward, but not when you flex your foot up and down or twist your ankle outward. Thus, bicycling—where your foot and ankle only bend upward and downward—will probably not aggravate the ankle problem. Whether you make this determination yourself or let a doctor decide will depend on the severity of the injury.

Most runners think in terms of replicating the muscle movements used in running in these alternate workouts. But the psychological contribution of these alternate sports is at least equally important—they keep alive the habits and routines of daily training.

Running has a profound psychological effect. Psychiatrist Thaddeus Kostrubala, M.D., felt so strongly about the mental benefits of running that he introduced it as a therapy technique in his book, *The Joy of Running*. Rather than giving medication to his patients, he went on runs with them and then used the physiological and mental changes associated with running to help them communicate their problems to him. He felt these changes from running helped improve their response to therapy.

Sometimes, though, you just have to swallow your pride and take some pure rest. For severe knee or ankle injuries, fractures and certain back injuries, your doctor may prescribe rest with *no* alternative activities. This is easier to accept if you recognize the profound contribution of this rest toward your goal—to heal completely and resume your normal running as soon as possible. And it may help to realize studies have shown that even after three months of inactivity, you lose only about 10 percent of your cardiovascular endurance.

Ice Is S-o-o-o Nice

Ice is one of the most important anti-inflammatory tools in your arsenal of treatments—and also the simplest and cheapest. The benefits of icing your injured area can't be overstated.

Although a Jacuzzi or warm bath might feel nice, it won't help you to heal. Heat *increases* the swelling and bleeding of your injury. Cold, however, can penetrate the barrier of skin and fat and

SO, WHAT WENT WRONG?

One positive way to wait out your injury is to do some soul-searching. Rather than sitting around bemoaning your fate, look back at what went wrong. Rather than blaming the gods of running, think about what *you* did to cause the problem.

In particular, try to assess your complete running profile. This includes mileage, speed, type of workout, running surface, time of day when you train, equipment changes, injury history and anything else worth noting. You should be regularly recording such information in your training log.

Now take out your running log and rethink the weeks preceding the injury. Ask yourself these questions:

■ Did you train excessively or not enough for a certain race?

■ Did you make a sudden change in your training program?

■ Did you change shoes?

■ Do you suffer from a lack of flexibility or imbalances of strength?

■ Did you fail to heed your body's warning signs or read them inaccurately?

Any small alteration in your equipment or training can lead to an injury. Even running at a different time of day or on the opposite side of the road can hurt you.

The quicker you recognize what happened, the sooner you can make peace with the result and the clearer you can see your way out of this morass. Better yet, you now have good reason to think this problem won't repeat itself later.

effectively reach the injured muscle, tendon or ligament.

Initially, ice works by decreasing the blood flow to an area. As that occurs, you notice the area turning white as blood is shunted around the injured site. After several minutes of icing, the available blood supply increases. Your body realizes that it has plenty of warmth and, to keep that part from freezing, it increases the blood flow locally. This brings in much-needed nutrients while flushing out the waste products of the injury. You know this is occurring because your skin now turns red.

Icing can be done immediately after a run or at least two hours before a workout. But *never* ice immediately before training. It has an anesthetizing effect and will block the pain response that gives you a warning signal of an injury.

As a general rule, ice the injury several times a day—for 15 to 20 minutes—starting immediately after you are hurt. Any time delay allows more inflammation to occur.

You can pack ice in a towel and hold it tightly to the injured area. Or you can massage a smaller area with ice. A convenient way to perform ice massage is to freeze water in styrofoam cups. You peel off the top half of the cup, exposing ice for the massage, while holding on to the bottom of the insulated cup. The cup helps keep your hand from getting frigid, while the injured area gets the full effect of the ice.

I don't recommend commercial ice packs, which tend to be either too cold or not cold enough. Commercial preparations that are too cold might cause skin and nerve damage. If they retain their coldness too long, they can "burn" the skin and even injure the underlying nerves. That never happens with real ice.

On the other hand, many of the "blue-ice" preparations lose much of their coldness after only 5 to 10 minutes. You are then left with a cool pack instead of an ice pack and "cool" isn't an effective treatment.

How Compression Helps

Inflammation and swelling cause fluid to fill the area surrounding the injury. Then after the swelling has diminished, your body still faces the task of eliminating all that fluid and other matter, such as dried blood, it had deposited in the area.

Healing is speeded if you minimize the amount of swelling that occurs in the first place, and this is where compression comes in. Compressing an injury as soon as possible after you're hurt helps decrease the amount of swelling that occurs, because it's harder for your heart to pump the fluid into an area that is compressed. Minimizing swelling minimizes pain and speeds your healing.

To compress an area, simply apply a uniform pressure. The simplest way to do this is with an elastic wrap such as an Ace bandage. There are also compressive tapes, compressive socks and neoprene sleeves.

The compression should be somewhat gentle. It also should involve a much greater area than is injured. For instance, in an ankle wrap the foot and lower one-third of the leg are included.

Lift Up the Injured Area

Some bleeding occurs within the tissues at the time of injury—and gravity helps pull the blood into that area. By elevating the injured part higher than your heart, you partly negate the force of gravity. The blood can't be pumped as hard to that part, reducing fluid buildup.

Elevate the injured area as much as possible during the first 48 hours post-injury. The best way to do this is to lie down with the injured limb elevated on pillows. After those two days, elevation provides little additional help.

At this point, you need to be thinking about long-term treatment and more lasting cures. These may include seeking medical advice, making changes in your footwear, altering your future training and supplementing that training with certain exercises—all of which are covered in subsequent chapters.

Chapter 7

PRODUCTS THAT WORK
(AND SOME THAT DON'T)

You're running well—everything is clicking, you're feeling good and your times are steadily getting faster. Then you get injured.

If it's your first injury, you'll likely ask your running friends for advice. Or you might seek help from the athletic store where you buy shoes.

You'll find a wide variety of remedies in both athletic stores and drugstores: everything from salves and ointments to innersoles and braces, all claiming to be exactly what you need. How do you know what will really work for your particular condition, which advertising claims are valid and which are not?

What follows is a buyer's guide to many of the pain-relief products available to you over the counter. Six categories are discussed:

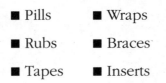

■ Pills   ■ Wraps

■ Rubs   ■ Braces

■ Tapes   ■ Inserts

Proceed Cautiously with Pills

The first instinct of many runners with any type of pain—tendinitis, muscle strain, ligament damage and even fractures—is to reach for an over-the-counter pill to lessen the pain. So there you are in the drugstore, gazing at shelf after shelf of pain relievers. How do you know what to buy?

Whenever you have an injury, you also have inflammation, which causes your pain. Simple pain relievers such as acetaminophen, however, only lessen the pain and do not have anti-inflammatory properties. They may make you *feel* better, but they don't deal with the underlying problem. These painkillers just fool your brain into thinking nothing is wrong—they block the pain symptoms rather than relieve the inflammation.

What you need is a pill that acts as both an anti-inflammatory and a painkiller. These medications reduce the fluid buildup, the redness *and* the pain. Over-the-counter anti-inflammatories include ibuprofen and aspirin, which also have some pain-killing effects.

You should use these products only as needed—to treat pain from an injury, or soreness immediately after a strenuous race or training run. The chronic use of these anti-inflammatories is *not* a good idea. Instead of medicating away the discomfort again and again, try to find ways to keep it from occurring in the first place—such as cutting back on running mileage or intensity, changing surfaces or wearing different shoes.

The problem is that anti-inflammatory medications can be brutal on your stomach, liver and kidneys and can cause a great deal of bleeding within your digestive system. Even nonaspirin anti-inflammatories such as ibuprofen can be hard on the liver. To minimize this, take them with a meal or with a lot of water. Even then, they can cause gastric irritation or worse.

One runner I know, Frank, began taking eight aspirin a day so he could continue running while injured. Although that is not an abnormally large quantity, he took them for such a long period of time (six months) that he developed a serious stomach ulcer. The last time I saw Frank, he was on his way to surgery for the ulcer.

So even though the medication is over-the-counter, that doesn't mean it can't harm you. Always be aware of the complications of any medicine you are taking: Read the label and insert, if there is one. Follow the directions on the label to the letter and never exceed the recommended dosages. (Never take more than 12 aspirin in 24 hours, and don't take them for more than 10 days, for example.) Remember that these pills are for short-term relief. Any pain that lasts longer than four or five days should be considered beyond the scope of the medication and you should seek professional help.

Rubs Aren't a Shortcut to Warming Up

Mary provides a good example of what warming rubs *don't* accomplish. Mary isn't what you would call a morning person. On race days, by the time she got up, dressed and had coffee, there was no way she could make it to the race in time to stretch and warm up properly.

Then she saw an ad in a running publication for an ointment (also called a "healing salve") that promised to end her problems. "Just rub it on before your run," the ad claimed, "and it will warm up your muscles and tendons within five minutes."

Mary thought it was working fine until she pulled her Achilles tendon early in a race on a cold day. My diagnosis: Because she failed to warm up and do flexibility exercises, Mary's Achilles was too tight. The sudden stress of the race had caused a slight tear in the tendon.

I don't believe that heating rubs or salves do much to warm the muscles of either a healthy or an injured runner. A fast walk or slow run will warm your muscles much more effectively than any of the commercial "heating" products. There aren't really any warmup shortcuts.

In fact, it is very difficult—if not impossible—for a topical heating agent to penetrate all the way down to your muscle. The warmth that you perceive when you rub on the salve is generally only superficial. (What you are really getting is a chemical irritation of the tissues, resulting in a sensation of warmth.) Your skin and maybe some superficial muscles warm up. But the bigger and deeper muscles that you really want warmed feel no effect. So you get a false sense of security that the muscles are warming and lengthening in preparation for your activity.

I also don't recommend using any of these heating agents after your run. After a workout you need to cool down, and heating up your skin or muscles would be pointless. A cooldown jog or walk will help decrease your heart rate gradually and return your muscles to their resting state gently.

And you shouldn't use these preparations for injuries. Even if they had their intended effect of warming up the deep tissues, this is exactly what you *don't* want when you're injured. Every injury involves inflammation and you want to cool that inflammatory process as quickly and completely as possible.

Treat injuries with cold, not heat. And the best cold treatment—as explained in the previous chapter—is ice.

Taping Can Supply Support

Frank Shorter, the 1972 Olympic marathon champion, used to tape his arches before any run of consequence to prevent arch pain by supporting his arches and the surrounding muscles.

Many runners tape to prevent injuries such as ankle sprains, particularly before certain events such as track workouts and races. You can also tape various recently recovered injuries to protect them during workouts and races. Use a porous athletic tape, which you can find at sporting goods stores and drugstores.

The taping itself can be tricky. Ask your doctor or therapist to show you the proper wrapping for your particular injury, then follow those instructions carefully. Don't make up your own design: You can do more harm than good by taping your foot or ankle at the wrong angle.

Tape can also cause irritation, blisters and allergic reactions. The first rule of taping: Never apply tape directly to your bare skin. The chances of a irritation and blistering are high when you mix tape, exercise and sweat. Putting tape on skin is also a problem if you apply it over hair. If you do, you'll learn a whole new meaning of the word "pain" when you remove the tape.

To avoid this problem, use a prewrap, a thin foam that goes on the skin before the tape. This prevents the tape from sticking to your skin and virtually eliminates the chances for irritation. (You can find prewrap at sporting goods stores and drugstores.)

The second rule of taping is that you first try it in a run with little at stake—not, for instance, a race.

Runner Larry broke *both* rule number one and rule number two. After he had registered for a 10-K race, he developed a mild arch pain. Not wanting to lose his entry fee, he taped his arch the morning of the race. To make matters worse, he used gray plumber's tape rather than medical tape, and didn't use any pre-tape.

When I saw him the next day, the skin had peeled away from his entire arch area. His foot was bloody and raw, with speckles of gray adhesive dotting his foot. Larry wasn't able to wear shoes for almost a month. It was two months before he could run again.

One final word of advice: retape daily. Tape begins to stretch and loosen as soon as 30 minutes after you put it on, even though it may seem taut. (It continues to provide some support, though not as much.) By the next day, the tape isn't doing much of anything, so retape. Leave the tape off for a few hours between tapings to allow the skin to breathe.

Wraps Have Their Role, Too

Elastic wraps, such as Ace bandages, primarily compress the injury. This stretchable material can be wrapped around an injured area to provide a small degree of support as well as compression. Wraps work best when used immediately after an injury: The compression of the affected area minimizes the inflammation in the injured tissues.

But many runners continue using these wraps even after the injury has healed and there is no inflammation. They wear them for "support"—but wraps provide very little of that. Most wraps can be pulled, twisted or otherwise distorted with only a few pounds of pressure; think what the forces of your weight while running will do.

Wraps will, however, help your proprioceptive ability—the part of your nervous system that lets you detect where you are in relation to the ground. Your proprioception can become confused following an injury. You might, for instance, start to resprain your ankle before your brain registers that an injury is in progress. A wrap, however, can serve as an "early warning system" to let you know that your ankle is twisting. The pressure from the wrap will increase as the ankle begins to turn, triggering the proprioceptive fibers in your skin.

PROPER WRAPPING TECHNIQUE

Wrapping an injured ankle with an elastic bandage will help compress the area and retard inflammation. Follow the directional arrows in this series of drawings.

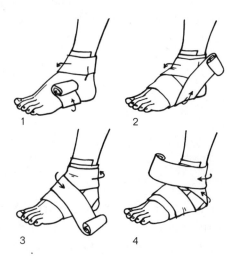

1

2

3

4

A good illustration of this: A patient of mine was playing basketball in high-top shoes when he came down from a rebound lopsided and his ankle started to twist. His brain registered the feel of the shoe material on his lower leg and immediately triggered a reflex that shifted his weight to the opposite foot. He ended up with only a minor ankle strain instead of a severe sprain. A wrap could have served the same purpose as the high-top shoe.

Neoprene sleeves perform a function similar to elastic wraps. These sleeves, made of wetsuit material, provide a little bit more compression than an Ace wrap and also provide some warmth around the affected area. Both wraps and sleeves can be found in sporting goods stores.

Braces Can Buttress Your Injury

Ankle or knee braces specially designed for athletes give even more support. You can buy some of these over-the-counter, but if

PROTECTIVE SLEEVE

A neoprene sleeve is shown here guarding an injured knee joint. Similar sleeves can be used on the ankle, calves or hamstrings while they heal.

you have an injury that warrants using a brace, you should see a sports-medicine specialist for treatment.

Braces are designed to keep lateral (sideways or twisting) motions from injuring the joints. Your knee and ankle joints are built to take all the flexing and extending you can give them. But they aren't created to handle much twisting or side-to-side movement. Braces allow the joints to flex and extend for straight-ahead movements but severely restrict side-to-side movements. They allow normal motions while minimizing abnormal motions.

If you sprain your ankle, your doctor might recommend a brace made of anything from soft canvas to hard metal stirrups to help keep you from respraining the ankle. Basically, the more severe your injury and the more support you need, the firmer or harder your brace should be. The firmer the material used for support, the more difficult it is for you to reinjure yourself.

Before you buy a brace, test it. Put it on and go through the motions of running very slowly and carefully. If the brace allows the movements that caused your injury, then obviously it won't do the job.

Also make sure that an ankle brace fits comfortably into your

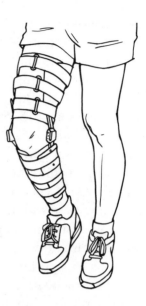

BRACING FOR INJURY

Braces give an extra measure of protection beyond that provided by tapes, wraps or sleeves.
Braces have stiffer reinforcing material and are
prescribed for more serious injuries.

running shoe and doesn't cause blisters or irritation. If your injury
and the merchant allow, go for a trial run with the brace on.

Inserts Give a Lift to Your Arches

For the *ultimate* in foot support and motion control, you need
custom-made orthotics—personally geared to your biomechanics,
foot type, specific injury tendency and the type of running you do.
Orthotics must be fitted by a sports-medicine specialist who works
with runners. (See Chapter 9.)

You can, however, buy inserts (these may be erroneously
called "orthotic devices") for moderate arch support. Those supports are readily available in sporting goods stores and pharmacies.
If your heel or arch becomes sore or you feel that you have a little
too much foot motion, inserts are a good and inexpensive first stab
at treatment. Spenco, Dr. Scholl's and Sorbothane all produce a relatively soft arch support.

Essentially the insert adds more material—whether Neoprene,
cork, leather or foam—under the arch area. As you run, your arch

pushes against the thick material of the insert to decrease motion and increase support. This may be all you need to ease your pain.

Many "off-the-shelf" inserts also have a built-in metatarsal support, seen as a "bump" at the forward edge. This ridge fits underneath and behind your metatarsal heads, just behind your toes, and alleviates pain in the ball of your foot. Certain nerve conditions, bone bruises and even metatarsal stress fractures can be helped with a metatarsal pad.

Most over-the-counter inserts wear out at about the same rate as your shoes. If you are using them more or less permanently, purchase a new pair whenever you replace your shoes.

A few companies sell do-it-yourself kits to make orthotic "inserts" for your shoes. Generally they supply a box of soft foam with instructions to step into it to make an imprint of your feet. You then send the foam box to the manufacturer, who supposedly fashions "custom" orthotics. In fact, I happen to know that most of these companies merely estimate your arch height and foot size from the molds, then send you a prefabricated insert. Usually these are plastic or other hard materials that aren't too suitable for running. The support you get is still a little better than the over-the-counter inserts give. But I don't recommend do-it-yourself orthotics: They occasionally work, but not reliably.

No mass-produced insert will be a panacea: The best you can hope for is a little extra arch support. But sometimes that bit of extra support can spell the difference between overcoming an injury on your own and seeking help from a doctor.

Chapter 8

WHEN YOU MUST SEE A DOCTOR

Jordan, a new patient, arrived in my office. When I asked him the reason for his visit, he took out a typed history of his injuries—five double-spaced pages.

That in itself wasn't *too* unusual. Runners often are compelled to document the course of their injuries and the various treatments they have attempted or had performed by health-care specialists. What was unusual about Jordan was that his injury was only two months old, yet he had volumes of documentation.

According to his log, he first paid a visit to his family doctor, who recommended that he begin taking an anti-inflammatory medication. Jordan wasn't sure he wanted to take those pills and, being somewhat on the cautious side, he sought the opinion of a different general practitioner.

This health specialist advised Jordan to stop running for a few weeks to give the injured area a rest. Jordan, like most runners, didn't like that advice, so he went to see an orthopedic surgeon. In fact, Jordan visited three orthopedic surgeons—all within a 10-day period! The treatments they advised ranged from anti-inflammatory medications to physical therapy to discontinuing running.

He opted for treatment by a physical therapist, who told him he had a gait imbalance and needed orthotic devices, which the therapist could make. But Jordan was concerned that he hadn't received a second opinion on *that* advice, so he went to a chiropractor. The chiropractor recommended adjustments, but was uncertain of the need for orthotics.

Four more visits to various health practitioners led Jordan to my office. And what was his problem?

A sprained ankle, and not even a bad one. All the doctors agreed on that. Jordan just wanted to find the *right* person to treat his injury—and preferably someone who would tell him it was okay to run.

His experiences had discouraged him. "Why can't any of you guys agree on what to do for my problem?" he asked. "What's wrong with health practitioners today?"

I would like to think that there is nothing wrong with us. But everyone in the medical field has different training, different experiences and different clinical abilities. Everyone also has different methods of treating certain injuries.

As Jordan learned, there are many possible treatments for any medical condition. Your task is to find the right professional for your particular problem.

Finding the Best Care-Giver

You should ensure that any medical specialist you see has sports-medicine training and experience. If a doctor spends most of the time specializing in geriatrics—treating elderly patients who may be physically challenged or bedridden—he or she isn't your best choice for a running injury. Likewise, your pediatrician may have helped you through many years of childhood illnesses and mishaps, but sports medicine is probably not that doctor's chosen practice.

Sports medicine is a demanding and intricate field. Your doctor must have knowledge of running mechanics, running shoes, and abnormalities that could cause problems in your gait and training. The doctor has to know how to put all these pieces together, like putting together a big jigsaw puzzle. And you need to know the extent of your doctor's training in this field.

I am reminded of a woman who came into my office complaining of frequent side stitches, pains in the side everyone who has ever run has had at least once. These nagging pains occur when you have overexerted yourself and allowed your diaphragm to go into oxygen debt, build up lactic acid and then go into spasm.

This runner had asked her OB-GYN about the pain, and reported that that doctor told her "Your insides are mixed up and you're not suitably built for running." In fact, merely slowing down her running and gradually allowing herself to build up her aerobic capacity resolved the problem. There was never anything wrong with her "insides."

Her doctor didn't have a sports-medicine background and really couldn't understand why this woman would want to run in the first place. If your doctor is like this, you'll find it almost impossible to get any help for running injuries.

This doesn't mean your doctor has to *be* a runner. I have known many excellent sports-medicine physicians who never ran a step. But they all understood not only the potential pitfalls of the sport but also what motivates runners.

Don't let looks fool you. Always consider the doctor's training, experience and, above all, personal recommendations from other runners who've received successful treatment from that doctor. Two excellent orthopedic surgeons I regularly work with don't run and aren't likely to be mistaken for runners—they weigh 450 pounds between them. John Beck, M.D., and Jeff Bronson, M.D., trained at some of the most prestigious sports-medicine institutes in the country. They are also among the most gifted and talented diagnosticians of athletes I've ever met.

All athlete-oriented practitioners should also belong to the American College of Sports Medicine (ACSM). The ACSM invites all medical specialists with a professional interest in this subject to join the society.

Your doctor normally will display a plaque indicating an association with the ACSM. If you don't see one, ask if he or she is a member. If not, you should seriously consider finding another doctor, whether it's your general practitioner or a specialist.

Never feel embarrassed to ask your doctors about the credentials that qualify them to treat you. Remember, it's your body they're treating—and you're the one paying for treatment. Just as you wouldn't allow a doctor not certified in open-heart surgery to perform such an operation on you, you shouldn't allow a doctor who lacks credentials in sports medicine to treat your athletic injury.

Involvement with sports-medicine groups helps keep the doctor up to date on the rapidly changing technology in this field. Many of the common practices of 5 or 10 years ago are outdated and no longer used. If your doctor is not aware of these changes, you are shortchanging yourself. You're liable to hear, "Well, if it hurts when you run, then just don't run." You certainly don't need to *pay* someone to tell you that.

Surveying the Specialists

My specialty is podiatry. Podiatrists, because they specialize in the feet—the starting point for most running injuries—have long been at the forefront of sports medicine, particularly as it applies to runners. But we're only one group of medical professionals available to you. Let's take a quick tour through the various professions, looking at what each one does (or doesn't) offer you.

General practice or family physician. Most people first seek treatment for an injury with their family doctor. After all, this is the physician they've known and trusted for years.

Nowadays, with the advent of health maintenance organizations, preferred provider groups and insurance company networks, many people are required to see their primary physician before being referred to a specialist. This is known as a "gatekeeper system"—your family doctor controls access to other physicians covered by your insurance plan. It's best if your primary doctor has some sports-medicine training and belongs to the ACSM. This way he or she can do a good job diagnosing your injury, treating minor ones and referring you to specialists for more complicated ones.

Generally, the family physician will guide you to another practitioner for specialized care. This will most commonly be a podiatrist or an orthopedic surgeon, though you might also be referred to a physical therapist, chiropractor or another practitioner with experience in treating runners.

Podiatrist. After four years of undergraduate training, a podiatrist undergoes four years of medical school and then up to three years of residency and/or fellowship. Podiatrists are experts on the foot and ankle, as well as the way the lower body moves as you walk or run.

Thus, all foot injuries from abrasions to fractures should be seen primarily by a podiatrist. And I'm not saying this just because I practice podiatry! Your podiatric physician can determine if you have a structural problem, a biomechanical problem or an injury that needs to be referred to another specialist.

Orthopedic surgeon. Podiatrists give most of their attention to the foot, while orthopedists are experts in the rest of the joints, muscles and bones. This includes your knee, hip and back.

A knee problem, for instance, should always be checked out first by an orthopedic surgeon. Although I have many runners come into my office with knee pains, a podiatrist is not really qualified to check out the inner workings of a knee. So I refer them to an orthopedic surgeon.

Podiatrists are thoroughly trained in biomechanics, however. A good, sports-minded orthopedic surgeon wouldn't hesitate to refer a patient to a podiatrist for a gait evaluation if there are no structural defects apparent in a knee injury.

Many orthopedic surgeons are conservative when it comes to surgery and offer options such as rehabilitation and rest. This is the type of person you want to treat your injury. Shy away from the orthopedist who suggests surgery after only a cursory examination. Granted, major injuries might need surgery, but the vast majority don't need it immediately. Other possibilities must at least be discussed.

Physical therapist. The physical therapist (PT) is one of the least utilized but most important health-care practitioners a runner can see. Physical therapists, who undergo two to three years of training after their undergraduate study, are specialists at treating musculoskeletal injuries. They do this with a combination of massage and manipulation, therapeutic exercises, hydrotherapy and various forms of electrotherapy and ultrasound.

I advise getting a physician's referral for physical therapy. (In fact, this is required in some states.) Most PTs I know aren't comfortable diagnosing problems. Once a diagnosis has been established by a doctor, the therapist has no problem with treatment.

Physical therapists are trained to treat soft-tissue, joint and muscle injuries. They evaluate your motion, strength and specific joint restrictions. Then they devise a treatment plan to return you to running as soon as possible.

When it comes to ankle sprains, tendinitis, muscle tears and strains and most post-operative care for running injuries, the therapist's office is the place to be. Ask for recommendations from other runners or at sport facilities such as health clubs. A good therapist will have a reputation for treating athletes successfully. You'll want a therapist who belongs to the sports or orthopedic section of the American Physical Therapy Association.

As with all other health practitioners, make sure your therapist works primarily with athletes. A therapist who spends most of the time treating patients in a hospital setting—say, accident victims or stroke patients—usually will not be as proficient at sports physical therapy as one who does little else.

Be wary of the "HUMmers"—an acronym for therapists who use Hot packs, Ultrasound and Massage and few other treatments. (Some nickname them "shake-and-bake artists.") Ask the physical therapist what type of treatments he or she uses. The answers you want to hear are one-on-one therapy, mobilization, massage, ice, ultrasound and electrical stimulation to help decrease swelling by driving out excess fluid. In general, avoid treatments involving heat.

I'm also not a big fan of the various rehab machines, such as Cybex and Lido, some physical therapists use. These are *workout* machines and will help measure certain strengths, but they don't really help much with rehabilitation.

The one-on-one approach is ideal. That way, the therapist can put you through the motions and exercises and constantly alter the resistance and repetitions depending on how you respond. A machine can't do that—at least not yet.

Chiropractor. Do you have a neck or back problem? A pain or ache that has started up in the last few weeks? A chiropractor's office is a good place to start looking for relief, especially while you're also working with a good physical therapist. The chiropractor restores mobility to the joints by manual manipulation while the therapist restores strength and function.

Chiropractors treat the entire body holistically without drugs or surgery. They do so by manual manipulation and the use of applied kinesiology. Their training teaches that most diseases are caused by interference with the nerve impulses and that they can be corrected with periodic adjustments. These specialists are well trained in kinesiology, the study of how you move. Their schooling involves an undergraduate degree, usually in a scientific field, and then three years in chiropractic school. Chiropractors are not allowed to prescribe medications or perform surgery.

In my estimation, chiropractors have much to offer within their area of expertise. However, my experience is that some of them try to go beyond the scope of their training. A prime example is the making of orthotics. This work is best left to a podiatrist who specializes in it.

Massage therapist. Masseurs can help work out sore areas and muscles that have been overused. Massage is effective after a hard workout or race, for instance.

Massage therapists with an interest in treating running injuries sometimes form sports-medicine massage practices. But for diagnosing an injury, you should really seek a health-care professional with diagnostic tools at his or her disposal rather than someone who will mainly massage whatever is ailing you.

First go to your medical practitioner for a referral to a sports masseur. Or find one through recommendations from friends *after* a specialist rules out certain illnesses.

Acupuncturist. Acupuncture has become an accepted part of Western medicine, but most of us understand very little about it. Acupuncture, which uses needles to stimulate various points in the body to correct energy imbalances, is designed to break a pain cycle. (Acupressure, which uses pressure instead of needles, works similarly.) When you feel pain, you will also experience inflammation and "guarding" of an area as your body tries to protect the injured part. That leads to even more pain, which in turn causes more inflammation. It's a vicious cycle.

One way to stop the cycle is to stop the pain. Once that's done, your body can start functioning more normally. This can assist in the healing process.

Remember, however, that pain also protects you. If you block the pain of a serious injury such as a muscle tear then you might do even more damage by wrongly assuming that you're cured.

Nowadays, many physicians practice acupuncture. If you're interested in this treatment, I recommend that you see an M.D. who is also an acupuncturist. This gives you the benefit of both traditional Western medicine and the Oriental philosophy of medicine.

Alternative-health professional. A wide variety of health professionals practice unconventional medicine. Basically, this means that they have not been accepted into the mainstream of Western medicine.

Their techniques include the Feldenkrais method, yoga, pilates, the Alexander technique, t'ai chi, herbal therapy and Rolfing. If you decide to utilize any of these therapies, I recommend they be done in conjunction with your physician rather than as an alternative. Unconventional health practitioners are largely unregulated and should be examined very closely to determine their suitability for treating your condition. Should you be inclined to pursue one of these options, your best bet would be to find an alternative-medicine practitioner who is also an M.D.

Also, there are few standards established to regulate the conduct of personal trainers, and there no licensing requirements. Anyone can call himself a "personal trainer" or "free-lance coach."

A good personal trainer helps you design and implement your training program. He or she also provides alternate exercises if you're injured. As for qualifications, a degree in exercise physiology is preferable. Otherwise, search for someone you can be comfortable with—and *not* just someone who sits and watches you work. You want an active trainer.

One word of caution: Many personal trainers are former top-class athletes and may expect more out of you than your body is willing to give. Make sure that both of you understand your goals completely before you start this trainer's program. His or her job is to improve your health and fitness, not to send you to one of the sports-medicine doctors' offices for repairs.

Chapter 9

WHAT THE DOCTOR CAN DO

Vicki was sold on our office before she ever stepped through the front door. "I scheduled appointments with two other doctors who listed themselves as sports-medicine specialists," she explained. "But after making my initial appointments, I called back and canceled them."

"What was the problem?" I asked. "A rude receptionist? An appointment too far in the future?"

"No," she replied, "the fact is that none of the other doctors' offices asked me to bring in my running shoes. How can they know what I am doing and how to treat a runner if they don't even look at my shoes?"

Good point. At my office, the receptionist always asks if the patient is being seen for an athletic injury. If the answer is yes, she asks the person to bring in their athletic shoes and clothing. Then I can watch you run, if necessary, or determine wear patterns of your shoes. This is a very important first step—and often the most important element of the visit. I don't just look at wear pattern of your shoes, but also their general condition. Broken-down, worn-down or unevenly worn shoes can provide essential clues as to why you're injured.

I also encourage runners to bring along their running logs. That way, I might discover how your training program has led to the injury. Overuse injuries are often easy to spot in a training log: Frequently, a detailed record of this injury's causes exists, in your own writing.

Although you might not appreciate the significance of all the questions I ask, everything has a bearing. Changes in shoes, changes in running surfaces, a race a week ago—all of these facts and more go into both the treatment of the current injury and the prevention of future injuries.

Next, I obtain a complete history of previous running injuries. I don't want to focus exclusively on the current injury, because I might miss a trend of recurring problems.

For instance, you might have had Achilles tendinitis which was resolved. Then a year later, plantar fasciitis might have developed. If I take shortcuts and fail to learn about the old Achilles injury, I might miss the cause of the current problem: The Achilles tendon pulls at the heel bone and puts a strain on the plantar fascia.

So you can see that the two problems might be directly related. The injury might have shifted from the back of the leg to under the foot. The symptoms may be different, but the cause is probably the same.

Then I'll probably videotape you running on a treadmill for one to two minutes. Next I play the video in slow motion so we can discuss your running pattern together. This way you can see exactly what I'm talking about as I point out any abnormalities in your biomechanics.

The videotape will answer these important questions: Do you overpronate or underpronate? Does your heel lift off the ground early? Do you toe in or toe out? Is your kneecap gliding evenly, or is it being pulled to one side or the other?

With this information we can piece together how the injury occurred, from a mechanical point of view. Then the treatment plan begins taking shape. Most importantly, because we discuss the videotape and clinical findings, you understand what has happened—or is continuing to happen—to cause your injury and why I am recommending the proposed treatment.

By the time you leave my office, I've tried to tell you exactly why your problem developed, what the solutions are and how to prevent a recurrence. You should expect nothing less at your doctor's office.

Don't Use Drugs as a Crutch

While taking histories on runners, they frequently tell me that in order to keep running they had to take medication ranging from aspirin all the way up to narcotic painkillers.

Use of pain medication for more than a few days is *not* a good idea, because pain is your body's best way of telling you that something is amiss. If you consistently block that pain, how can you possibly know what is going on?

Taking pills to help you run is like sticking your head in the sand to keep from looking a problem in the eye. You're masking a message that your body is trying to get through to you. This is not wise.

Use painkillers with care. Pain relievers are often prescribed to help a patient through an injury, and they certainly have their place. A fracture can be excruciating; even a stress fracture can be extremely painful. To ease the pain while the healing process is occurring, pain relievers might be prescribed to help the patient get on with everyday life and get a good night's sleep.

After all, there is more to life than running—such as working, taking care of a household and even just going to the restroom. Pain relievers can let you carry on without being in severe pain, but these drugs should not be used as a crutch. Never use them to keep running. Along with the medication, the doctor should give a clear warning as to what activities are safe and when you can resume running. Follow your doctor's advice to the letter.

Anti-inflammatory medications also are often prescribed to reduce swelling and pain. As with all drugs, they're only meant to give an early respite from the worst pains. They are *not* meant to let you continue running.

Beware of injected medications. Injections involve using a needle to deliver medication to a specific area of your body. For athletic injuries, the medications are usually an anesthetic or a steroid.

Anesthetics block pain and might break the pain cycle. Steroids, such as cortisone, are anti-inflammatory medications which reduce your body's normal reaction to injuries and stress. When the inflammation is reduced, healing can occur faster.

While these can be used for some muscle and tendon problems, injectable steroids should never be used around a fracture or an infection; the inflammatory reaction is absolutely necessary to allow healing in those cases. Also, there have been cases of tendons rupturing when injected with cortisone. Those areas need special precautions—especially non-activity for 48 hours following the injection.

Every doctor in sports medicine has heard horror stories of athletes being injected with painkillers or anti-inflammatories to complete a game. We normally see this in professional sports, but unfortunately the practice now seems to be spreading into college and high school athletics. I believe that *no* single game or event is important enough to place yourself in a potentially crippling situation.

Almost all pain relievers (especially the narcotics) affect your central nervous system. In a sense, your brain is not allowed to work correctly. Your reflexes are slowed and your perception is dulled. If you run while on medication, you might not see the curb that "springs up" in front of you until it is too late and you have fallen and sprained your ankle.

Other systems in your body, including your respiration and temperature-regulating ability, are influenced by narcotic painkillers. If you can't sweat and breathe properly, you can do serious and permanent harm to your body.

Forget about DMSO. Early in my career I treated a woman on the U.S. Olympic track team who had a nagging Achilles tendon strain. But with important track meets to compete in, she applied a substance called dimethyl sulfoxide (DMSO) to her tendon.

DMSO is an industrial solvent, also used in veterinary medicine, that penetrates the skin and has anti-inflammatory properties. It has the potential for transporting medications such as aspirin and cortisone through the skin. Using DMSO on humans for medical purposes is also illegal in this country (for good reason). You don't really know what harmful substances might travel through the skin into your blood supply.

When I first saw this runner, heavy use of this solvent had burned her skin severely. She also had suffered a good-sized tear of her Achilles tendon.

After several weeks in a cast and considerable physical therapy, she was able to run again at her previous level. She was lucky. The consequences could have been much greater since she came extremely close to having a complete tear of that tendon, an injury which probably would have ended her career.

Orthotics for Faulty Feet

Like many runners, Jean put off making her first appointment to my office. The reason: She was afraid I would tell her to stop running.

In fact, she did a 10-mile run the morning she first came to see me. She explained, "I ran today so my injury would be good and painful and you could really get to see what is wrong."

This didn't make much sense to me—her problem was plantar fasciitis and it hurt *all* the time. Later she confessed, "I was afraid I'd have to stop running after you saw me and I wanted to get one last run in."

She was surprised when I taped her foot on the initial visit and told her to go out and run. "Great," she said somewhat sarcastically. "First I delay making this appointment for two months, resign myself to stop running and you tell me to run. What kind of a doctor are you, anyway?"

I'm the type who wants to keep runners running unless there's a compelling reason not to. The taping allowed Jean to continue while I fashioned a more permanent solution for her in the form of orthotics.

The Right and Wrong Way
to Make Orthotics

Orthotic devices can control abnormal motion such as excessive pronation and relieve pressure from anatomical and biomechanical irregularities such as improper foot placement. However, "orthotics" is a very broad term.

Almost anything that fits into a shoe has been called an orthotic. This includes parts of the shoes themselves, commercial innersoles, arch supports and, yes, even socks.

Here I will concentrate on true orthotics, which are inserts that fit into your shoe and help improve your running gait. These are custom fitted to you from an impression of your foot. They are constructed of thin and light, but strong, materials such as polypropylene.

There are many different ways to take this impression. Some methods are outdated, such as tracing an outline of the foot onto some sort of material or stepping down into a box of foam in order to duplicate the shape of the foot. Once the patient has stepped into a box of foam and an imprint is made, the foam is filled with a material that gives an impression of the foot as it appears with weight on it.

The problem with this—or any weight-bearing method of making an impression of the foot—is that the biomechanical problem the orthotic is supposed to correct occurs *when* weight is put on the foot. If the individual's arch is prone to collapse, it will collapse when the person steps on the foot; if there is excess pronation, that too will occur with a weight-bearing impression. The impression of the foot is made with the arch collapsed or the foot pronated excessively. The orthotic made from this impression then fails to give the degree of support you require. What you need is an orthotic that *prevents* the arch collapsing or the excessive pronation—and what you get is one that allows it.

The method most widely used by biomechanical experts and sports-medicine physicians for taking an impression of the foot is non-weight-bearing. Plaster of Paris is wrapped around the foot while the patient is sitting or lying down. The foot shape is then duplicated without the forces of body weight or gravity causing it to change. Essentially, your foot is "captured" in the ideal biomechanical position.

Because the non-weight-bearing technique captures the arch in its resting position—without the normal motions or gravity acting on it and without the arch collapsing—a much more detailed biomechanical evaluation is necessary than with the other method of taking a foot impression. This evaluation involves taking measurements of the foot and leg to determine how much correction to put into the orthotic. This determines the type of abnormalities you may have in your foot in either the takeoff or landing phase.

The negative impression is then filled with more plaster to produce a positive shape of the non-weight-bearing foot. The orthotic is formed over this mold and corrections are made based on a biomechanical evaluation.

The materials used for orthotic devices, which are designed to control abnormal motion and relieve the pressure from anatomic variations, tend to be thinner yet more supportive than over-the-counter arch supports or weight-bearing orthotics because they're made of better materials and are form-fitted.

Polypropylene is one of the preferred materials. This substance provides stability and has some "give" to it for moderate-to high-impact sports. Perfect for running, polypropylene orthotics are fairly lightweight and dissipate heat well. They fit easily into running shoes.

MAKING AN IMPRESSION

To make an orthotic, the sport-medicine practitioner first applies plaster of Paris to the runner's foot in a naturally relaxed, non-weight-bearing position. This creates a mold from which the orthotic can be fashioned.

Graphite or TL61 is a composite material used to provide a great deal of support. It can be made extremely thin and firm, so that a graphite orthotic can fit into women's fashion shoes and men's dress shoes, as well as tight-fitting shoes such as those used for bicycling and ice skating.

Graphite's main disadvantage is the precision required to cast the foot accurately and make corrections. With such firm material, a small error ends up creating pain and discomfort for the patient. Graphite is also much more brittle than other materials and breaks easily, so graphite is rarely used when impact is a factor—such as in running or court sports.

As a general rule, the more control you need, the firmer the material required for the orthotic. Conversely, the more impact involved in the sport, the more flexible the material should be.

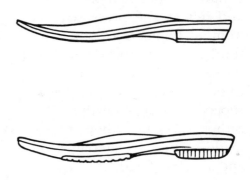

FINISHED ORTHOTICS

Orthotics are made from various materials for individual requirements. Sometimes a runner will have a rigid orthotic (*top*) for work shoes and a more flexible one (*bottom*) for running and other sports.

Casting for a Cure

Some injuries—usually certain fractures and severe ankle sprains—absolutely must be immobilized to heal correctly.

If your doctor says you need a cast, don't fight it. I know of no doctors truly involved in sports medicine who place runners in a cast without an absolute need. That need might extend to a patient I am fairly certain is going to be uncooperative. Ron is a good example.

No matter what his injury, Ron will continue to run as if nothing were wrong. He won't back off his training one bit. I might place someone like Ron in a cast for a few weeks to allow his injury to heal. I hate doing it because it's so inconvenient and restrictive, but it's for his own good.

Casts have changed a lot in the last few years. We once used plaster of Paris casts that were heavy, took several hours to harden and needed to be kept dry even after they set.

Then synthetic casting material was developed, which hardens in minutes, is about one-third the weight of the plaster and can be immersed in water for a shower or swim. This makes it a superior immobilizer for athletes.

Even better for athletes are removable casts. These can be taken off to shower or air your leg. But the patient must only take the cast off occasionally, when no force or stress will be placed on the injury. Some patients—because they can't be relied on to follow these restrictions—would never qualify for a removable cast.

When All Else Fails—Surgery

Sometimes even the best conservative treatments fail. We just run out of options. The runner is still in pain and surgery might be necessary.

Many people fear surgery. But nowadays techniques have greatly improved the success rate of all surgeries while significantly shortening the recovery time. Remember Joan Benoit Samuelson. She underwent arthroscopic knee surgery, performed by prominent orthopedic surgeon Stan James, M.D., only 17 days before she won the U.S. Women's Olympic Marathon Trial. Joan then proceeded to win the marathon at the Olympics in Los Angeles later that summer. Without the surgery, Joan wouldn't have even reached the starting line in L.A., much less won the first marathon gold medal ever awarded to a woman.

Arthroscopy has been called the most significant medical discovery of recent years. The arthroscope is a sophisticated set of instruments that allows the surgeon to make an extremely small incision and yet have a complete view of the area to be operated on.

A miniature camera and light are placed in an area like the knee or ankle through a very small incision. The light source is fiber-optic, about the thickness of a pencil. Then very small tools are inserted into the joint to either cut away injured tissue or repair it. The healing period is much shorter than it would have been with conventional surgery because less tissue is damaged.

Traditional surgeries have also been improved with better instrumentation and post-operative techniques. Even *where* doctors perform the surgery has changed greatly. When I graduated from podiatry school, for example, bunion surgeries were performed in a hospital where patients remained for two or three days. The surgeries were almost all done under a general anesthetic.

Now those same surgeries are performed in an outpatient surgical center under a local anesthetic. The patient comes to the center an hour before the surgery and leaves for home a few hours later.

Post-operatively, portable electronic devices are used to help block pain and reduce inflammation by electrically blocking nerve conduction. Certain electrical waves also help reduce swelling and fluid buildup. The result is less down time after the surgery.

Before you undergo surgery, you should know as much as possible about the operation—including possible risks and complications. I recommend getting a second opinion for elective surgery; most insurance companies will pay for the additional information and this gives you more criteria on which to make a sound decision.

If your doctor tells you that there are "no risks" involved in the surgery or the results are "guaranteed," don't believe it. Success rates vary from procedure to procedure and surgeon to surgeon, but none is 100 percent. You should also be told the alternatives to surgery, the possible pros and cons of different surgical procedures and your anticipated recovery time.

Chapter 10

SKIN AND TOENAIL DAMAGE

Probably the most common yet least discussed injury to runners is sore or blackened toenails. Nails can become irritated or bruised when they hit either the front end of the shoe or the top of the shoe.

Blisters run a close second to sore toenails in frequency of occurrence to runners, and other skin problems you may encounter include athlete's foot and calluses.

While these may sound like minor problems, they aren't always small matters. Damaged toenails can be painful, and there's a risk of infection. Likewise, blisters are a common source of infection, and even athlete's foot can curtail your running time.

Here are stories of runners who wholeheartedly wish they had had their "minor" foot problems treated earlier. These case histories may give you—or your doctor—some ideas on how to avoid or treat these problems.

How Not to Drain a Blood Blister

I once consulted for a company called Compute-a-Shoe. This was in the early days of portable computers, and Charles Boyer, a

(continued on page 110)

SKIN AND TOENAIL DAMAGE

Here's what can happen:

Sore or blackened toenails. Nails become irritated or bruised when they hit either the front end of the shoe or the top portion of the shoe. The usual cause is an improperly fitting shoe.

A shoe that's too tight or short is an obvious culprit. But too large a shoe can also cause damage by allowing the foot to slide around and irritate the toenail from the constant banging and jamming.

COMMON FOOT PROBLEMS

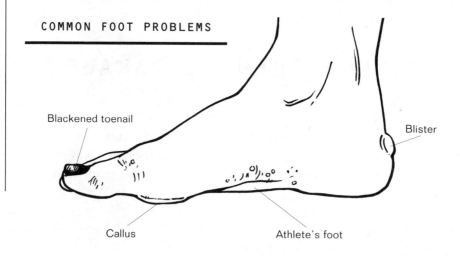

Blackened toenail

Blister

Callus

Athlete's foot

Occasional or slight irritation to the toenails will only make them sore. This soreness is normally temporary and will disappear in a day or two. But it's a warning that if you go longer distances, you will further traumatize your toenails. With increased running (and trauma), bleeding can occur underneath the toenail. This will make your toenail look purplish-blue and can be excruciatingly painful.

When the bleeding occurs beneath the toenail, it takes days, weeks or even months for the blood to work its way out. Compounding this problem is the fact that the blood is a perfect growth medium for bacteria. The risk of infection makes this an injury that should not be ignored.

Blisters. We've all experienced blisters, which are caused by heat buildup from friction or pressure. As the skin heats up, the outer layers can separate, with fluid filling in the gap. The fluid causes more pressure and, of course, pain.

When greater skin trauma occurs, blood can fill in the gap—bringing about even more pain. As with black toenails, blood blisters are susceptible to infection. Blisters generally take several days to go away on their own. But if you continue running, you may tear the outer layers of skin, delay the healing and develop complications.

Athlete's foot. This condition, caused by a fungus, can cause burning or itching anywhere on the foot, but usually under the arch and between the toes. You can see little red spots or rashes wherever the athlete's foot infection has occurred. For the most part, athlete's foot is not very serious. It can be quite uncomfortable, however, and should be treated promptly.

Calluses. Calluses are another common skin problem that can annoy runners. A callus is your body's way of building up areas of abnormal motion or increased pressure to prevent blistering.

Calluses usually occur either under the ball of the foot, on the inner side of the big toe or around the heel. Sometimes your body can overdo the callusing, causing so much thickening of the skin that it becomes painful. You can treat calluses at home. Soak the foot 10 to 15 minutes to help make the callus softer, then gently file it down with a pumice stone or emery board. Don't file it all the way down, and *never* use a razor.

high school computer-science teacher and track coach, came up with the idea of combining his two areas of interest.

His computer matched runners' characteristics with the available shoes on the market and recommended the appropriate model. What became obvious fairly quickly was that certain injuries were mileage related—in particular, black or sore toenails. Almost everyone who ran more than 25 miles per week had suffered from this problem at one time or another.

So it came as no surprise when Mark came to my office complaining about chronically blackened big toenails on both feet. Mark was a veteran marathoner who, over the past few years, had scaled back his mileage to 35 miles a week.

He told me, "My toenails become black and fall off, or sometimes become really thick. When actively training for marathons, I used to put in 60 to 70 miles per week.

"I figured that by cutting the mileage in half my toe problem would get better. But it didn't."

Mark was blaming his shoes for the toenail problem and becoming annoyed at shoe manufacturers. It didn't matter whether he bought shoes big, small or "just right." His big toenails would still suffer.

He said, "I've become adept at heating up a paper clip and pushing it through the toenail to drain out the blood blister that accumulates underneath it. I know this sounds gross, but it helps relieve the pain and lets me continue training."

When I examined Mark's shoes, I noticed an indentation in the upper fabric where his big toe was pushing into the toe box area. In fact, he told me that in many of his shoes his big toe would actually poke a hole through the nylon mesh material in that area.

It didn't take a rocket scientist to figure out that it wasn't the length of the shoe that was causing Mark's problem—it was that big toe hitting the top of the toe box. This is normally the case with runners who suffer from bruising of their toenails.

When I examined his feet, I noticed that his big toe didn't lay flat on the ground like his other toes, but was cocked up a bit higher than his other toes. This created pressure from the toenail pressing into the upper fabric of the shoe—and caused his sore and sometimes bloody toenails.

So we needed to take corrective action with either Mark's shoe or his toe. The shoe is much easier to alter than the toe, as Mark quickly agreed.

We could have simply cut a big hole in the nylon fabric over the big toe of each foot and significantly eased this problem. But this shoe surgery doesn't look very good, and lets dirt and water into the shoe too easily.

Instead, I showed Mark a lacing method that works extremely well for this problem. Essentially, this lacing lifts up the toe box area of the shoe, elevating the front of the shoe and giving extra room for the toes. The method will work for all of the toes—but especially the big toe, which is the most likely one to get injured.

My last piece of advice to Mark: Keep your toenails trimmed nice and short. If nails are allowed to grow too long, they have a greater tendency to push against the end or top of the shoe. A shorter nail resists the excess pressure that causes injury. Ideally, cut nails even with the end of your toes. Any longer than that and you risk trauma.

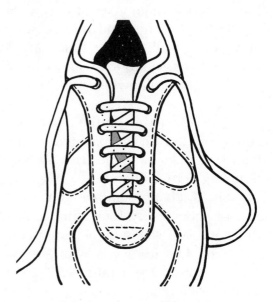

A BETTER WAY TO LACE UP

Sometimes something as simple as changing the way you lace your shoes can solve the problem that causes your black toenail. Weave the lace starting from a top front eyelet all the way down and then back up to the opposite top eyelet. This pulls up the toebox of the shoe, relieving pressure on the toe.

The advice on lacing his shoes and cutting his toenails solved Mark's problem. His mileage increased as the damage decreased.

And he no longer needed to jam a hot paper clip through the nails after each race, then wait for them to fall off.

The Blister That Wouldn't Quit

Gayle seemed almost embarrassed to be visiting my office. "As I sat in your waiting room, I saw people who have had surgery, people on crutches and one person who looked like he had run into a brick wall," she told me. "My problem seems so minor I was even embarrassed to tell your assistant."

She practically whispered, "It's only a blister. But I can't get rid of it."

The blister was on the inside of Gayle's big toe, and it had recurred off and on the past five years. Every time she trained more than four miles, it came back. Whenever she raced, it would start troubling her well before she reached the finish line.

She'd left no self-treatment untried—including buying a new pair of shoes every four months. "I've tried every home remedy I can think of," she said. "I've applied Vaseline, K-Y jelly and A&D ointment. I've used every anti-blister insole available—even one that I ordered from Europe. Two-layer socks haven't made the slightest difference."

The recalcitrant blister was taking the joy out of running, to say the least. "If you can't solve this problem, I'll just have to give up running," she concluded.

Talk about putting pressure on your doctor! Looking at her blister, I had to admit that it didn't look like much of a problem. It was no bigger than a penny and was located around the inside portion of her big toe.

But after further questioning I learned that the blister chronically became infected. Gayle had to take several months off running each year because of pain and infection. Her family doctor hadn't been able to solve the problem, so he referred her to me.

We know that blisters result primarily from heat buildup on the skin. There are other causes, such as certain infections and diseases, but generally pressure, friction or both cause that "hot spot."

So first we had to figure out whether pressure or friction was the major cause of Gayle's problem. In her case, the blister developed on the side of her toe where there were no excess bony prominences such as bone spurs, calcium deposits or bones that were out of place. Everything was well aligned in that area. So pressure from natural causes wasn't the culprit. This made clear that many of Gayle's self-treatments—the ones that involved bandages and padding—could not have helped.

I then checked her shoes to make sure that they fit properly. They did, so this ruled out another possible cause.

Gayle's frequent shoe changes proved a great help in determining the origin of her blisters. As she had tried so many shoes (and she brought most of them to the office!), we could assume that shoe pressure wasn't the cause of her problems. Shoes vary so widely in their construction that it would have been extremely unlikely for all of her shoes to have rubbed in exactly the same spot on her relatively normal foot structure.

Having ruled out pressure as a cause, we could assume that friction from increased motion in that part of her foot was causing the hot spot. In runners, excessive motion can be either forward and backward (as in a too-large shoe) or pronation and supination caused by a biomechanical abnormality.

It was unlikely that forward and backward motions were the cause of Gayle's complaint, based on the 20 different pairs of shoes she'd worn in the past five years. It's highly unlikely that they *all* fit improperly.

By process of elimination, the cause of her blistering was found to be abnormal pronation and supination of the forefoot. Her foot "rocked" inside her shoe, creating a tremendous amount of friction between her big toe and the side of the shoe.

Here is where the patient's history provided vital clues. Gayle told me, "The problem doesn't occur unless I run farther than 3½ or 4 miles."

That is why other self-treatments didn't work. Applying lubricants such as petroleum jelly gave her a few comfortable miles, but eventually the Vaseline liquefied and provided no further benefit. She needed a more lasting solution.

The answer was an orthotic to stabilize Gayle's forefoot. My assistants and I were able to make it very thin and light, with only enough correction to stop the excess motion. Her blister problem was alleviated, and her running became enjoyable again.

When the Shoe Doesn't Fit

The blister problems of a runner named Madeline weren't as easily solved. She has a relatively long but slender foot: It was about size 10 in length, but AA in width. Madeline found it almost impossible to find a shoe to fit.

"Whenever I find a shoe that fits snugly around my heel, it's too short," she complained. "If I buy a pair of shoes that are long enough, my heel slips up and down. I can't win."

Madeline first came to see me with a blister on the back of her heel. Adding to her problem was the fact that she had a high-arched foot with a "pump bump" on the heel (an enlargement of the heel bone near the Achilles tendon).

So Madeline's blister had two causes: up-and-down movement of her foot within the loose-heeled shoe (since the current pair had been picked for its length) and pressure on the extra bump of bone at the back of her heel. It was almost "too loose" and "too tight" at the same time.

"I'm in agony," she told me. "I don't want to put on any shoes, much less go running."

First, as with Gayle, I drained the blister. The fluid underneath the blister provides a perfect growth medium for infections, so great care must be taken when draining a blister.

I liberally applied an antiseptic solution to the blistered area before poking a couple of drain holes in the blister with a sterilized needle. I then left the skin flap in place, and covered the blister with a sterile dressing. Anything less than that can lead to an infection, especially for do-it-yourselfers.

Now Madeline and I set about trying to prevent future blisters. Our initial attempts included finding shoes that were narrower-lasted than her previous pair. But while this helped minimize the friction in that area, it caused more pressure—which equaled more pain.

We also tried accommodating the heel bump by applying various felt and foam pads to Madeline's shoe and foot to relieve the pressure. But this had little effect on the up-and-down motion of her foot within the shoe.

In addition, her dress shoes created havoc. They didn't allow enough room for her heel, let alone any padding material.

Conservative treatment didn't pan out in this case, and the end solution was surgery. I scraped that pump bump from the back of her heel. Then after recovery Madeline found running shoes that were snug enough in the heel area to prevent the excess motion that had caused her blister.

Six weeks after surgery, Madeline was running pain-free again. As a bonus, she was now able to slip into her dress shoes without gritting her teeth.

Madeline saw me at a race about a year after her surgery. "I don't know why I didn't get medical help sooner," she said. "I just figured it was too small of a problem for a doctor."

Eradicating Athlete's Foot

Few problems are more chronic and annoying to runners than athlete's foot.

This type of infection likes moisture and dark areas. Since runners tend to sweat a lot more than less active people, their feet are often damp. The combination of damp feet and dark shoes creates an environment that is athlete's foot heaven.

This is how Terry's problem started. Terry considered himself a "jogger" rather than a "runner" because he never ran more than three miles at a time and tended to plod along. But he told me, "My feet sweat a lot. They always seem to be wet."

Because Terry didn't view himself as a real athlete, he didn't think that the itching and redness on the bottom of his feet was athlete's foot. So he hadn't tried any of the commercial preparations available for his problem and, like many sufferers, just let it go.

Eventually, the itching got the best of him, and he started scratching his feet. Whenever he had an opportunity, he would pull his shoes off and scratch. He eventually scratched so hard that his feet bled.

Suddenly Terry developed an infection as bacteria got into the wounds he had created with his incessant scratching. This condition brought him to my office—unfortunately not right away. He waited until the infection became serious. By the time he saw me, there were red streaks heading up his leg.

First we had to clear up the bacterial infection. This was more serious than the fungal infection and the most debilitating.

SKIN AND TOENAIL DAMAGE

You may have this problem if you experience:

- Blackened toenails

- Blisters

- Athlete's foot

- Calluses

Your doctor may prescribe:

- Change of lacing style

- Moleskin and padding

- Change of shoes

- Antifungal medication

- Orthotics

- Neoprene insoles

What you can do to avoid these problems:

- Keep nails trimmed straight across

- Wear shoes that fit properly

- Wear dual-layer socks

- Use a neoprene or other anti-blister insole

- Keep feet dry

We treated this with warm-water soaks and oral antibiotics. Within a week, we had the infection pretty much under control and could then turn our attention to his athlete's foot.

The trick in treating this fungal infection is to use clear solutions. It doesn't really matter which preparation you use as long as it is a solution, ointment or gel. Avoid creams, powders and sprays at all costs. Creams cake up too much and quickly lose their effectiveness. Powders and sprays aren't really efficient in dealing with athlete's foot.

But the solutions work extremely well at eradicating the fungus. Whether the solution is an over-the-counter item or (as in Terry's case) a prescription medication isn't all that important. They all work almost equally well.

After I gave Terry his prescription for the antifungal solution, he told me that he had tried using it before. "It worked for a little while," he said. "But within a month or two, the redness and itching returned." He wanted something more permanent. "I don't want to continue applying this stuff for the rest of my life," he told me.

The problem, I explained, was that he had applied the athlete's foot medication only until his redness, itching and burning had gone away. Then he'd figured the condition was cured and stopped using the medication. That was his mistake. Because the fungus that causes an athlete's foot infection is a microscopic organism, it remains on your foot even after all of your symptoms have cleared up. It's simply waiting to multiply again and cause more problems.

The trick is to continue applying the solution for *two full weeks* after all the signs and symptoms are gone. Then you are sure to have eradicated all of the fungus and given yourself the best shot at a permanent cure.

In the last two years, Terry only had one brief recurrence of his infection, and that was after a week-long camping trip where he practically lived in heavy, nonbreathable hiking boots.

Chapter 11

METATARSAL INJURIES: BEHIND THE TOE BONES

Fernando had been running for 22 years. Like many masters runners, he hadn't started until he turned 40. He'd weighed close to 250 pounds at the time and by his own definition was a "serious couch potato."

But that all turned around one summer day in 1972 when he watched Frank Shorter win the Olympic gold medal in the marathon. As the American runner took his victory lap, Fernando realized that his own inactivity had taken a heavy toll on his mental and physical well-being.

He decided right then and there to get fit. He was going to emulate his new hero, Frank Shorter, and run a marathon someday. To seal his commitment, Fernando threw out his half-eaten bag of chips on the spot and poured the rest of his can of beer down the drain.

Fernando's "Bone Bruise"

Seated before me now was a completely different-looking man from that obese fellow of two decades earlier. Here was a fit-looking gentleman in his early 60s, weighing a trim 150 pounds at 5 feet 10 inches.

Running had become Fernando's passion and had changed his whole outlook on life. But he had recently begun to develop a problem that threatened his running—and his mental well-being.

"I feel like there is a rock underneath the ball of my foot," Fernando told me. "No matter how soft the shoes are and no matter how much cushioning or padding I put in, I can't shake it." In fact, it didn't matter whether he ran or not. The sensation was always there.

"It started a few months ago as a little bruising feeling," he continued. "At first, I thought it was a wrinkle in my sock or a small nail in my shoe, but it wasn't.

"I didn't want to see you because I didn't want to give up running. I know how you doctors are. It's always the same thing: 'If it hurts, stop running.' "

Years of trial and error had led Fernando into a very sensible training program. He had more than accomplished his original goal by running more than two dozen marathons, and he now ran six miles four or five times a week. Over the last few months, in large part due to his injury, he had been doing most of his running on a soft track or around a golf course.

When I first looked at Fernando's foot, nothing was obviously wrong. He was wearing good shoes with adequate cushioning. When I checked him on the treadmill, his gait pattern looked pretty good. In fact, Fernando had an almost ideal gait.

I then pressed the area beneath each of his metatarsal heads. When I touched the second one (next to the big toe), Fernando nearly jumped out of the chair.

The X-ray showed that one of Fernando's metatarsals (the second, of course) had fallen below the level of the others. That one metatarsal was taking the brunt of the force that normally would have been distributed more evenly across the entire ball of his foot. Essentially, he had developed a bone bruise that wouldn't go away.

METATARSAL INJURIES

Bruising pain under the metatarsal heads is a common complaint of runners. Metatarsalgia (pain somewhere underneath the metatarsals) is usually caused by one of your metatarsals collapsing.

Just as your regular arch can fall, so can the lesser-known metatarsal arch, formed by the metarsal heads, that makes up the ball of your foot.

When a metatarsal falls, it places excess force beneath that one metatarsal head. Usually it is the second head (the counting starts with the big toe), but it can also be the third or fourth. A callus will often develop under the fallen metatarsal.

Metatarsal stress fractures of the second, third or fourth metatarsals are, unfortunately, extremely common. The metatarsal bones are relatively long but thin. With repeated pounding and stress, they tend to get sore as the body tries to "remodel" the bone to make it thicker.

That is, the bone first breaks down and then builds up again as bone tissue is lost and replaced. If you continue to train during this breakdown period, then—seemingly all of a sudden—a microscopic fracture can occur.

The fracture usually occurs just behind the metatarsal head in an area called the "neck" of the metatarsal. This is the area of the bone that is the thinnest and, therefore, the weakest.

Another possible problem is that runners with a high-arched foot may develop tendinitis over the first metatarsal. Normally this

I see this problem quite frequently. The fallen metatarsal is usually the second, but it may be the third or fourth. We don't really know why these metatarsals collapse. But we know it doesn't happen suddenly: It is a gradual process that takes months or even years.

is caused by a buildup of bone at the base of the metatarsal and appears as a bump in that area. The tendon may rub over that spot and become very painful.

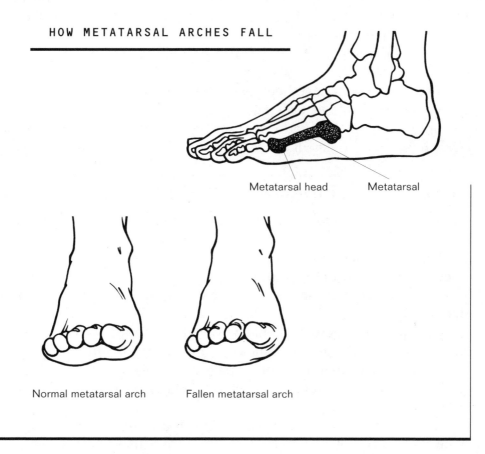

HOW METATARSAL ARCHES FALL

Metatarsal head   Metatarsal

Normal metatarsal arch   Fallen metatarsal arch

It's similar to the deterioration of your eyesight. You don't have 20/20 vision one day and suddenly need glasses the next. The muscles around your eyes weaken slowly. Likewise, the metatarsals fall gradually. Then, "suddenly," the symptoms develop.

Fernando's treatment was relatively simple. I cut a U-shaped pad out of felt and attached it to his foot with a mild adhesive. This immediately took the pressure off the painful metatarsal. I then told Fernando, "Go out and run." This unexpected advice thrilled him.

He returned to the office three days later. His running had been pain-free at first, but on his last run the soreness had started to return.

That was simply because the felt pad had compressed down to about a quarter of its original thickness. But now we knew that padding the painful area would work, so I merely had to fashion a more permanent pad that he could easily slip into his various shoes.

Orthotics would have been overkill for this injury. Instead, I attached cork and rubber material—which compresses very little—to a neoprene insole. Fernando only needed to wear this simple device when he ran to get all the relief he required.

Brian's Stress Fracture

Brian, who also felt pain under his metatarsal area, was not as fortunate as Fernando. When Brian's pain appeared, he was increasing his distances to train for a 10-K race. He normally ran 10 miles per week, divided into three workouts, and was now running 5 or 6 miles four times a week, for a weekly mileage of 20 to 24 miles.

This was an overuse problem waiting to happen—Brian had increased his mileage too quickly. Only a week into his new training program, Brian developed pain under his fourth metatarsal head. Not only did he refuse to back off; he actually kept increasing his mileage.

Then he felt pain over the top of his fourth metatarsal as well as on the bottom of that metatarsal. When he came to see me, he was limping, and his foot was swollen in the area of the fourth metatarsal.

When I pressed below the fourth metatarsal, Brian grimaced in pain. Then when I barely touched the area on top of that metatarsal, he let out a big yelp.

"Hey, not so hard!" he shouted. "What are you trying to do, break my bone?"

An X-ray confirmed that Brian had suffered a stress fracture of his fourth metatarsal. This type of fracture is a microscopic crack in the bone. The fracture itself is rarely if ever visible on X-rays. But within about 10 days to two weeks after the cracking occurs, bone callus builds up around the fracture; the callus is visible with an X-ray.

Basically, Brian had waited too long. He, like Fernando, had a dropped metatarsal. But instead of heeding the pain on the bottom of metatarsal as a warning sign, Brian ran even harder. This was a major mistake. The bone, unable to handle the stresses of running, fatigued and cracked.

So now we actually had bad news and good news for Brian. I gave him the bad news first:

"You're not going to be running for another month. This means your all-important 10-K race is out. We don't really have much choice—we must wait for the bone to heal and we can't rush that."

I also warned him to make sure his nutritional habits were sound. Many people become depressed when they're injured and lose their appetite, or deliberately lower their caloric intake because they're worried that they're getting too fat from the few weeks of layoff. But all undereating does is make it harder for the body to heal the injury. These people actually need to *increase* the amount and quality of food they eat to speed up the healing process.

Now I gave Brian the good news: "You essentially fixed the structural problem by breaking that bone." I explained that a collapsed metatarsal had been a cause of his injury. When the bone fractured, it was due to the pressure from the metatarsal head pushing upward.

This caused it to crack in an upward manner. Since the bone was slightly elevated from the fracture, it would heal in a more elevated position.

"That is a tough way to correct a problem," I told him. "Not only is it painful, but the potential side effects of a fracture are severe. The fracture might heal poorly, or it might create scar tissue that would be extremely painful for years to come."

Fortunately for Brian, he didn't need to be in a cast. A special shoe helped keep the broken metatarsal at a level approximately even to the other metatarsals as it healed. The stress fracture healed normally and he had no further problem with that foot.

However, Brian later developed a pain under the same metatarsal on the *other* foot. That didn't surprise me, since the body tries to be symmetrical. It doesn't always succeed, but it tries.

This time, Brian took a more cautious approach. He used accommodative padding and backed off from his training, and the injury didn't progress to the fracture stage. And he didn't jeopardize the healing process by entering any races.

Ellen's Big-Toe Injury

Ellen considers herself both a dancer and a runner. She has danced since she was five years old and loves to take classes in aerobics, jazz, tap and ballet.

She also began running several years ago to help keep herself in shape for dancing. She found, however, that she liked running for its own sake and has kept up the habit.

Ellen developed a pain under the ball of her foot, directly behind the big toe. Since she takes so many dance classes but also runs 15 miles a week, she was not sure exactly what triggered her pain or what aggravated it. She just knew that it hurt no matter what her activity.

She tried wearing softer shoes for running, but that didn't help. She tried Viscoelastic innersoles to further cushion the ball of her foot. That only helped slightly.

Her dance shoes were more difficult to modify. She was able to put a neoprene insole in her jazz and tap shoes, but again she didn't achieve noticeable relief.

Ellen was an interesting case, similar to that of a triathlete whose injury hurts whether he or she runs, bikes or swims. Which activity is causing the trouble?

To find out, I could have asked Ellen to stop one of her activities for a couple of weeks. If the injury improved, I could have then assumed that the other activity caused the problem. But if it didn't improve, I could surmise that the sport she'd continued was to blame.

Ellen, however, didn't want to give up either running or dancing. So I studied her foot type. She has a very high-arched and rigid foot, which is great for ballet dancing but lousy for running. It doesn't absorb shock: It slams down to the ground, then the shock is transmitted through the foot up the leg.

My exam revealed another structural problem. Ellen's first metatarsal was lower than the others. Usually the first metatarsal has some motion to it, so that it can move up out of the way when you step down. But Ellen's was rigid. When she hit the ground, it froze. Thus, the majority of force in the forefoot from Ellen's running and dancing occurred beneath the big toe joint.

This force is worse during dancing than in running, since much of the movements of dancing are up on the ball of the foot. Although Ellen's feet weren't particularly well designed for running, in running most shock is at the heel, and the shoe Ellen ran in helped cushion the impact.

Another possible complication of this problem involves two small bones, called the sesamoids, underneath the big toe joint. These little guys help support the long tendon of the big toe and give leverage to it. One or both of the bones can become inflamed and can sometimes, in cases like Ellen's, even crack or break. She was lucky—X-rays showed no fracture.

I couldn't change her foot type, so I did the next best thing by using an accommodative pad. It took force off of the big toe joint (especially the sesamoid bones) and put more force on the second through fifth metatarsals.

This pad compensated for Ellen's structural problem by putting more pressure where it was needed and by relieving pressure where there was too much. We were able to incorporate this pad in most of her shoes and to apply sticky felt directly to her feet when she danced in ballet slippers or barefoot.

Ellen is back running and dancing without any problems. Now she's thinking of adding bicycling to her already crowded fitness schedule.

Marla's Morton's Neuroma

Marla walked into my office with a somewhat confusing story. She said, "I've been running for only two years, two miles every other day. I run primarily to lose weight. I still haven't felt the 'runner's high' but hope to experience it someday."

The unusual part of her story was that she preferred to run barefoot. "Whenever I put on shoes," she told me, "I feel like they're constricting my foot to the point where it's painful."

It didn't matter which brand of running shoes Marla used. They all hurt, as did her dress shoes. She *had* to wear shoes to work. But she could run barefoot on a soft track in a grassy park.

Marla came to see me primarily because she was getting so many weird looks and comments from other runners who saw her run without shoes. She thought it was time to look for shoes she could tolerate.

Initially, she just asked, "Which are the widest shoes? I want a pair that won't hurt my feet."

Her foot was a little bit wider than normal, but not so wide that she couldn't find a shoe that fit. As I questioned her more about the discomfort, she told of experiencing "a burning pain at the bottom of my foot."

She pointed to the metatarsal area and said, "Sometimes when I'm wearing shoes the pain gets so bad that I have to take them off and massage the area. But it never hurts when I'm barefoot."

When I touched the area between her third and fourth metatarsals, Marla nearly went through the ceiling. She reported feeling "a tingling sensation" that radiated to the end of her third and fourth toes.

When I squeezed her foot from the big toe to the little toe, there was a "click" around the third toe. These symptoms are all characteristic of a Morton's neuroma.

This neuroma is a nerve inflammation, and sometimes scar tissue occurs around the nerve, primarily in the area of the third and fourth metatarsals. The nerve tends to get squeezed by the metatarsals, which is why shoes cause more pain than going bare-foot. No matter how wide the shoe is, it will always cause more pressure on the foot than going without shoes. Neuromas are much more sensitive to even pressure than to shock or jarring.

We aren't really sure what the cause of a Morton's neuroma is—only that it makes the nerve inflamed, that the inflammation lasts a long time and that scar tissue forms around the nerve. Once the area is scarred, the situation becomes difficult to resolve.

The first line of treatment is to reduce the inflammation around

MORTON'S NEUROMA

This nerve inflammation usually results in pain that may radiate out to the third and fourth toes. Tight shoes make the problem worse.

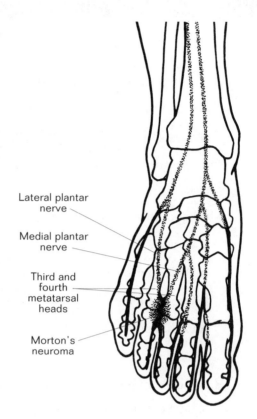

Lateral plantar nerve

Medial plantar nerve

Third and fourth metatarsal heads

Morton's neuroma

the nerve. This is primarily done by injecting a steroidal anti-inflammatory medication. If the inflammation hasn't persisted too long and scar tissue hasn't taken hold, a single injection can work well.

But Marla had waited too long. She had let the problem go untreated for a few years and the injections didn't help.

Gait analysis of Marla revealed a lot of pronation in her loose, excessively mobile feet. So I made her orthotics with good metatarsal support to stabilize her foot and reduce the movement of the bones around the neuroma, thereby relieving the irritation.

I hoped that the orthotics with additional forefoot support would work, since the last option involved a surgical procedure to remove the scarred nerve. Although it is a relatively simple surgery, with minimal down time, I like to exhaust every effort before resorting to surgery.

METATARSAL INJURIES

You may have this problem if you experience:

- Pain that feels like a stone bruise

- Swelling, tingling or burning in the ball of the foot

Your doctor may prescribe:

- Ice

- Injected anti-inflammatory

- Wider shoes

- Padded insole

- Cross-training

- Orthotics

- Casting

How you can help prevent this problem:

- Use metatarsal pads

- Use insoles or arch supports

- Wear a softer shoe (with more cushioning)

Fortunately, the orthotics worked. Marla's symptoms took about two months to disappear completely, but she noticed steady improvement during that period.

She is now much more comfortable running with shoes than without them and can't believe that she used to be a barefoot runner. Her colleagues at work are happier, too, as she no longer takes off her shoes during meetings.

Chapter 12

TARSAL TUNNEL SYNDROME: A NERVE PROBLEM

Jeff Bronson, M.D., struck me as rather imposing when we first met. He stood 6 feet 2 inches and weighed about 220. But what amazed me more than his size was the intensity with which he watched patients walk.

I had never before seen an orthopedic surgeon so interested in biomechanics that he would routinely evaluate a person's gait. He also had an uncanny ability to pick up details at a glance that I could only see in slow-motion video analysis. Dr. Bronson had made a special study of kinesiology (human mechanics and anatomy), and he knew foot surgery. So he could look at gait from more than one viewpoint. Rather than just looking at the motions of the bones and joints, as is traditional in biomechanical analysis, he also could evaluate nerve responses to an injury.

Initially I found this an odd way to analyze a gait. It certainly hadn't been taught in any of my courses, nor could I find this approach in medical literature.

Dr. Bronson, however, was convinced that if a nerve was injured, it would create a very different gait pattern than a muscle, joint or tendon injury. He had come to my office that day to watch

TARSAL TUNNEL SYNDROME

Tarsal tunnel syndrome is one of the newest injuries diagnosed in runners. Essentially, it is an injury to a nerve that runs along the inside of your ankle. It is similar to carpal tunnel syndrome in the wrist, which is pain usually associated with repetitive motions such as typing.

We used to think that numbness or tingling along the inside of the ankle or on the bottom of the foot was needed to confirm tarsal tunnel syndrome. But now we know that pain felt while pressing just behind the ankle bone is enough to signal this problem.

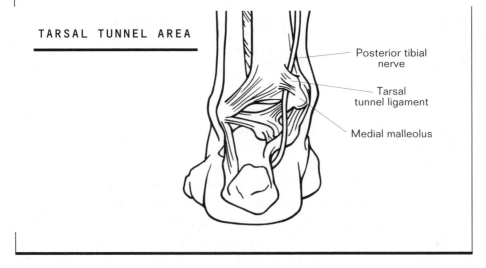

TARSAL TUNNEL AREA

Posterior tibial nerve

Tarsal tunnel ligament

Medial malleolus

me work with patients. He arrived just in time to watch a gait analysis of a young female runner, Leslie.

Investigating an Injury History

Leslie was a 20-year-old collegiate cross-country runner who had been bothered by shin splints on and off for the past 2½ years. She had tried all the normal treatments—icing, resting, taping, changing shoes, strengthening exercises and orthotics.

Her injury history also included knee pains, several occurrences of plantar fasciitis and chronic soreness of her Achilles tendons. I had seen her almost monthly and was getting a little frustrated with my lack of success at correcting her problems.

When Dr. Bronson arrived, I was evaluating Leslie's gait (for probably the fifth time) to see if I'd missed something or if perhaps some abnormality had developed since the last time I'd seen her.

There was, in fact, something amiss with Leslie's gait—abnormalities that I hadn't seen in biomechanics textbooks. In particular, Leslie had an "early heel-off." Her heel just didn't want to stay on the ground. Almost as soon as it touched down, it immediately lifted up again.

Usually your heel stays on the ground for about 20 percent of the stance phase of gait, the time your foot is flat on the ground before it's propelled forward. Leslie's heel was staying down for maybe 5 percent of that phase.

The most common cause of an early heel-off is a tight Achilles tendon. When that tendon lacks flexibility, it causes the heel to lift off the ground very quickly. But I'd determined that Leslie had plenty of flexibility in her Achilles.

I'd detected another strange motion while viewing videotapes of Leslie's running. She wobbled with her weight-bearing foot. "Wobbled" might not be an accepted medical term, but it aptly describes how she ran. After she touched the ground at heel strike, her foot rolled in briefly as it should. But then it quickly rolled out again, then back in and finally back out again. This happened within a few tenths of a second. It was almost as if she were walking on hot coals, or had accidentally stepped on a hard object and was trying to avoid contact with it.

This was definitely an unusual gait. But I could find no explanation for what was happening.

A Diagnosis from an Expert

Dr. Bronson didn't say much during my examination of Leslie. But when we sat down later, he said, "That patient of yours has had knee problems, hasn't she?" In fact, she had, although I didn't understand how Dr. Bronson could know that.

Then he asked, "Has she ever had Achilles tendon pains or plantar fasciitis?" I stared in amazement—once again, he was right.

"Okay, how did you know that?" I asked. "And as long as you're at it, maybe you could also help me figure out why Leslie keeps getting shin splints."

"That's easy," stated Dr. Bronson. "She has tarsal tunnel syndrome."

This confused me—at least at first. At the time, most doctors who knew about this condition looked for specific symptoms of nerve irritation.

Tarsal tunnel syndrome classically involves pain on the inside of the ankle, which then usually radiates down through the arch and the bottom of the foot. The symptoms normally include pain, burning and tingling sensations as the injury to the nerve becomes more acute.

But Leslie had none of those symptoms. Through all of her different injuries, she had never experienced pain on the inside of the ankle.

"But how could you possibly think that's the problem?" I asked Dr. Bronson, like Dr. Watson quizzing Sherlock Holmes. "You never even examined the patient."

He asked me to do a thorough evaluation for tarsal tunnel syndrome. He said his limited look at Leslie's gait had suggested that was the best diagnosis, but there was always the possibility there might be additional problems.

Naturally I was somewhat skeptical. But I examined Leslie for tarsal tunnel syndrome—including palpating that tibial nerve. Sure enough, she jumped when I touched the area on the inside portion of her ankle where the tibial nerve is the closest to the surface. It is also the area where the nerve most likely will become entrapped or irritated, because it's where the least fat and other soft tissues surround it. I still wasn't 100 percent sure until I ordered a special nerve conduction test. The results showed definite nerve damage.

Dr. Bronson was exactly right: This patient had tarsal tunnel syndrome. The reason she hadn't experienced any pain around the nerve was that her body was compensating for it. Those unusual gait patterns were Leslie's mechanism for dealing with the nerve injury. She was compensating by lifting her heel up early in her gait cycle to keep pressure off the rear portion of her foot. That decreased the pressure on that injured nerve.

But it takes a lot of work to lift your heel up off the ground when your entire body weight is pressing down on it. You can't really do this without the cooperation of some of your other muscles, particularly those around your knee and hip, which must "weaken" for your heel to lift up like that.

When those muscles stop operating normally, other muscles pitch in and try to take the load. They must do their previous work plus the added work of covering for the weakened muscles. As you can imagine, this creates tremendous muscular imbalances that can lead to all sorts of injuries.

Dr. Bronson also had a ready explanation for Leslie's wobbling gait: "Initially, she pronates—which is normal. But in the act of pronation she pushes the bony part of her rearfoot [back foot] into the nerve and her body reacts by supinating—rolling away to take pressure off the tarsal tunnel. That leaves her unstable, so she starts to pronate again, starts to irritate the nerve, and then supinates again."

This accounted for her rocking motion. Based on this new diagnosis, her weird gait actually made sense.

In fact, Leslie's current symptoms of shin splints were now easy to explain. The muscles on the inside of her leg were trying to pull the foot up and keep it from rolling inward each time her tibial nerve was in danger of being irritated. That's a lot more work than those muscles are used to, and they just fatigued.

The knee problems she had experienced earlier had been a result of the excess torsion that occurred at each step because of all that "wobbling" (pronation and supination). Her knee didn't know which way the forces were going to come because the direction was changing so fast.

She endured the additional insult of her quadriceps muscles weakening to allow that early heel lift. This created further imbalances in an already unstable situation as her kneecap was tugged off center due to the abnormal pull of the quadriceps.

I'll never forget that day when I thought I was showing Dr. Jeff Bronson (who has since become a national authority on tarsal tunnel syndromes) how to analyze gait. He taught me that no matter how much I think I know about biomechanics, there's always something new to learn.

On the Road to Recovery

Leslie was lucky that Dr. Bronson had chosen that day to "observe" my treatment of patients. Without his specialized neuro-orthopedic knowledge, I would have treated the shin splints in a mechanical way rather than focusing on the real cause, just as most other sports-medicine doctors would have.

Once we had confirmed Leslie's tarsal tunnel syndrome, I set out to resolve it. The first step in treatment involved limiting the motion at the back of her ankle so the bones in the rear portion of her foot wouldn't push into the nerve. This required a special type of orthotic, designed to protect the nerve, rather than a traditional biomechanical one. We used the same non-weight-bearing method of casting as for regular orthotics, but built in more correction in the orthotic to take the stress off the nerve. This was done with a lift to raise the heel a bit in Leslie's case.

Physical therapy is also extremely important in treating tarsal tunnel syndrome. With Leslie, we used a treatment called phonophoresis around the tibial nerve, which combines ultrasound with hydrocortisone cream to help calm the inflamed nerve.

The therapist also attempted to reeducate Leslie's muscles (and brain) to break the compensation patterns she had learned and to get her walking and running normally again.

Because tarsal tunnel syndrome usually goes on for many years before symptoms develop, her bad habits couldn't be unlearned overnight. But significant improvement began to appear after only three or four weeks of treatment.

Once Leslie's nerve condition was resolved, the shin splints went away like magic. Her total treatment time was less than one month, and her cure occurred even though none of our efforts were directed at treating the painful shins themselves.

This gratifying and eye-opening treatment occurred many years ago. Except for an occasional blister or toenail complaint, Leslie has only stopped by the office to say "Hi"—and to show off her latest running award.

The "Protective" Reaction

I now see runners quite often who come to the office with a multitude of other symptoms but in fact have tarsal tunnel syndrome. Formerly, these runners would have received traditional treatments for their primary complaints—and then would have suffered recurring injuries because we had failed to solve the real problem.

We now know that tarsal tunnel syndrome can cause a multitude of abnormalities. And probably the *least* common complaint is pain in the nerve that's responsible for this whole mess.

Tarsal tunnel syndrome shows how pain is not a primary sensation like sight, smell and hearing. Pain can be blocked out or altered—or your body can seem to "choose" one injury over another.

It's as if the body has a priority system that says "Protect the nerve at all costs." So your body will sacrifice muscles, tendons, joints and sometimes even bones to protect certain nerves. You can get shin splints, knee or Achilles tendon problems or plantar fasciitis without even knowing that your tarsal tunnel nerve is injured.

Imagine having a little pebble under your heel inside your shoe. It irritates the bottom of your foot, and you naturally start limping. That's a natural and almost involuntary reaction as you make every effort not to put full weight on that pebble.

After a while, your heel might not even hurt, but you probably will develop pain somewhere else—such as the other leg—because you are now overusing it. The protective mechanism has gone astray.

Now let's say the pebble is removed after several days. Believe it or not, you will still limp because your brain still thinks that it needs to favor that foot. Physical therapy, however, can help you retrain your body to function normally.

Before we can accurately and completely diagnose tarsal tunnel syndrome, we run special nerve-conduction tests. Standard nerve conduction testing isn't particularly valuable because it generally doesn't show an injury to the nerve until it is pretty far gone or shows actual pain, numbness, burning and tingling.

The state-of-the-art nerve testing methods include Somatosensory Evoked Potential (SSEP), which tests your sensory nerves, and the more common Nerve Conduction Velocity (NCV), which stimulates the motor nerves. The good news about this testing is that no needles are involved: The nerve is stimulated by a surface electrode.

The feet must be tested in three different positions: neutral,

TARSAL TUNNEL SYNDROME

You may have this problem if you experience:

- Shin splints

- Sore Achilles tendon

- Plantar fasciitis

- Burning or tingling on inside of ankle

- Bone spur

- Discomfort that increases with movement and decreases with rest

Your doctor may prescribe:

- Arch supports

- Orthotics

- Physical therapy

- Casting

- Surgery

How you can help prevent this problem:

- Wear supportive shoes

- Massage the ankle

- Do towel exercise, page 145

- Take warm baths

flexed upward and flexed downward. Those are the motions you go through when you are running, and commonly only one of the positions causes the problem. If testing is done in only one position and it's the wrong one, the diagnosis might be missed.

When the test is interpreted by a qualified neurologist, it becomes apparent whether or not this condition exists. If it does, we can use this information to interpret the symptoms and actually cure conditions we could only treat symptomatically before. This means that *both* the patient's and my frustration levels are decreased.

Janet's Bone Spurs

Now that I'm able to diagnosis more tarsal tunnel syndromes, I have noticed some variations. One of the most important occurs when there is a bone spur against the tibial nerve behind the ankle.

Janet had one of these. Whenever she ran (or walked), that bone spur, called an os trigonum, would jam into the nerve. This created scarring around the nerve to the point that it looked like Swiss cheese.

In Janet's case, neither orthotics nor extensive physical therapy would solve her problems. Surgery was necessary. The conventional treatment for tarsal tunnel syndrome is merely to cut the laciniate ligament that surrounds that tibial nerve so the nerve has room to move.

But we now have a secret weapon when we operate: nerve testing *during* the surgery. The nerve comes back to life almost immediately when it is freed, and the testing can tell us instantly—before we close up the surgical site—whether or not we've been successful.

When Janet's laciniate ligament was cut and the nerve released during surgery, nothing changed on the nerve-conduction test. But when I and my associates went in further and scraped away the bone spur, suddenly the nerve conducted normally.

In other cases, we've had to remove enlarged veins (called "leashes") surrounding the nerve or scar tissue that adheres to the nerve. But in nearly all such surgeries, we have to do more than simply open up and release the laciniate ligament.

Janet needed a few months of physical therapy before she could run again. Then, unfortunately, a bone spur on the other foot led to a similar condition that required a second operation. The good news is she returned to running this time with no further complications.

Chapter **13**

PLANTAR FASCIITIS:
ARCH PAIN

I would wager that just about every runner has heard of this injury. Plantar fasciitis is the most talked-about, most written-about and possibly most dreaded injury in running.

Statistically, plantar fasciitis (pulling and tearing in a fibrous tissue in the foot) affects no more than 8 percent of runners. Yet it sometimes seems that everyone has either experienced it or knows someone who has. Some runners will tell you that once you have plantar fasciitis, you can never get rid of it; your running days are over.

The Japanese Olympic team trainers once invited me to examine a number of runners who had retired due to their injuries. I was astonished to find that almost 60 percent of them had quit the sport because of plantar fasciitis pain.

They'd given up an activity they loved or excelled at because they could find no treatment to solve their problem. As we shall see, there are answers. But they're often difficult to uncover. As the following case histories demonstrate, this is one of those injuries that you almost never resolve without proper treatment. Time off

PLANTAR FASCIITIS

The plantar fascia is a long, fibrous band of tissue that begins at the heel and travels forward under the arch. It then splits off and attaches under the metatarsal heads at the ball of your foot.

A HIDDEN BAND

You can't see your plantar fascia, but if you could, you'd see a dense, fibrous band reaching from the back of your foot to your toes.

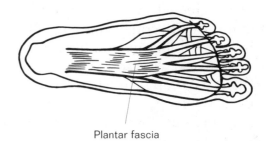

Plantar fascia

In many ways, the plantar fascia resembles a tendon or ligament. When you pronate excessively or your arch begins to fall, the plantar fascia takes the strain and tries to help your foot. Since it pulls at one location into the heel (rather than the five locations up on the ball of the foot) you will normally feel the strain under the heel bone.

Because the plantar fascia doesn't have much ability to stretch, it tears under the stress of pulling. The tears always heal with scar tissue, which easily becomes inflamed. This becomes an unpleasant cycle: Because scar tissue is even less elastic than the original tissue, it has less ability to resist the excessive pull on the plantar fascia and even more tearing results. Also, scar tissue isn't a neat little patch; it's a dense network that adheres to other tissues. This causes further pulling from other parts of the foot.

Chronic low-grade stress to the plantar fascia also may cause a heel spur to develop—the body's way to try to strengthen the heel bone where the plantar fascia inserts.

The pain from plantar fasciitis, most often directly under the heel, is most severe when you first get out of bed or after you sit for a long period of time. The pain may fade as you walk or run.

will seldom heal it, nor will simple changes in your footwear or routine.

Unraveling Joe's Problem

Joe's case was a particularly complex one. Joe, an attorney who likes to run to stay fit, hadn't been able to run for two years when he came to see me.

Pain greeted him as soon as he stepped out of bed in the morning. He described the pain like that of a bruise under the heel—one that lingered day after day, week after week, month after month. He said, "It also just kills me when I've been seated awhile and then stand up, like when I'm at the movies." He couldn't even walk without limping.

Placing cushioned insoles and soft heel cups in his shoes hadn't helped, nor had several cortisone injections he'd received from another doctor. Joe knew his problem was plantar fasciitis, and one of his running co-workers whom I had successfully treated for the same problem finally referred him to me.

He appeared pessimistic about my chances of helping, but wanted to try one more doctor before admitting that his running days were over.

Joe was now a bit overweight from his lack of activity, but otherwise he was in basically good health with no serious biomechanical problems. He had a flexible foot, which *does* stress the plantar fascia. But the flexibility—and the overpronation and collapsing arch that result from this condition—didn't appear to be severe enough to cause such a painful, lingering condition.

After studying an X-ray, I saw a small bone spur where the plantar fascia inserted into his heel. Bone spurs don't occur without a reason. In this case, the pulling of the plantar fascia at its attachment into the heel probably caused the spur to develop. Usually a spur itself doesn't cause pain, however—it's just a long-term effect of stress on the plantar fascia.

One of Joe's previous doctors had discussed surgery to remove the bone spurs. But Joe wasn't convinced he wanted such drastic action. Plus, he had heard through the running grapevine that "those surgeries usually fail, anyway." And because bone spurs rarely cause pain, it isn't usually necessary to remove them.

PLANTAR FASCIITIS

You may have this problem if you experience:

- Pain like a bruise under the heel

- Pain first thing in the morning that diminishes during the day

Your doctor may prescribe:

- Ice

- Taping

- Oral or injected anti-inflammatories

- Heel pads

- Orthotics

- Physical therapy

- Flexibility exercises

- Surgery

How you can help prevent this problem:

- Wear supportive shoes

- Do towel exercise, page 145

- Do calf stretching exercises, pages 246 and 247

- Ice the heel area immediately after activity

- Use arch supports or heel cups

- Do plantar fascia stretch, page 145

- Do toe raises, page 145

While examining Joe's foot, I felt a thickening of hard, fibrous tissue where the plantar fascia inserted into his heel, probably scar tissue built up from years of inflammation and stress.

Besides having a flexible foot and a tendency to overpronate, Joe also had a relatively tight Achilles tendon. He should have been able to flex his foot upward from his ankle about 10 or 15 degrees, but could move it only about 5 degrees. That tightness translated into even more pulling at the plantar fascia.

To help take stress caused by overpronation and a collapsing arch off Joe's fascia, I taped his foot during the first visit.

"We can't expect complete relief at this juncture," I told him. "But you should feel at least a 50 percent improvement from this taping."

But when he returned to the office three days later, Joe reported glumly that the taping hadn't helped. "It didn't work," he said. "The pain is as bad as before." Even though he didn't say so, I could imagine his unspoken thought "—and I knew it would be."

Unlike Joe, however, I wasn't dismayed by the news. The fact that the taping hadn't worked told me a lot. Treatments that don't work can often tell us just as much as those that do. Because the taping hadn't given relief, I knew that a supporting orthotic wouldn't either, at least in this phase of treatment. This further disappointed Joe, as a co-worker of his who'd had plantar fasciitis had told him that orthotics had solved her problem.

Now I turned my attention to Joe's scar tissue. I suspected it was preventing his injury from healing, so I prescribed physical therapy.

This included ultrasound to help soften the scar tissue and a technique known as "friction massage," where the therapist attempts to break the scar tissue's attachment with other tissues and "remodel" that tissue so it pulls in the direction the muscles move rather than haphazardly. The therapist also worked on Joe's lack of flexibility in his hamstrings and calf muscles and helped him strengthen the supporting muscles in his feet and legs that had weakened in the past two years because of lack of use.

After nine therapy sessions, the scar tissue was definitely more pliable. Joe's pain had localized to one smaller area instead of spreading across the bottom of his foot—but it was as intense as before.

Now that Joe's scar tissue was reduced and he had regained some muscle strength in this foot, the next task was to get rid of the inflammation.

I injected cortisone directly into the area of Joe's pain. It took some selling to convince Joe to try this, since his previous cortisone injections hadn't helped.

But we were playing on a different field now. The previous injections hadn't stood much chance of reducing the inflammation because of all that existing scar tissue.

A single injection of cortisone almost completely relieved Joe's symptoms. He could now walk without any discomfort, and could jump out of bed in the morning without that agonizing pain. He was ecstatic (he's a skeptic by nature), but still not convinced of the likelihood of finding a permanent cure.

At this point a taping job that supported Joe's collapsing arch and helped resist his tendency to overpronate gave even more relief. Now the solution was obvious: orthotic devices. With the complicating factors of scar tissue and inflammation gone, the orthotic corrected Joe's overflexibility and prevented the strain on the plantar fascia.

I'm happy to report that Joe has no more pain, is on a walking program and will be running again soon. His case was a tough one—but it shows the need for patience and perseverance with some injuries. Instant cures aren't always possible!

Racing against Time for a Cure

Julie Brown had been on the 1980 and 1984 Olympic teams, and wanted to qualify for the 1988 Olympic marathon. As a member of a past team, she didn't need to qualify for the Olympic Trials. That was fortunate, because debilitating plantar fasciitis had plagued her for almost a year.

Julie's case illustrates how stubborn plantar fasciitis can be, as well as all the different treatment methods. Julie had tried ice massage, soft heel cups, cushioned innersoles and soft shoes, but her symptoms persisted. When she came to see me, she was running out of time. The Trials were only a few months away.

We made her two different types of orthotic devices, one for her athletic shoes and the other for her everyday shoes. The everyday orthotics were a little stiffer, while the running orthotics had more "give" to them. They helped a bit, but not enough.

We next tried an oral anti-inflammatory medication combined

with icing. For two weeks, she iced her heel six times a day (for 20 minutes each time) and took the medication. This treatment was unsuccessful.

Then she had a month of physical therapy: ultrasound and friction massage, plus workouts to increase her strength, flexibility, balance and coordination.

Her pain continued to worsen, however, as she tried to keep training. Then I gave her a couple of cortisone injections at the area of pain around the insertion of her plantar fascia. I followed these with ultrasound to disperse the cortisone through the tissues.

But nothing was working. Julie's pain still prevented her from training—and the thought of competing in the Olympic Trials was rapidly disappearing as we were running out of options.

I had tested Julie for other potential problems such as a stress fracture of her heel, tarsal tunnel syndrome or another nerve injury. All were negative. I even thought about a bursitis underneath the heel, but this wasn't the case.

We were down to our last resort: surgery. This procedure is called plantar fascial release; the plantar fascia is separated from its insertion into the heel. Without the fascia pulling into the heel, the symptoms generally resolve (the surgery works 8 times out of 10).

This surgery is done on an outpatient basis, under a local anesthesia. The patient goes to a surgical center an hour or so before the operation, then leaves about an hour afterward.

With Julie, I made an inch-long incision to expose the plantar fascia and then performed the needed work. She began physical therapy within a few days to keep the scar tissue from forming incorrectly, as well as to keep the inflammation and swelling down to speed the healing.

Within three weeks, Julie was pain-free in her plantar fascia. With the Trials rapidly approaching, she resumed running—slowly at first. Since the heel wasn't hurting, she probably added distance and speed more rapidly than she should have.

The plantar fascia held up well. Unfortunately, a few weeks before the Trials, Julie developed a stress fracture in her foot, and her chances of qualifying for the Olympics disappeared.

Although we usually have pretty good success with these injuries, it is impossible to predict everything else that might go

TOWEL EXERCISE

To strengthen your foot, lay a towel in
front of you as shown, then gradually
move the towel by scrunching your toes,
pulling it toward you (without moving
your leg), releasing, then reaching out
with your toes to "grab" more towel.
When you have pulled the whole towel
toward you, reverse the procedure and
push the towel away from you.

To vary this exercise, lay the towel to the
left of your foot. Pivoting with your ankle,
grab the towel with your toes, pull it
around to the right of your foot, and continue until you've reached the end of the
towel. Then reverse the procedure by
pulling the towel around to the left of
your foot.

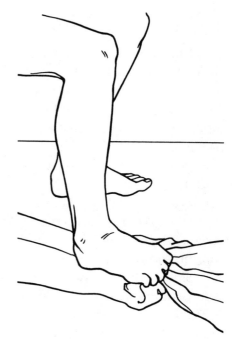

PLANTAR FASCIA
STRETCH

With the knee bent and the ankle flexed
toward you, pull the toes back toward
the ankle. Hold for a count of ten, and
repeat 10 times throughout the day.

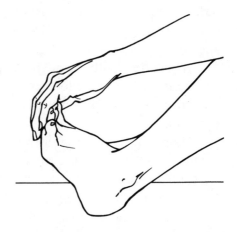

wrong—such as Julie's stress fracture, which probably resulted from her sudden increase in training intensity.

Taping Solves Jim's Troubles

Jim was a sub-2:30 marathoner before his plantar fasciitis slowed him down. He operates an athletic-shoe store, and had heard plenty of advice about his injury from other runners.

It had never dawned on him to see a doctor. Other than trying different shoes and innersoles, he was just trying to live with the problem.

When I visited his store, he mentioned his 18-month ordeal with plantar fasciitis. I performed a quick exam on the spot and confirmed his self-diagnosis.

Like Joe, he had a very flexible foot type, with an arch that collapsed down to almost nothing. I taped his arch to relieve pressure on the plantar fascia.

Since I didn't have the recommended cloth tape and foam pre-tape padding available, I put a plastic tape directly on his skin. This *isn't* the best thing to do, because this tape can cause blisters and irritation, but it was the best we could do at the time, and Jim was anxious to try anything.

I told Jim to leave the tape on for a day, which usually is the maximum time it remains effective. He called me a week later and said, "Doc, I don't have any more pain in my foot. It's completely gone! I can't believe it!" (He also admitted that his foot was still taped.)

When he finally took the tape off, he remained symptom-free. He could run in complete comfort after a year and a half of pain. Jim didn't bother to come to the office for the orthotic devices I'd recommended.

Then a few years later, his plantar fasciitis returned. He immediately came to my office this time—not for orthotics but just to be taped again. Again, the pain went away while the tape was on, but slowly returned after he removed the tape.

So he decided to be fitted for orthotic devices. These were made of polypropylene (as are most of today's sports orthotics) to support the foot while still having enough "give" for the impact of running.

Jim didn't like the idea of orthotics at first. He was a "purist" who wouldn't even wear socks when he ran. And he had heard that the orthotics would make his feet weaker.

I showed him that his feet were already weak and that he needed orthotics to run, just as he needed glasses to read. The orthotics wouldn't make his feet any weaker, but would let him continue running.

We covered the orthotics with neoprene so he could wear them in his shoes without socks. That finally made Jim happy. Of course, so did his anticipation of years of pain-free running.

With most cases of plantar fasciitis, the quicker treatment is initiated, the better your chances are for a complete recovery. Jim was lucky that his problems were so easily remedied. Generally, the more treatment is delayed, the harder plantar fasciitis is to resolve.

TOE RAISES

Slowly raise yourself on your toes, then lower your heels to the floor. Repeat 10 times.

Chapter 14

ACHILLES TENDON PROBLEMS

In mythical lore, Achilles was the strongest and fastest of the Greek heroes. Every part of his body was invulnerable—except one small area on the back of his heel.

As the myth goes, during the battle of Troy an arrow struck him in the heel, the only place he could possibly be injured. Thus, the term "Achilles heel" came to represent a weakness in the human body.

And as it turns out, the Achilles tendon is the weak spot in many runners. Like Achilles, many runners start out thinking that they, too, are invincible—until this heel injury strikes, putting them face to face with their own vulnerability.

"Streaking" Can Be Risky

Ann was what I call a "streaker." By this I mean she kept count of the number of days she could run without taking a day off. She trained 7 days a week, 365 days a year. Running wasn't a passion for her; it was an obsession.

Ann's normal training course was five miles, starting from her front door, going through her neighborhood and ending up back at

ACHILLES TENDON PROBLEMS

The Achilles tendon connects two big muscles of the calf—the gastrocnemius and the soleus—and attaches them into the back of your heel bone. These muscles are designed to forcefully pull your foot downward, while allowing enough flexibility to bend your foot upward when running.

SEVERE ACHILLES INJURY

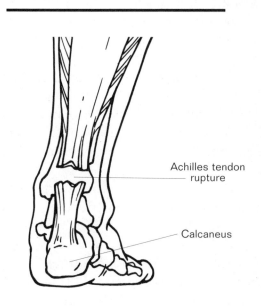

Achilles tendon rupture

Calcaneus

The gastrocnemius and soleus allow you to propel yourself forward. But running tends to cause these muscles—and hence the Achilles tendon—to tighten up. Without proper flexibility, the Achilles is forced to do much more work than it can handle.

This causes the tendon to become inflamed (that's tendinitis) and it can tear or rupture if you continue to work it. The Achilles, like all tendons, heals its injuries with scar tissue. This makes it weaker and more susceptible to further injury. You must treat Achilles injuries quickly, before too much tearing or scarring occurs.

her house. She rarely entered races and only competed against the clock (and herself) during her runs.

Ann's streak had lasted six years without mishap. Rain, sickness or minor surgery—nothing had stopped her. Thank goodness she hadn't become pregnant during this time!

Then a construction project along Ann's regular route caused her to alter the course. While she'd previously run three-fourths of the distance on trails and one-fourth on hard surfaces, she now had to run almost entirely on asphalt and concrete.

Near the end of a day's run, she felt a slight soreness in her left Achilles tendon. The pain appeared two to three inches above her heel bone and it really hurt when she squeezed the tendon.

Although she hadn't experienced pain in this location before, Ann had run through plenty of other minor aches and pains. She figured this, too, would pass.

So Ann continued her running streak. Predictably, her Achilles tendon grew more and more painful from day to day.

Before long, she found herself limping—not only while she was running, but also when she was walking around during the day. The pain was worst early in the morning and after she'd been sitting awhile.

She tried icing her Achilles, but that didn't help much. She bought new shoes, to no avail. Ann then tried ibuprofen tablets and wrapped an elastic bandage around her ankle and tendon. Nothing slowed the escalation of her pain.

Now Ann faced a dilemma. She certainly didn't want to tear her Achilles tendon, which is what her running friends had suggested might happen. But she also didn't want to break her streak by taking time off.

Ann finally scheduled an appointment with me three months after her pain started—in the afternoon, so she could fit in a run in the morning. That way, if I told her not to run, she already would have gotten in that day's workout. Then she would have until the next day to figure out how to ignore my advice and keep her streak alive.

When Ann first came into my office, she was limping badly. Immediately I could see this wasn't a small problem: She had a major-league injury.

The back of her ankle was so red and swollen that I couldn't even see her Achilles tendon. I could feel a "creaking" sensation in the tendon, like a rusty door hinge, whenever she flexed her foot up and down.

I was disappointed to find a big deficit in the tendon—an actual hole in the Achilles where tendon material should have been. This almost always indicates a rupture of tendon fibers. By the size of the defect, I guessed that a large percentage of the tendon had been ripped.

I ordered magnetic resonance imaging (MRI) to get a clear picture of the extent of Ann's injury. In this painless test, Ann laid in a tube while a magnet passed around her ankle, measuring the signals put out by her various tissues. The MRI showed more than a 90-percent tear of her Achilles tendon. That meant that it was almost literally hanging on by a few fibers. A few more runs—or possibly even a slip walking off a curb—and she would have completely ruptured it.

No question about it—Ann's streak was broken. There was no way I could allow her to run until her problem was corrected.

Ann sobbed with disappointment as I placed her in a cast. I explained to her, "A partial rupture of the Achilles tendon—no matter how severe—is always better than a complete rupture. Your recovery time will be much shorter if we take care of this problem now."

I kept her ankle in a cast the next two months (although I changed it several times). This allowed the fibers to heal with scar tissue. Had she completely torn the tendon, surgery would have been her best recourse.

Ann was like a horse champing at the bit, ready to run as soon as she came out of the cast. But I held her back, only allowing her to swim and bicycle.

She needed another six more weeks of physical therapy to minimize the scar tissue and reduce the swelling before she was ready to run. Even then, she had to start with a walk/run session every other day.

Finally, Ann is back to running at her normal pace and distance. But, to her credit, she has given up the idea of streaking and now takes occasional days off. She even allows herself to stay in bed when she has the flu.

Burt's Problem: Too "Busy" to Stretch

Achilles tendon mishaps are not always as dramatic as Ann's. Burt's case is more typical.

Burt tried to run four days a week, totaling about 20 miles. He didn't always reach his mileage goals, and when he failed he felt a little guilty. So he'd push a little harder the next time to make up the deficit.

Burt didn't practice any flexibility exercises, saying, "I don't have the time." Since he normally ran during his lunch hour, he barely had enough time to change, get his run in, then shower and gobble down a quick sandwich before returning to his desk. This frantic routine also meant Burt didn't warm up or cool down properly.

He began feeling pain in his Achilles tendon about a year before he first came to see me. He rationalized, "It's only a dull ache and seems to warm up when I run, so it can't be too bad."

Some days the pain would be worse than others, but it never became so sharp that he had to stop running completely. A few days off would ease the pain enough for him to resume training. Then the guilt factor would take over. On his next run, he would try to make up by running farther than normal.

After one such run, his Achilles tendon acted up more than before. He immediately stopped running and walked home, but the pain persisted. His foot hurt the next day as he walked and it didn't get any better the next week.

Burt took a month off from running. When he returned, the sharp pain returned. That's when a friend of Burt's suggested that he see me.

When Burt came to my office, he wasn't limping—always a good sign. When I examined his Achilles tendon, however, I could feel several small lumps. A tendon should be nice and smooth, not bumpy like Burt's.

Those little lumps—each about the size of a pea—indicated scar tissue. Scarring can be both friend and foe. It's the material the body uses to heal wounds, but it also is a sign of inflammation and pain.

The scar tissue in Burt's tendon indicated that over the previous year he had suffered micro-tears. These certainly weren't as bad as Ann's injury, but they still showed that fibers of the tendon had been torn and scar tissue had filled it in.

As you might guess, I found that Burt had a problem with flexibility. Normally you should be able to hold the foot at a 90-degree angle to the leg and then flex the foot upward about 15 degrees more. Burt could barely get his foot to that 90-degree angle, let alone that extra 15 degrees. All those years of running without stretching and warming up had taken their toll. Burt's calf muscle and Achilles tendon were too tight for running. In fact, they were even too tight for normal walking, which also aggravated the tendon problem.

I told him not to run for a while, to keep a rather minor injury from turning into something a lot bigger. I suggested alternate activity. Given his history of avoiding stretching, warming up and cooling down, I wasn't surprised when he resisted.

"I don't have time for anything else at lunch hour," he said. "And when I get home at night, I need to spend time with my family."

When I suggested that he exercise in the morning, Burt replied, "I'm lucky to get to work on time." I mentioned the possibility of walking at lunch time, but he said his fellow runners would consider that "a sign of weakness."

I persisted, suggesting that he and his family might take a walk of up to an hour after dinner, thus combining a gentle workout with family time. He agreed this might be possible and I put a heel lift in his shoe to keep pressure off his tendon.

Fortunately, it turned out that Burt and his family enjoyed these strolls. Besides getting exercise, they enjoyed the time they spent together.

The next step was to decrease the symptoms around Burt's Achilles tendon with icing and anti-inflammatory medication. He iced for 20 minutes at lunch time and after his evening walks.

Next, we went to work on his scar tissue. A physical therapist employed ultrasound and deep-tissue friction massage to realign and reshape this tissue.

Finally, we tackled the cause of the whole problem—Burt's lack of flexibility. The physical therapist gave Burt lessons in correct stretching exercises for his Achilles tendons, calves and hamstrings. The exercises only took him about 10 minutes daily, and Burt found them easiest to do at night while watching television. This was a good time because his muscles were already a bit warmed up from the day's activities.

A little over a month after he suffered the injury, I gave him the green light to run again. But I cautioned him to include warming up, stretching and cooling down.

"Run less distance if that's what it takes," I told him, "But you must do your exercises and you must warm up and cool down. It's better to have a shorter run than risk another Achilles tendon injury."

My final words of advice to him: "*Never* try to make up a 'lost' run. Forget about it. Nothing serious is going to happen just because you missed a run or two. But, as we've seen, serious things *can* happen if you try to do too much."

Nowadays, Burt only runs once or twice a week at lunch hour. He does his other runs with his family before dinner. They had enjoyed the evening walking so much that they all began a running program.

Each family member runs his or her own distance and pace. But they all stick together for the initial warmup period, then regroup at the end of the run for cooldown exercises.

A Tendon Pushed to Its Limits

Some runners, unfortunately, really let their Achilles tendon problems get out of hand—and for some reason these people are almost always men.

Kenneth is a great example. Besides being a runner, he's an avid all-around sportsman. You name the sport—he's played it, everything from hockey to rugby. He likes to think of himself as a "macho man."

But running was his favorite activity. For several months, he felt a pulling or tugging in his Achilles tendon during his runs. The problem gradually worsened, but he wouldn't give up any of his activities—especially running.

During one very hilly 10-mile run, Kenneth felt a stabbing pain in his Achilles. But he was running with his friends, so he toughed it out to the finish.

He then tried to walk off the pain, but it became progressively worse. As he was walking to his car, his foot gave way as he stepped off a curb, and he fell to the ground. He wasn't in much pain, but he'd lost all control over that foot.

ACHILLES TENDON PROBLEMS

You may have this kind of injury if you experience:

- Soreness in tendon

- Stabbing pain in tendon

Your doctor may prescribe:

- Heel lift

- Oral anti-inflammatory

- Cross-training

- Change of training

- Casting

- Physical therapy

- Flexibility exercises

- Surgery

How you can help prevent this problem:

- Wear supportive shoes

- Do calf stretching exercises, pages 246 and 247

- Decrease hill training

- Decrease speed workouts and track workouts

Kenneth's friends literally carried him into my office. By this time, he was starting to think that his buddies had made too big a deal about his injury. He was protesting, "I don't really need to be here. I could get up and walk out."

I performed the calf-squeeze test. Normally, when the muscle is squeezed the foot moves downward. Kenneth's foot didn't budge. That's about the worst sign you can have with an Achilles tendon injury: It told me that his tendon was completely ruptured. How much pain a person feels isn't an accurate indicator of how much damage has been done to the Achilles, but lack of the ability to flex the foot downward certainly is.

I and my associates operated on Kenneth the next morning, and found that his tendon looked like spaghetti. Years of overuse had taken a tremendous toll, until finally the Achilles was completely torn apart.

To repair the tendon properly, I first had to cut away all the bad spaghetti-like tendon to find two good ends. Then I lengthened the tendon by partially "splitting" it (a procedure called a Z-plasty) and sewed the whole thing together.

Since tendons don't have the good blood supply needed for quick healing and the Achilles tendon needs to be very strong to support the entire body weight, I kept Kenneth on crutches and in a cast for almost two months. Then he went through another three months of rehabilitation therapy. Only at that point, six months after his injury, could he slowly move back into running.

As was to be expected, years later Kenneth's Achilles tendon is still quite thick from the surgery and the buildup of scar tissue, and frequently gets sore. The repaired Achilles is definitely weaker than the tendon on his good leg—and always will be. He'll always have to baby it, because it's more susceptible to strain and injury than the other tendon.

Kenneth is able to run and participate in other sports, but not to the degree that he once did or to the degree that he'd like. However, he is realistic about his injury and now takes much better care of himself.

He now knows how important it is to be a smart athlete, rather than a "macho" one.

Chapter 15

ANKLE SPRAINS

Whenever a runner enters my office on crutches, my heart sinks. Few running injuries are so severe that a runner can't walk unaided.

And while I certainly commiserate with runners when they must decrease or stop training because of an injury, it's even worse when their condition is so serious that it affects everyday living.

One injury that can get to this point is an ankle sprain. These can involve various degrees of inflammation and tearing of the ankle ligaments, and how you treat them initially can make a difference in how the injury heals. These two cases of ankle sprains illustrate how important it is to treat these injuries promptly and correctly.

The Cost of a Moment's Inattention

Kathleen hobbled into the examining room on borrowed crutches. This 20-year-old recreational runner had competed in a 10-K race the previous morning.

"It was a beautiful morning for a run," she told me, "and my

ANKLE SPRAINS

Because you normally strike the ground on the outside portion of your heel, your foot makes every effort to pronate or roll inward so it can be flat on the ground. But occasionally your foot might accidentally roll to the outside. This causes an inversion-type ankle sprain or strain.

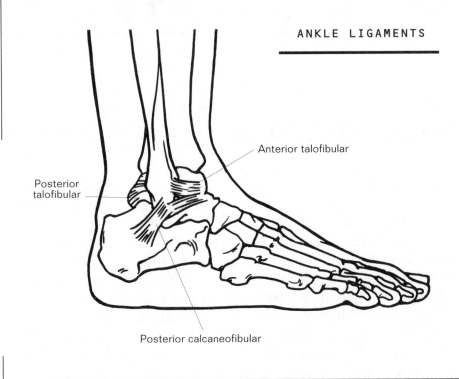

ANKLE LIGAMENTS

Anterior talofibular

Posterior talofibular

Posterior calcaneofibular

mind was more on the blue sky and the trees than on where I was going." Five miles into the race, she tripped on a speed bump in the road.

"One moment, I was staring off into the trees," she said. "The next moment, I was flat on my face."

She had twisted her ankle. Taking the advice of some well-intentioned bystanders, she alternated walking and jogging and was able to limp to the finish line.

The opposite type of ankle injury is called an eversion sprain. This is where your ankle rolls to the inside; it is much less common.

Ankle sprains are graded according to how much pain and disability they cause. A Grade I sprain, with stretching and inflammation of the ligaments, causes mild pain and slight swelling and normally resolves within a few days.

A Grade II sprain is more severe and involves tearing or partial tearing of one or more of the ligaments. It takes weeks for scar tissue to heal the tear. Since scar tissue isn't as pliable as the normal ligamentous tissue, the ankle will always be somewhat weak and prone to reinjury.

The Grade III sprain is the most severe, involving a complete tear of all three ligaments. This creates a completely unstable ankle and in an active individual usually necessitates surgery.

A sprained ankle can cause other conditions, including a tear of the joint capsule and, more commonly, a fracture of one or more of the bones around the ankle. Usually it is the fibula (the small bone in the lower leg) that breaks, but it can also be the base of the fifth metatarsal. This is why we doctors always X-ray the foot and ankle when a major sprain has occurred.

It can be difficult for you to tell how serious your injury is. But a good physician can tell you quickly and suggest appropriate treatment that can help it heal quickly and prevent recurrences.

But by the time she arrived home, her ankle was significantly sorer. She knew she was supposed to apply either heat or cold, but couldn't remember which. Since her Jacuzzi seemed much more inviting than a bucket of ice water, she chose that.

Later that evening she couldn't put any weight on her ankle, and the outside portion was swelling quite a bit. When she got up the next morning, the top of her foot and the outside of her ankle were almost completely discolored, plus the foot was badly swollen. Her toes felt cool and she could not put any weight on her ankle.

Now she was worried. She called her mother, who lived nearby, and Mom brought her crutches and drove her to my office.

Kathleen was wearing a sock but no shoe on the injured foot. She was in so much pain it took us nearly a minute to remove that sock.

As she told her story, she noticed my frown when she got to the Jacuzzi part. "Hot water might feel good at the moment, but it can really aggravate a fresh injury," I told her.

Submerging the injury in warm or hot water caused more bleeding and swelling than if she had done nothing at all. In most ankle injuries, ligaments and soft tissues tear and bleed. That is why the black-and-blue (or purple-and-blue) coloration occurs. Generally, the deeper and darker the coloration, the greater the amount of bleeding.

Immediately after an injury, icing is really the only sensible treatment. Ice helps decrease the bleeding, reduce the swelling, cut down on the inflammation and diminish the pain.

Icing is, of course, a component of the acronym RICE, which stands for Rest, Ice, Compression and Elevation. RICE is the best first aid for a sprained ankle, ensuring quicker healing and fewer complications.

Unfortunately Kathleen's Jacuzzi treatment had been the wrong choice. So now we had to deal with more bleeding and swelling than normal. This made her ankle more painful and difficult to examine.

I took an X-ray to rule out a fracture and found nothing broken. While this sounded like good news to Kathleen, I viewed it as a mixed blessing. Sometimes it's better to break your ankle than to sprain it: With a break, there's a definitive diagnosis and a specific treatment. For a broken bone, the runner gets a cast, the bone mends, and within a few weeks that person is back on the roads. Unless the bone doesn't heal, there are relatively few complications or residual problems.

But with a sprain all sorts of problems may go undiagnosed. There are usually tears to the lateral (outside ankle) ligaments—and sometimes to the medial (inside ankle) ligaments. There are also muscles and tendons that get pulled, torn or strained, and the ankle-joint capsule can get stretched or ripped.

Some of these injuries are very difficult to detect. Or one particular soft-tissue injury can be so severe that it overshadows another. Swelling adds to the difficulty of finding all the injured areas. And each specific problem that isn't diagnosed fails to get appropriate treatment, which can cause residual scar tissue and pain.

Because I couldn't examine Kathleen's ankle thoroughly due to the tremendous amount of swelling and pain, we conducted magnetic resonance imaging (MRI) on her ankle. This test revealed a complete tear of all three lateral ligaments in her ankle but no tearing of the medial ligaments, and significant swelling within her ankle joint and along various tendons of her foot and ankle.

This accurate diagnosis left us with a major decision to make. There are two primary ways to treat a complete tear of all the lateral ligaments.

The most conservative involves casting and physical therapy. The patient is placed in a cast for several weeks to allow healing of the ankle ligaments. Then a physical therapist works on the ankle for a period of four to eight weeks to reduce scar tissue and restore strength and function.

With a runner, however, this conservative approach isn't always successful. The ligaments almost always remain looser than before the injury and many runners later suffer another severe ankle sprain.

So our other option is a surgical repair of the ligaments. The person still needs a cast and physical therapy. But by the end of treatment, which takes about the same amount of time as the nonsurgical route, the ankle is much tighter and significantly less likely to be sprained again.

Kathleen opted for the surgery. She knew she would face months of casting and therapy anyway, and she wanted the end result to be an ankle as strong as possible so she could continue her running and other sports, including soccer.

I operated on her ankle along with John Beck, M.D., a prominent orthopedic surgeon. He, too, is a firm believer in post-operative physical therapy, and pointed out prior to the surgery, "If a first-year resident were performing the surgery and sent Kathleen to

BALANCE BOARD EXERCISE

This disk, which rolls on a semi-sphere, is used to help improve balance while recovering from ankle injuries.

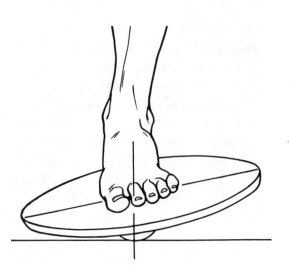

BAND EXERCISES

With your knees, feet and ankles together, tie a rubber exercise band loosely around your feet as shown at top. Pull the front of your feet apart, then relax. Repeat 10 times. Then tie the band around your feet with the ankles crossed, as shown at bottom. Push one foot out to the side, and relax. Repeat with the other foot, then relax. Repeat 10 times. (You can use a bicycle inner tube in place of an exercise band.)

physical therapy afterward, the result would be better than if I operated but no therapy were subsequently performed." That's quite a statement to come from a grand master of ankle surgery.

The surgery went well, as did Kathleen's rehabilitation. She has returned to her normal running regime—and although she still "smells the roses" on her runs, she also remembers to watch where she's going.

The Case of the Recurring Sprain

The vast majority of ankle sprains aren't sudden, debilitating sprains like Kathleen's. Chronic ankle pains, which occur as a result of several minor sprains, slow far more runners.

Laurie fits that second mold. She's a 35-year-old mother of two who has been running for about eight years. She runs around her neighborhood—five times a week, four miles at a time.

Laurie came to see me for pain on the outside of her right ankle. It had been recurring for the past five years. "It seems that every couple of years I sprain my ankle," she explained. "The pain lasts for about six months and then everything seems to clear up.

"I'll be fine for another year or so, then for no apparent reason my ankle just twists under me. I'll be laid up again for several months."

She recalled her first ankle sprain: "It was in college during our annual Sorority Olympics. During the sack race, I twisted my ankle and it swelled up pretty badly."

Friends took her to the student health facility, where the campus nurse just told her to rest and ice the ankle. Since it wasn't broken, the nurse figured there wasn't much else to do. Whenever Laurie reinjured the ankle later, she did the same thing—rested and iced it, plus wrapping it with an Ace bandage.

"I'm here today," she told me, "because I sprained it again a few weeks ago and I'm just getting tired of this. I sprained it on my normal run and when I got home I just sat down on my front porch and cried.

"I wasn't crying because of the pain—well, maybe a little bit— but mainly because I was so frustrated. Every time my running starts going well, this happens and I feel like I'm going to have to start building my training up all over again. I don't want to spend another half-year recuperating from this sprain—only to have it happen again."

Laurie's injury reminded me of a period when I held clinic hours at a local university's student health center. I noticed that many of the nurse practitioners and doctors would see students who had suffered ankle sprains.

Unfortunately, their diagnosis was usually limited to ruling out a break, then recommending icing and an elastic wrap. No matter how much I tried to impress upon these practitioners that their patients would have more problems down the line (as Laurie did) unless more aggressive action were taken, they said they didn't have the time or finances to do more.

Ankle sprains such as Laurie's are very common, and subsequent sprains and strains will almost certainly occur without adequate initial treatment. Yet the majority of runners receive only cursory care for the first sprain.

When Laurie first sprained her ankle—years before coming to see me—she undoubtedly tore some of the ligaments on the outside of her ankle. These help hold the ankle together and give it stability.

When the ligament fibers are torn, scar tissue fills in the gaps and "heals" the injury. But the ligaments normally heal looser than they were before, thus reducing the ankle's stability and strength. In addition, with your foot and ankle in a new position because of the ligament looseness, you might not be as aware of changes in footing.

So the next time Laurie hit an uneven surface, her ankle sprained more easily than it should have. After her second ankle sprain, even more scar tissue filled the new tear and even more of the weaker fibers were laid down in an effort to heal the new injury. The cycle continued as Laurie's ankle became weaker and less stable with each new sprain.

But fortunately there was a way to break this cycle and improve the integrity of her ankle.

Laurie experienced most of her pain over the anterior talofibular ligament on the outside of her ankle, one of the three ligaments on that side of the ankle and almost always the first one to tear. To a lesser extent, there was pain at the calcaneofibular ligament, generally the second one to tear. There was no pain in the third ligament, the posterior talofibular.

A strength test on Laurie showed that the muscles on the outside of her legs—the peroneals—were very weak. Because this muscle group helps roll your foot so it is flat and stable on the ground, the muscles help resist ankle sprains. Or at least they're *supposed* to.

If the ankle has been sprained, these peroneal muscles and tendons have failed at their job, and they likely were injured while trying to do it. When muscles are injured, your body tries to rest them to avoid further damage and allow healing. As a result, the strained or injured muscles aren't used very much and lose strength. The weakened muscles allow your ankle to sprain easier. This is exactly what happened in Laurie's case.

I prescribed physical therapy for Laurie. With an ankle sprain, this is absolutely the most important aspect of treatment.

Laurie's therapy took place at a clinic called Progressive Sports Therapy. The therapist evaluated Laurie's ankle and found that there was, indeed, major weakness around the lateral (outside) side of her ankle. She determined this by having Laurie stand and balance on her injured leg, with her eyes closed. Normally Laurie should have been able to do this for 60 seconds, but on that day she couldn't last 5 seconds!

In addition, the therapist confirmed a looseness of the ankle due to the repeated sprains and tears of the lateral ligament over the years. In fact, she was surprised that Laurie had not suffered a major sprain.

The treatment started with work to reduce the swelling around the ankle—thereby lessening pain and improving function. (Swelling prevents the ankle joint from going through its full range of motion as it guards against further injury.) This was accomplished with electrical stimulation as well as icing, compression and gentle massage. The stimulation involved interferential electrical stimulation, which uses specific electrical wave patterns that create a "pumping" effect to help drive the excess fluid out of the ankle.

The therapist next worked on the scar tissue, using ultrasound and cross-friction massage. The ultrasound softens the scar tissue so

ANKLE SPRAINS

You may have this problem if you experience:

■ Turned ankle

Your doctor may prescribe:

■ Rest, Ice, Compression, Elevation (RICE)

■ Physical therapy

■ Wearing a brace

■ Casting

■ Surgery

How you can help prevent this problem:

■ Do towel exercise, page 145

■ Do alphabet exercise, opposite page

■ Do band exercises, page 162

■ Do not run on unstable surfaces such as beaches or a grassy field

it can be reformed with massage to gain strength and to line up in the direction of force.

Next, the physical therapist went to work on improving Laurie's range of motion. The initial exercise was merely "tracing out the alphabet" by pointing with her toes and moving the whole foot three times a day. This was to actively work all of the muscles around the ankle joint. The exercises became more specific and intense as her ankle improved.

The therapist then helped Laurie increase her balance and coordination. After an ankle injury, these abilities are lost and the joint tends to become clumsy. By increasing specific coordination, Laurie

ALPHABET WRITING

Use your big toe as a "pen" to write the alphabet in the air, moving your ankle to form the letters. Repeat 3 times.

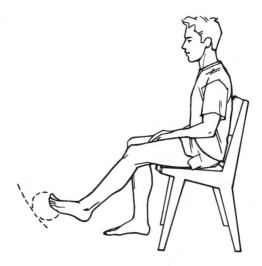

guarded against future sprains merely by improving her awareness of her ankle's position.

One of the ways the therapist did this was to have Laurie balance on a circular board that rests on a half sphere. This is called a BAPS (Biomechanical Ankle Platform System) board (see page 162). While balancing on the board, Laurie flexed her foot in all directions. As her ankle became more accustomed to this exercise, she graduated to bigger and bigger half spheres on the bottom of the board, which made it increasingly difficult to perform those circular motions and significantly improved her balance.

After six weeks of therapy, Laurie was ready to return to her normal activities while continuing her exercises at home. Her ankle was strong, her pain was gone and her balance, proprioception and strength were excellent.

We treated her over five years ago. Laurie hasn't had any more ankle pain in all that time. She now sends other patients to our office when they complain to her of chronic sprains or pains in their ankles. She realizes that without treatment their injury days would come to outnumber their running days—as they once did for her.

Chapter 16

SHIN PAIN

Of all the medical terms I routinely hear, "shin splints" is my least favorite. In fact, I intensely dislike this phrase.

Runners (as well as many doctors) use this term as if it were a definitive diagnosis. To me, it's a *non*-diagnosis that doesn't tell me anything. It can describe almost anything related to leg pain. You might as well say you have "foot splints," "knee splints" or "back splints." All this term tells me is the general location of the pain, not its cause.

Shin splints can actually be any of a half-dozen problems ranging from stress fractures to tendinitis to nerve irritation. Proper treatment starts with a specific and accurate diagnosis.

Sensible Sam and His Careful Routine

Sam thinks of himself as an "average" runner. He puts in about 25 miles a week and trains sensibly. He doesn't suddenly increase his mileage or speed, and enters only two or three 10-K races and maybe a couple of 5-K races each year. He buys new shoes every six months, always warms up before running and does his flexibility exercises religiously. Whenever he has a pain or injury, he rests until it gets better.

Sam is my idea of a model runner who tries to do everything correctly. So when Sam began to experience what he thought were shin splints, he did what he thought was logical.

He cut back on his training mileage and bought a new pair of shoes—the softest available. That way, he figured, there wouldn't be as much stress to his shins. He then bought shock-absorbing Viscoelastic insoles to give even more cushioning.

Unfortunately, his "shin splints" persisted. He went a step further in his softness crusade and started running only on the grass of a golf course.

But his problem got worse. Being the careful fellow he is, Sam stopped running and scheduled an appointment with me.

He gave me all the details, then added: "As I run, I seem to block out the pain and not feel it very much. But by the time I drive home and step out of the car, the pain has returned." Sam, who is a computer operator, said that when he got up from his chair for a break at work, his shins would also hurt.

When I examined Sam's leg, I determined that all his pain was on the inside of his shin bone. It radiated from about an inch above his ankle to about two inches below his knee.

He had very flat feet and was slightly bowlegged. Gait analysis on the treadmill showed that he also overpronated. His flexibility was excellent, but with Sam's cautious nature—which prompted him to stretch carefully—I would have expected that.

I explained, "It's obvious that your primary injury is tibial tendinitis. Tendons warm up and become longer as you use them more, then become tighter and hurt more when they're cold. That's why you feel less pain while running and more when you've been sitting."

Sam's overpronation was putting a big strain on the muscles and tendons on the inside portion of his leg. Because of the increased rolling motion, the tendons that help to resist that motion became stretched and strained, inflamed and painful.

Another key in diagnosing Sam's problem was his response to his various treatment programs. Everything he tried involved

SHIN PAIN

Shin splints can mean any pain around the front, inside or outside portion of the lower leg. (Medical specialists consider "shin splints" a garbage-can term. We don't like it, but many of us keep using it anyway.)

What we call shin splints can be any of the following:

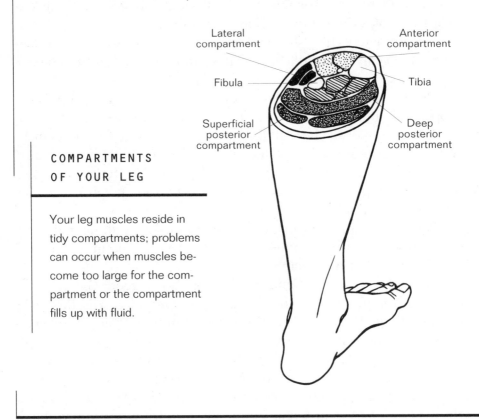

COMPARTMENTS OF YOUR LEG

Your leg muscles reside in tidy compartments; problems can occur when muscles become too large for the compartment or the compartment fills up with fluid.

moving toward softer surfaces and more cushioning. The soft shoes, cushion insoles and grassy surfaces did significantly decrease the amount of shock and jarring, but these experiments also increased the amount of motion his foot went through. This meant he was aggravating his problem instead of relieving it, because he already had too much motion.

Tendinitis of the lower leg. This can occur from over-stress or excess pronation. The pain will normally be felt along the inside of your shin bone, but may occur on the front or outside portions.

Inflammation of the bone covering. Periosteum is the material that covers your bones. When there is too much shock or jarring, it becomes inflamed, generally along the inside of the shin bone.

Stress fractures. These can occur in the leg or the foot. Normally, the fracture will appear low on the fibula, where the bone is thinnest.

Nerve irritation. The tibial nerve runs down the inside of the leg and around the inside of your ankle. It can become inflamed on the lower portion of the leg if it gets caught between muscles or veins that have become enlarged.

Compartment syndrome. The muscles, tendons, nerves, veins, arteries and bones of the leg run through four different com-partments. Each is tightly wrapped with a cellophane-type fascia. When fluid builds up in a compartment or muscles enlarge too quickly, pressure builds up there, and can diminish blood flow and cause pain.

The solution for Sam was to minimize overpronation. To do that, I prescribed sports orthotics made of polypropylene for him to wear while running.

He also added ice massage for 20 minutes twice a day, and some leg strengthening exercises to his routine. Two weeks after getting his orthotics, Sam resumed running and has had no complaints since. I'm sure that conscientious Sam continues to do what's right: follow a careful training program and pay attention to his body's complaints.

The Weekend Warrior Syndrome

Sam's story contrasts sharply with Mark's. The president of a Fortune 500 corporation, Mark wasn't the most sensible runner in the world.

He ran exclusively on the weekends, the only time he could fit running into his busy schedule. His entire weekly training schedule consisted of a six-mile run on Saturday and another on Sunday.

To help keep himself motivated, he entered races about twice a month, almost always 10-Ks. He would run them as hard and fast as he could. His 10-K times never seemed to improve very much, but this only motivated him to try harder at the next race. In fact, he set the stopwatch on himself with every training run and pushed to the limit.

When Mark came down with "shin splints," he tried to run them out. Monday morning, he went work with a severe limp. By Saturday, his shins felt better so he resumed his intense weekend training.

This cycle went on for about a month, until finally the pains became so severe that they didn't go away by the weekend. Mark went to see a sports masseuse, receiving leg massages three times a week. The pain persisted, however, and he came to see me.

When I examined Mark, I noticed he had very high-arched, rigid feet—feet that do not absorb shock well. Because of their lack of motion, almost all of the shock at each heel strike is transmitted straight up the leg, with only minimal cushioning.

Mark also had an extreme lack of flexibility in his calf muscles. He should have had 10 to 15 degrees of upward flexion of his ankle (with his knee straight): I was generous in giving him credit for 1 degree.

I took an X-ray of his leg and found he had periostitis running up and down the leg. This is an inflammation of the periosteum, the sheath that covers the bone.

Many of your tissues are surrounded by some type of wrapper.

Tendons have a tendon sheath, muscles have a muscle sheath and bone has periosteum. When bone is jarred too much, the sheath becomes inflamed and actually pulls away a little bit from the bone. This was apparent from Mark's X-ray.

His periostitis was due to excess shock; essentially this was an overuse problem. Although massage can be excellent therapy for many soft-tissue problems, it will only make periostitis worse by further inflaming the bone covering. I told Mark to discontinue the massage treatments immediately.

Our initial goal was to calm down the inflammation around the bone and periosteum. I placed Mark on anti-inflammatory medications and heavy-duty icing treatments. He had to ice his entire lower leg four or five times a day, no matter how busy his schedule. In addition, he had to stop running until the bone inflammation subsided.

This was also an excellent opportunity to reeducate Mark on the elements of a sensible training program, as well as improve his flexibility. I immediately started him on stretching exercises so that when he did return to running, he wouldn't have further problems due to the tight calf muscles.

In the meantime, Mark could cross-train, because periostitis would allow him to practice a nonpounding activity. I offered him the choice of swimming, using a cross-country ski machine, cycling and in-line skating. Not surprisingly, he decided to skate because he could go fast while not jarring his bone.

When Mark did return to running, he changed to soft, cushiony shoes. He had been wearing supportive, motion-control shoes—precisely the wrong choice for his type of foot.

Within a few weeks, Mark's bone inflammation resolved. Then he had another decision to make: How would he train in the future?

"If you only want to run twice a week," I told him, "you can do that. But you must reduce the intensity and run no more than three or four miles at a time.

"And no racing unless you change your training!" I admonished. "Two days a week of training doesn't give you an adequate base for racing." This was the main reason why he could never cut his 10-K time.

As it turned out, Mark still runs a few miles on the weekends.

But he came to enjoy his in-line skating so much that he now skates several times during the week and enters skating races rather than running events: I never thought to tell him not to enter *that* type of race! But at least he isn't continuing to injure himself with the jarring of running.

The Fracture That Wasn't

Beverly, a 27-year-old flight attendant, came to my office complaining of repeated stress fractures in her right leg. She said that every time she developed shin pain, her doctor would tell her she had a stress fracture and she'd have to stop running for three months.

The first stress fracture occurred a couple of years earlier, then again about a year later. Now her doctor was telling her she had developed another. All of the "fractures" were in approximately the same spot on her leg. She had pain even while working and was worried she might lose her job because of the frequent absences her injuries necessitated.

She said X-rays showed no break, and the pack of 15 X-rays she brought along confirmed this. There was no visible evidence of a fracture or of the normal resulting bone callus on any of those X-rays.

In fact, her doctor had made the diagnosis of a stress fracture using a nuclear medicine bone scan. Beverly's hot spot, indicating what the doctor thought was a fracture, had shown up as clear as day at the upper inside portion of her tibia.

But there would have been bone callus if there were a fracture. It was also doubtful that Beverly would get a stress fracture in that particular area of her tibia, since it is awfully thick up there. A fracture is most likely to occur at the bone's thinnest point.

The diagnosis of a fracture was incorrect. Beverly did have pain in the area of the "hot" bone scan, but it was not due to a fracture. The posterior tibial tendon and the soleus tendon insert at the top portion of the tibia, and I suspected tendon strains.

An exam showed that Beverly's calf muscles were extremely tight and she overpronated extensively. This combination had put such a strain on the muscles that the soleus tendon actually started pulling away from its attachment into the bone. As this separation occurred, the tendon pulled the bone covering (the periosteum) away from the bone as well. This caused an intense bone irritation—and hence the hot spot on the bone scan.

Beverly's treatment was relatively simple. We placed her on an aggressive flexibility program—with particular emphasis on the calf muscles and her soleus. This reduced the stress to that muscle at its attachment into her tibia.

We also switched her into a firmer, motion-control shoe. The new model was board-lasted, had a dual-density midsole and a supportive outersole. Then my assistant and I fitted her for two pairs of orthotics to control her excess motion and overpronation. One set was for running and one for work, because in her job as a flight attendant she had to do a great deal of walking up and down the airplane aisles.

Within a month, Beverly's symptoms completely disappeared. She has suffered no further "stress fractures."

Beverly's story illustrates how we must treat the body as a whole, rather than just the specific areas of pain. Without knowing her biomechanics, flexibility and mechanisms of gait, I would have never been able to solve her chronic problem.

When Things Go Very Wrong

One particular shin injury, known as compartment syndrome, can have disastrous consequences if an accurate diagnosis isn't made within a very short time. Just ask Terry.

Terry, a nationally ranked runner, was leading the pack in his first marathon when he felt a severe pain in his right leg.

The pain became so intense that he was forced to start walking at the 18-mile mark. After a few minutes, the pain decreased and he tried to run again—only to have it recur. He was forced to drop out of the race with what he thought was "the worst case of shin splints known to man."

Within the hour, he noticed his right foot was becoming colder and purple-blue. Terry knew he had a problem of major proportions and called me at home.

As soon as I saw him, I knew he had compartment syndrome,

SHIN PAIN

If you have pain at the front or sides of your legs, your doctor may prescribe:

- Oral anti-inflammatory

- Ice

- Taping

- Orthotics

- Flexibility exercises

- Strengthening exercises

- Change of shoe type

- Physical therapy

Warning: If foot becomes cold, purplish or blue, seek emergency treatment immediately.

How to help avoid this problem:

- Wear the proper shoes for your foot type (see chapters 4 and 5)

- Increase mileage no more than 10 percent per week

- Add speedwork judiciously

- Don't increase mileage and speedwork simultaneously

- Do band exercises, page 162

which occurs when too much pressure builds up in the leg. You have four compartments in your lower leg, each wrapped very tightly with a sheath—kind of like a plastic wrapping. When you have overdone an activity, either the muscles can become too big for that compartment or fluid from muscle and tendon strains can fill up the compartment. Pressure results because the compartment can't expand.

With the increased pressure the nerves, arteries and veins become compressed. This not only causes severe pain, but also pushes on the blood vessels and decreases the blood flow to the lower leg. That lack of blood flow creates an emergency situation. Without blood, Terry could have lost his foot.

We elevated Terry's leg and applied both ice and electrical stimulation. Gradually, the color returned to his foot and the pain diminished.

ACHING SHINS

Inflamed tendons, such as the tibialis posterior, can lead to shin pain.

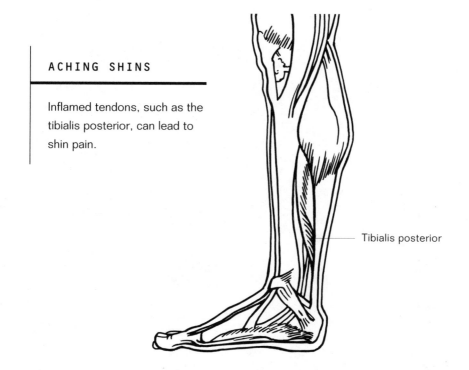

Tibialis posterior

Many times surgery is necessary to create holes or slices in the fascia to let the fluid escape and decrease the pressure. Fortunately, Terry didn't need that drastic a measure, but a number of runners have, including two-time world champion Mary Decker Slaney.

Terry was slowly able to return to running, but the symptoms kept recurring. He had to modify his training schedule significantly.

He did a great deal of cycling, which didn't aggravate that compartment. Gradually, the symptoms took longer to appear during his runs and were less severe.

Six months passed before Terry could get back to normal training. Fortunately, he has remained free of this problem. But his case exemplifies the tremendous stresses that can be exerted on the leg and the potential consequences of ignoring a problem that too many runners (and some doctors) still dismiss as "a simple case of shin splints."

Chapter 17

CHONDROMALACIA PATELLA: RUNNER'S KNEE

My running career started on a bet. Looking back almost 20 years ago, I realize that probably wasn't the best incentive. But at the time, several of my classmates thought I would have a reasonable chance at beating one of our medical school's senior residents in San Francisco's Bay to Breakers race.

My training for this 7½-mile event consisted of running two miles to school in the morning and two miles back home at the end of the day. I did this for six weeks, occasionally throwing in track workouts on weekends. I thought I was ready.

Unfortunately, my opponent was a real runner who had been running for years and knew how to train properly. Even though I started in the front of the pack of 10,000 runners and he started somewhere in the middle, he still caught me at the halfway point and never looked back.

From that irresponsible beginning, I have logged more miles and races than I care to remember. While I've tried to train sensibly, I too have had my share of running injuries. None is more memorable than the one that's so common that it's called "runner's knee."

This condition isn't limited to runners—tennis players call it

CHONDROMALACIA PATELLA

Chondromalacia patella, or "runner's knee," is a softening of the cartilage covering the underside of the kneecap and gliding against the thigh.

This generally occurs because the kneecap is not tracking as it should. It is supposed to glide easily up and down the leg as it helps the quadriceps muscles achieve good mechanical leverage. But with excess pronation, the patella deviates to the inside.

RUNNER'S KNEE

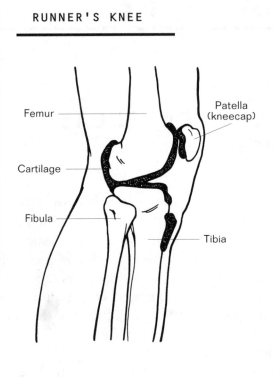

Femur

Cartilage

Fibula

Patella (kneecap)

Tibia

When this happens, the cartilage that lines the surface underneath the patella (kneecap) erodes or breaks down. Under stress, the cartilage softens and then slowly develops tears and cracks. This can result in a crunching, clicking or rough-feeling motion of the patella—and, of course, pain.

Unfortunately, eroded cartilage can't heal or be replaced. It's gone forever and the damaged knee is now an arthritic knee that will become inflamed because the cartilage can no longer provide adequate cushioning to protect the joint as the kneecap moves. The degree of damage, of course, depends on how badly the cartilage was affected. A surgical procedure known as a patellar scraping removes debris from the kneecap, and in some cases relieves a degree of pain.

"tennis knee." The medical term for it is chondromalacia patella; it means a softening or breakdown of the cartilage beneath the kneecap (patella).

When the Doctor Becomes the Patient

My personal introduction to this injury came while training for the Boston Marathon. I was totaling around 65 miles a week and I thought that I was doing everything sensibly and by the book.

Then, in the middle of a hilly 18-mile run, I felt a twinge under my kneecap. The pain wasn't sharp or debilitating, but the thought that I might have chondromalacia patella gave me a sick feeling.

As you know from reading this book, I should have stopped running on the spot. But as luck would have it, I was running a loop course and was about as far away from the finish of it as I could be. I was also training with a half-dozen other runners and didn't want to show any weakness. So I completed the run.

The next morning I could hardly get out of bed. As I limped around, I could feel a crunching sensation beneath my kneecap. A bad sign! I felt a lot of emotions, but denial wasn't one of them. It was obvious that I had chondromalacia patella and something had to be done about it right away.

This injury normally comes on slowly. It doesn't happen all of a sudden unless you receive a major blow or trauma to your knee. It's an insidious process that typically takes months or years to produce painful symptoms. I do remember having had a little post-run achiness around my knee, which I didn't think too much about. But now I know it had been a sign that this problem had been developing ever since I increased my training and started doing hill work. I realized that while I'd been increasing my mileage, my knee cartilage had been gradually softening and eroding undetected.

In medicine, we have a saying: A doctor who treats himself has a fool for a patient. Though I desperately wanted to solve my own problem, I knew I'd make a lousy patient for myself.

By chance, I was scheduled to give a lecture at the Portland Marathon the next day. My flight to Oregon was fine, but trying to stand up after sitting for 2½ hours on the plane was pure agony. It felt like someone had thrown grit and rocks under my kneecap.

Walking down the stairs from the aircraft into the terminal was even more difficult. The other passengers must have wondered as I hobbled down the stairway, supporting myself by holding onto both sides of the ramp.

This embarrassing deplaning convinced me to seek treatment from an old buddy and former classmate, Jay Goldstein, D.P.M., a sports-medicine podiatrist in Portland. Jay and I had worked together filming runners while we were in medical school.

One reason doctors make terrible patients is that we think we know everything and we want to impart that knowledge to whomever is treating us. I tried to "help" Jay perform his examination, but he would have none of it. "I'll let you tell me your history," he said. "But after that I'm the doctor and you're the patient."

After hearing my tale of woe and listening to me explain the importance of my upcoming marathon (boy, did I sound like *my* patients!), he took a thorough history. Then he examined my knee.

He asked if I could perform a squat. Forget it. My knee crunched loud enough for both of us to hear.

Then he performed the all-important test: He had me sit with my legs straight in front of me and held onto my kneecap while I contracted my quadriceps muscles. That produced more crunching and a great deal of pain.

Another strong indication of chondromalacia patella is weakness in the hip flexors. Generally, when chondromalacia patella occurs, the muscles that flex the hips weaken to avoid putting too much stress or pressure on the kneecap. You don't notice this unless you specifically test for it. To do this, Jay had me sit on the edge of the examining table and try to extend my leg upward while he applied resistance with his hand. I was so weak I couldn't lift my leg against as little as 10 pounds of force or less.

He also tested the flexibility in my various muscle groups. To test my hamstring flexibility, Jay had me lie on my back and—with my leg straight—lift the leg up as high as possible. I should have been able to make a 90-degree angle between the table and my leg, but I fell 20 degrees short of that.

The hamstrings play an important part in knee function: Any tightness in this muscle group can hamper the ability of the knee to go through its normal range of motion. My calf muscles were also fairly tight, as were my quadriceps, iliotibial band, and the muscles that flex the hips. Combined with my tight quads and hip flexors, there was just no way my knee could function normally.

By this time my knee was feeling pretty achy. I asked Jay, "Are you about finished with the exam?"

I had forgotten how thorough he is. Despite my protests, he insisted on doing a gait analysis. I had to admit that I had never had my gait checked by another podiatrist. He checked my gait, both running and walking.

I was wearing a motion-controlling shoe, but still over-pronated. Jay classified my overpronation as severe, and that alone can lead to chondromalacia patella. The patella (kneecap) is designed to ride smoothly in a groove in your femur. It should glide easily and with an equal amount of pressure on each side as it moves up and down.

But excessive pronation leads to abnormal torsion of the knee. These forces cause your patella to be twisted medially (toward the inside). This creates uneven pressure on your patella, which erodes the cartilage.

Additional abnormal pressure comes from the quadriceps muscles. In an effort to keep your kneecap tracking as normally as possible, the lateral portion of the quadriceps pulls harder while the medial quadriceps relax their pull on the patella. These forces pull the kneecap out of its groove, causing further damage.

Jay suspected that faulty biomechanics had laid the groundwork for my injury over a period of many years. One way to verify his suspicion was to check the angle formed by the quadriceps muscles and the patella.

This is the Q-angle that I explained in chapter 1. The normal Q-angle for a man is 10 degrees or less, and mine measured 21 degrees. With my high Q-angle and the tremendous amount of pronation, I was surprised I'd never dislocated my knee!

The Road to Recovery

Now Jay proposed his treatment plan. Due to the pain that my travel had aggravated, he placed me on Motrin—a nonsteroidal anti-inflammatory medication—to be taken immediately *after* my run (so the pills wouldn't mask the pain of my injury). He also told me to ice the knee. Next, he fitted me with orthotics.

Then he ordered me to lower my mileage by at least half, which meant limiting my weekly distance to 30 miles, with no workout longer than 6 miles.

That was a pretty bitter pill to take, with the Boston Marathon only two months away. But I figured that I'd already damaged my knee enough: There was no sense in being stupid and destroying it for the rest of my life.

The knee is easy to ice: You just fill a plastic bag with ice and use an elastic wrap to hold it to your knee. I iced three or four times a day for 20 minutes each time for the next two weeks.

Fellow passengers on airline flights looked on with sympathy as I iced my knee. They asked, "Have you been in an accident?" When I told them with some embarrassment that it was a nontraumatic running injury, their sympathetic looks vanished.

When I returned home, I immediately filled the final part of Jay's prescription: putting myself in the hands of a sports-minded physical therapist. She, too, warned me to be not the doctor but the patient.

The therapist was surprised that I had managed to train for so long at the mileage I'd been doing. She immediately began a program to restore strength to the medial part of the quadriceps muscles, which was virtually not functioning. In addition, she devised a program to strengthen my hip muscles.

Included in my rehabilitation prescription were exercises designed to retrain my quadriceps muscles to control my patella and allow it to pull evenly instead of at an angle. These strengthening exercises included quarter squats and step-downs, as shown on the opposite page.

Finally, the therapist worked to improve my flexibility, especially in my quads, hip flexors and hamstrings. These exercises have been a part of my running program ever since.

Two months after my original injury, I was back to about 35 miles a week, my normal mileage before I started training for the marathon. I ran my first 8-miler since the injury at just about the time the starter's pistol was announcing the beginning of the Boston Marathon. But at that point I was happy to be able to run at all.

In fact, I was able to run the Boston Marathon the next year. I'm certain that my increased strength, flexibility and coordination helped me train for it injury-free and record a satisfying finish time.

QUARTER SQUATS

Stand upright, with your back straight. Then bend the knees slowly to a quarter squat, as shown. (In a full squat, your thighs would be parallel to the floor.) Repeat 10 times, making sure your knees pass directly over the toes instead of bending out to the sides.

STEP—DOWNS

Stand on a box 4 inches high and tighten your quadriceps, with particular attention to the vastus medialis oblique, a muscle that runs down the inside of your knee. Keeping this muscle tight in one leg, lower the other leg slowly toward the floor and back up to the box. Relax and repeat 40 times. Switch to other leg and repeat.

The Peril of Ignoring Pain

Many people who have chondromalacia run with neoprene sleeves or braces. They believe this helps their knee track better. Most importantly, these runners insist that those supports allow them to run without pain.

While I don't doubt that these devices help psychologically, they do very little functionally. They're a poor substitute for biomechanical corrections and for strengthening and stretching exercises.

Remember, whenever you have any running injury you should look for a cure, not a crutch. Sooner or later the crutches fail, and you usually end up in a worse condition than when you started.

Jim is a good example of a runner using a shortcut to treat an injury. He developed chondromalacia patella while training for the New York City Marathon.

He trained between 50 and 55 miles per week. About a month before the marathon, he developed the same type of grinding knee pain that prevented me from running the Boston Marathon.

But instead of seeing a sports-medicine specialist, Jim went to his local athletic-shoe store and bought a tube of a deep-heating rub and a neoprene sleeve. He then limped through the rest of his training program, usually ending his runs in severe pain. There just wasn't time for him to rest since he felt he *had* to compete in this event. His only compromise was to shorten his long runs, because they'd become too painful to tolerate.

Jim's biggest hint that he wasn't ready for the marathon occurred when he arrived in New York City. After eight hours of flying, he literally couldn't get up out of his seat. Airline personnel had to help him off the plane in a wheelchair. He didn't have the nerve to tell them that he was about to attempt a marathon.

After resting in his hotel room for two days, Jim made it to the starting line for the race. He managed to run eight miles before the pain was too much. It was all he could do to hobble to the side of the road and sit down. Since it was a rainy day and all he was wearing was his shorts and T-shirts, hypothermia started to set in.

Luckily, a kind spectator helped Jim into a taxi. So there he was, shivering in a cab, unable to walk, feeling sick, in a strange city with no money. This wasn't what he had in mind when he sent in his New York City Marathon entry.

CHONDROMALACIA PATELLA

You may have this problem if you experience:

- Pain under kneecap

- Pain around kneecap

Your doctor may prescribe:

- Oral anti-inflammatory

- Ice

- Knee brace

- Orthotics

- Flexibility exercises

- Strength exercises

- Physical therapy

- Change of shoe type

- Change of training

How you can help prevent this problem:

- Wear proper shoes

- Do quadriceps strengthening exercises (quarter squats and step-downs), page 185

- Do quadriceps flexibility exercises, page 241

- Do hamstring flexibility exercises, pages 239 and 240

- Avoid running downhill

Somehow, he was able to get to the finish line, find his girl-friend and receive medical attention. But it was a *long* plane ride back home the next day.

His doctor discovered that Jim had a severe case of chondro-malacia. Jim was immediately placed on anti-inflammatory medications and referred to physical therapy. He underwent six weeks of physical therapy and rehabilitation to strengthen the muscles around his knee. While his condition improved greatly, Jim eventually gave up running. The cartilage was damaged beyond repair and could not withstand the stresses of running.

Given his intense training schedule and the time restraints of his upcoming marathon, Jim, of course, should have seen a sports-medicine specialist as soon as he experienced pain. Although giving up the dream of competing in the New York Marathon would have been painful, it might have meant saving Jim's running career.

Jim hasn't returned to New York since that aborted marathon. The memory of it is still too painful.

Yet he has framed his race number. It hangs in his den along-side the discarded neoprene sleeve as reminders to exercise better judgment in the future.

Chapter 18

ILIOTIBIAL BAND SYNDROME: A TRICKY KNEE PROBLEM

The iliotibial band, also known as the iliotibial tract, can be a tricky little devil. Composed of muscles and fascia (fibrous tissue surrounding muscles), it runs from your pelvis down the outside of your thigh, where it connects to other fascia, muscle, and rough edges or bumps on your leg bones.

Three different factors can leave the iliotibial band (ITB) inflamed and tender: overpronation, underpronation and inflexibility.

Regardless of the cause, the symptoms are pretty much the same: pain on the outside of the knee. And trying to pinpoint the cause can sometimes drive both doctor and patient crazy.

The Runner Who Refused to Stretch

Dina, a 38-year-old runner, trains sensibly with one exception: She never does any flexibility exercises.

When she meets with her running friends, Dina purposely shows up late so she won't feel obligated to stretch with them. She

ILIOTIBIAL BAND SYNDROME

The iliotibial band (ITB) runs down the side of your leg from your hip to just below your knee. One of the areas where it attaches (through a muscle called the biceps femoris) is the head of the fibula, the smaller of the two major leg bones. That area is most often the source of pain when this band is injured.

One major cause of an ITB injury is too much pronation in the foot and ankle. This happens because the ITB's attachment to the front and outside portions of the leg tries to give lateral stability to your knee and to resist internal rotation of your lower leg. The resultant pain from the ITB's attempts to resist this excessive motion almost always occurs at the point where this band pulls the biceps femoris muscle—the head of the fibula.

The ITB is also very susceptible to the forces from underpronation—when the foot moves too little when it strikes the ground and doesn't absorb much shock. The ITB not only helps stabilize the knee, but also helps the knee absorb shock. With a foot that underpronates, the ITB is subjected to more shock than normal, which causes inflammation and irritation at the head of the fibula.

The third major cause of ITB problems is lack of flexibility in this band, which can be the result of weakness in some hip muscles. Even though fascia has little ability to stretch, the muscles which attach to it—including the big gluteus maximus of your but-

told me, "I find stretching so boring that I just can't bring myself to do it."

Dina had been running for eight years and, except for the usual minor aches and pains, had never been injured. Then she ran a 7-K race on the beach. Beach runs are uncommon—for good reason, in my opinion. Running on a soft surface does ease most of the shock and jarring of heel strike. But it also gives almost zero

tocks—are able to lengthen. But because the exercise designed to stretch the ITB, which is described on page 244, is somewhat awkward, very few people incorporate it into their flexibility routines.

KNEE JOINT SHOWING
ILIOTIBIAL BAND

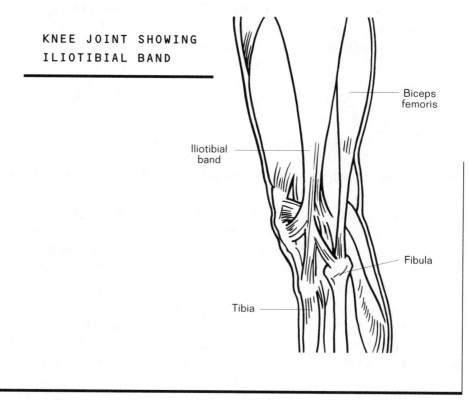

Biceps femoris

Iliotibial band

Fibula

Tibia

"energy return"—that is, the surface absorbs energy while giving virtually none back. A certain degree of shock absorption is good (which is why you buy cushioned shoes). But you also need some springiness. Because the beach gives none, you have to work harder just to keep moving.

In addition, the sand on the beach is slanted toward the water. This means that you are running on a banked surface, making one leg compensate by acting as if it's longer than the other. The leg closest to the ocean pronates less than normal due to this camber, while the upward leg pronates more. The beach run was Dina's undoing. Her upper leg created her problem because of the forced overpronation (this was a one-way race). She described a pain right on top of the head of her fibula that extended upward to a spot on the outside of her knee. Although she thought it was her knee that hurt, it actually was the area of the ITB's point of attachment to the muscle and fascia—well below and to the outside of the knee.

Dina thought her problem was a bone bruise, and it's true that the ITB inserts at a bony prominence. As I reminded her, however, bones don't have nerve endings; the soft tissue of the ITB and supportive muscles does. "It's those nerves that sense your pain and let you know that something is wrong," I told Dina.

Because the injury had occurred while she was running on a soft surface, I could be fairly certain that Dina did not have a shock-related problem. A mechanically induced problem was more likely.

I checked Dina's gait on the treadmill using our video analysis equipment. Sure enough, she overpronated a lot: 12 degrees in her rearfoot, at least twice the normal angle. When I moved Dina's foot into the position of maximum pronation, I could feel the tightness where the iliotibial band connected, and above it.

Moving Dina's foot also reproduced the pain she'd been feeling. So I was confident that we'd discovered the major cause of her ITB syndrome. But I also needed to check her flexibility, although I thought I knew what I'd find based on her refusal to stretch.

Boy, was I surprised! Dina's calves and hamstrings were a bit tight, but probably not enough to have triggered her ITB problem. Then I performed a very specific test to determine the flexibility of her iliotibial band, which I described in chapter 1. It's called the Ober test.

Dina laid on her left side, keeping her hip and knee flexed, while I held her right leg (the painful one) above and slightly behind the left leg. I then released her right leg. It easily fell to the level of the bottom leg—as it should.

When the iliotibial band is too tight, the tested leg remains hanging above the other leg even when dropped, due to the tight pull of the ITB. So, despite her reluctance to stretch, Dina didn't have a tight ITB.

Passing all her flexibility tests made Dina a bit smug—but now I knew her overpronation alone had caused the problem.

Our treatment plan was relatively simple. First, I told her not to run on the beach anymore. That alone decreased her overpronation and took a load off her ITB.

Next, we took a close look at her running shoes. Dina was running in very soft shoes—exactly the wrong type for her. As an overpronator, she needed a motion-control shoe instead of a cushioning one.

To make matters worse, her shoes were at least a year old and had definitely seen better days. I told Dina, "You've received your money's worth out of these worn-out shoes. Retire them—permanently—and buy a new, more appropriate shoe."

Dina bought new shoes—this time with a firmer midsole, rearboard lasted and with motion-control devices built into the midsole. She came back the following day and I again watched her run on the treadmill. This time her gait showed much better alignment—the new shoes worked as intended.

Within two weeks, Dina's ITB problem disappeared. I never was able to convince her that she needed to stretch, and so far she's able to get along without stretching. She continues her normal running and only skips one race a year—the beach run.

Setting the Stage for Injury

Girard arrived in my office complaining of a pain just below his knee, on the outside of the leg. Normally, Girard ran 40 miles per week, but recently he'd jumped to 50 to prepare for a marathon.

Unlike Dina, his pain hadn't suddenly appeared after a race but had developed slowly over a four-week period. The problem had first shown up halfway through a 12-mile training run.

This surprised him. "I've increased my mileage pretty sensibly," Girard told me. "I've had occasional, mild discomfort in this area throughout my four-year running career, but a change of shoes usually solved the problem quickly."

He replaced his running shoes every two months, no matter

what their condition. He didn't want to take the chance of having them break down and cause him painful symptoms.

Over the years, Girard had tried a number of different brands, models and styles—whatever was popular at the moment. But his unwritten two-month rule for shoe changes seemed to work no matter what brand or model he bought.

When the pain started this time, Girard again tried switching shoes. Unfortunately, his pains didn't respond. In fact, they worsened.

Given his area of injury, it was obvious to me that Girard had pain in his iliotibial band. In direct contrast to overpronator Dina, Girard's gait analysis showed a *lack* of sufficient motion.

His biomechanical measurements showed that his ankle joint flexed only two degrees after his heel hit the ground, while between four and six degrees is needed to absorb shock adequately. Girard also has a very high-arched, rigid foot.

Girard was also a bit inflexible in his calf and hamstring muscles, although I wouldn't have classified them as tight. But he failed the Ober test miserably: His iliotibial band was extremely tight.

We added a post-run stretch to Girard's flexibility routine. This consisted of him turning sideways against a wall after his run and, with his legs crossed, pushing his hip into the wall. He held this position for 30 seconds and repeated it five times per leg. (See page 244 for diagram.)

This is an exercise that few runners do. In fact, unless you've had an iliotibial band problem, you have probably never heard of it. But if you're susceptible to this injury, it's an excellent specific exercise.

To make better use of the time he spent stretching, I instructed Gerard to stretch *after* his runs, instead of before running, to maximize the benefits.

The combination of an underpronating foot and a tight ITB explained Girard's inability to absorb shock. It also was the reason he needed to replace his shoes every two months. Since his shoes, not his legs, provided most of his shock absorption, they would break down after a couple of months' use. When the shoes could no longer dissipate the impact, knee pain resulted.

To make matters worse, the shoes Girard selected were all

ILIOTIBIAL BAND SYNDROME

You may have this problem if you experience:

■ Pain on the outside of the knee

Your doctor may prescribe

■ Ice

■ Change of shoes

■ Change of running surface

■ Cushioned innersole

■ Orthotics

■ Flexibility exercises

■ Strength exercises

■ Physical therapy

What you can do to help prevent this problem:

■ Wear correct shoes

■ Avoid running on banked surfaces such as beaches or tracks

■ Do the iliotibial band stretch, page 244

■ Do calf flexibility exercises, pages 246 and 247

■ Do hamstring flexibility exercises, pages 239 and 240

wrong. While Dina had chosen a shoe that was too soft for her, Girard had selected a firm, motion-control shoe rather than the softer model he required.

Why? Because one of his running buddies recommended it.

Although that model worked just great for his friend, who had flat feet, Girard's high-arched feet weren't getting what they needed. The additional 10 miles of training a week—in the wrong shoes— had triggered his ITB problem.

I also noticed from his training log that Girard had moved shortly before he was injured. Previously he had been putting in most of his mileage on asphalt roads and hard-packed dirt trails; now he was running almost exclusively on concrete sidewalks, a harder surface.

So everything seemed to be working against Girard and favoring his injury: the increased mileage, the firmer shoes and the firmer surfaces.

It was an easy matter to put Girard into the correct, softer, slip-lasted shoes without motion-control devices. Much to the delight of the personnel at his shoe store, he continues to buy shoes every two months. To help further absorb shock, I prescribed a cushioned, Viscoelastic innersole. Girard also altered his running so that he'd be on a softer surface at least half the time.

Shock-related problems generally take longer than motion problems to resolve, however. It is pretty easy to control or minimize excess motion. But with a rigid foot, it's a matter of lessening the amount of shock in small increments.

We also placed Girard into physical therapy for three weeks. The therapist used ultrasound and cross-friction massage to help increase the circulation into the injured area and to remodel any scar tissue that might have built up. In addition, Girard was given more exercises for flexibility, strength and coordination.

Girard's injury took about a month to heal, and he was soon back on the roads. He was able to run his planned marathon—and told me later, "It was the most exciting experience of my life."

Chapter 19

PLICA AND MENISCUS INJURIES: MORE KNEE WOES

Since the knee is the biggest joint in your body, it also earns the distinction of being the joint runners injure the most. In fact, it is the most commonly injured joint in almost all athletic endeavors.

The reason for all of these knee injuries isn't so much the size of this joint as the responsibilities the knee carries. It supports your body's weight *and* is the prime joint for moving you forward.

The knee is also your main shock absorber. Running is basically a series of crashes, and at each footstrike your knee joint has to absorb the pounding impact of several times your body's weight.

So whether you have a problem in the knee joint itself, or the supporting muscles, tendons, ligaments or cartilage, all injuries around your knee must be taken very seriously. While you might shrug off certain pains, those affecting your knee should almost always warrant immediate attention. Otherwise, you might suffer permanent and irreparable damage to this important joint.

PLICA AND MENISCUS INJURIES

All joints have cartilage and fluid to separate the bones so bone doesn't rub against bone. That would be like running your car's engine without oil. There would be all sorts of scraping and grinding, and the entire joint would deteriorate quickly.

The synovium, the inside of the joint capsule of your knee, acts as a self-lubricating ball bearing. It secretes synovial fluid that lubricates the joint surface and allows your bones to glide smoothly over each other. For additional cushioning there are various bursae, fluid-filled sacs that contain synovial tissue, around your knee joint. If everything works well, this system provides a smooth, gliding surface so there is no erosion or irritation of the joint.

But sometimes things go very wrong inside the knee joint—producing a lot of pain and taking all the joy out of running. Two knee injuries that can plague runners are plica syndrome and problems with a cartilage called the meniscus.

Plica syndrome. The plica are folds of soft tissue that sit within the knee, on either side of the kneecap. If the plica becomes irritated or inflamed because of injury or biomechanical problems, it can produce a great deal of pain.

Meniscus problems. Another vulnerable tissue within the knee is a cartilage called the meniscus. Its jobs are to provide shock absorption within your knee, to help the knee function

Don't "Run It Out"

Stephanie ran track and cross-country at college. With her team, she entered 5-K races. She didn't particularly like these events because her coach insisted that the team run together during the race. He would always say, "The team that runs together wins together."

Stephanie wasn't one of the team's faster runners. In fact, she

smoothly, to improve your weight distribution and to protect the outside borders of your knee joint. Usually runners injure the medial meniscus rather than the lateral meniscus. It's usually injured by a twisting motion or a blow to the side of the knee.

Don't let a knee injury put an end to your running career: These types of injuries require treatment by a professional.

A POTENTIALLY TROUBLESOME FOLD

The plica is a fold of soft tissue that sits aside of the kneecap. Falling on the knee or twisting with the foot planted can cause the plica to become inflamed and painful.

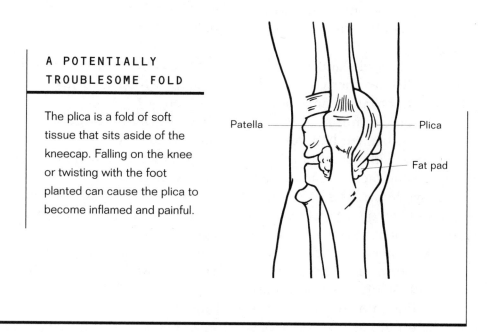

Patella — Plica — Fat pad

had to struggle to keep up with her teammates. But not wanting to slow down the whole team, she ran one particular race as hard as she could—and perhaps harder than she should have.

The night after the race, she went to a movie—which happened to be a long one—and at the end she literally couldn't get out of her seat. Her left knee had stiffened so badly that her friends had to help her stand up.

A friend told her, "You probably just overdid it during the race this morning and should take a couple of days off." Unfortunately, her coach had other ideas. He told her she was just stiff and needed to "run it out."

So the next day Stephanie ran the normal workout with her team. She began thinking that her coach was right, since her knee did feel much better at the end of that training session. But after her 30-minute drive home, she couldn't step out of her car without pain.

She put up with this discomfort for the next two weeks, continuing to train with her team. Every time she sat down for any length of time, her knee would refuse to cooperate. Friends who saw her hobble around school couldn't believe she was still running.

The school's athletic trainer noticed that her hamstrings were very tight but otherwise could find nothing wrong with her knee. He sent her to the team's orthopedic surgeon.

After examining her knee, the orthopedic surgeon told Stephanie that she had developed a plica syndrome. Any condition that ends with "syndrome" usually means there are a number of contributing factors leading to the final symptoms. In the case of a plica syndrome, this is especially true. For a host of reasons, this area can be come irritated, scarred or inflamed. When that happens, you experience symptoms just like Stephanie's.

After her orthopedic surgeon examined the knee, he referred her to me for a biomechanical evaluation as well as to a physical therapist. Stephanie was confused.

"I don't understand it," she told me. "I have a knee problem, but here I am at a foot doctor's office. I also have this prescription for physical therapy. The physical therapy I can understand, but I have a more difficult time relating my problem to your specialty."

I told her that I would answer her questions *after* I performed an examination. I first performed a flexibility test. Not only were Stephanie's hamstrings tight, but so were her calf muscles and the muscles around her hips. Stephanie said she did stretching exercises "once in a while"—when she had to with the team or when she thought of it, which wasn't too often.

Stephanie's gait analysis told me quite a bit about why her orthopedic surgeon had referred her to me: Stephanie pronated excessively. You could even see the effect of this pronation on her shoes. They were the best shoes she could buy—excellent motion-control ones. Yet the whole heel counter of her left shoe had broken down to the inside.

Her biomechanical evaluation showed that she overpronated almost 10 degrees. That amount of excessive motion really takes its toll on the knee when combined with the shock of running.

Adding to Stephanie's woes was the fact that the medial portion of her quadriceps muscle—known as the vastus medialis oblique (VMO)—was so weak that I couldn't even get her to contract the muscle.

To piece together Stephanie's problem, I showed her what was happening to her knee when she ran, and why she was in pain. "Your tight posterior muscle groups and the excessive overpronation caused the kneecap to track poorly and restrict its normal motions," I explained. "This caused the fold in the joint capsule—our friend, the plica—to become irritated and inflamed. This is what led to your pains.

"When you have a plica syndrome, it is very common to have a great deal of pain and stiffness of the knee after it has been flexed for quite some time. This often happens, as it did with you, at movie theaters or after you've taken a long drive. It generally doesn't hurt when you wake up in the morning because your legs have been straight at night."

Stephanie was already icing and taking oral anti-inflammatories prescribed by her orthopedic surgeon to quell the inflammation at the plica. I fitted her with functional orthotic devices to control her excess pronation, which would then take the stresses away from her knee.

Her physical therapy program was geared primarily toward decreasing her plica's inflammation via ultrasound, deep-tissue massage and more icing. The therapist also worked to increase the strength in her VMO and improve her flexibility—plica syndromes almost always go hand in hand with hamstring tightness.

Stephanie's pains eased within a few weeks, and she only

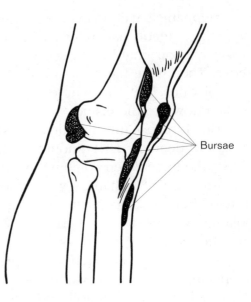

Bursae

missed a couple of relatively insignificant cross-country meets. Her coach now realizes that you can't just "run through" every injury. At least not a plica syndrome.

What Happens When You Ignore the Pain

For many runners, however, this problem comes on slowly and runners put up with the discomfort for far too long. When the condition goes unchecked, the chronic inflammation causes the plica to thicken and scar. Once that happens, the conservative approaches of anti-inflammatory medications and physical therapy have less chance of succeeding.

Symptoms can include sharp pains (rather than the dull aches Stephanie experienced). In some cases, runners will step off a curb after a run and have the knee collapse on them.

Lester was a runner who allowed this condition to go unchecked for more than four years. Not only would his knee occasionally buckle, but by the time he sought treatment his knee would "catch" periodically and sometimes even lock up. On his frequent business trips Lester had to fly first class so he had enough room to keep his leg straight.

PLICA AND MENISCUS INJURIES

You may have this problem if you experience:

- Knee pain

- Knee stiffness after sitting still

- A knee that "catches"

Warning: If your knee "catches" or buckles, see a doctor promptly.

Your doctor may prescribe:

- Ice

- Oral anti-inflammatory

- Orthotics

- Flexibility exercises

- Surgery

- Physical therapy

How you can help prevent this problem:

- Do quadriceps strengthening exercises, page 185

- Report knee pain to your doctor

His condition became so severe that the anti-inflammatory medications and physical therapy his orthopedic surgeon prescribed didn't work. Surgery was required to remove the thickened and inflamed plica. (You can get along without the plica just fine.) Following the operation, Lester needed six weeks of physical therapy to rehabilitate his knee and restore muscle strength.

He's now back to running, a lot wiser for the experience. Lester will be the first to tell you that if an injury persists for longer than a few weeks, seek professional help. "Four years is definitely too long to wait," he says.

Lester's only problem now is that he's back to flying coach with the rest of his company's employees.

That Tricky Meniscus

As a teenager, Cheryl was an avid soccer player. However, one day during a game as she came down ready to kick the ball, her cleats stuck in the ground. As she kicked the ball the leg twisted, causing a tear of her medial meniscus, a cartilage in her knee.

Though Cheryl avoided surgery, this was the end of her soccer career. Later she took to running to stay in shape. She generally ran less than 15 miles a week at a nine-minute-per-mile pace. But she was always aware of her "trick knee."

From time to time when Cheryl turned suddenly or twisted, her knee would seem to "go out" on her. She often felt like something was caught in her knee joint, and at those times she was unable to completely extend the knee.

As it turned out, that's exactly what was happening. A torn piece of cartilage became wedged between the joint surfaces and prevented her from fully straightening her leg. Then the cartilage would slip out of the way and allow her to function normally.

But one time her knee gave way and she was in such excruciating pain that her running partners had to carry her back home. Her orthopedic surgeon diagnosed a tear of her medial meniscus. Within three days, he performed arthroscopic surgery on her knee to repair the meniscus. After the procedure, the doctor gave Cheryl a videotape of her surgery so she could see the severe tearing of her medial meniscus.

Through the miracle of arthroscopic surgery she was able to walk (although with a noticeable limp) just a few days after the procedure. It only took a few weeks of physical therapy before she was back to running.

She still babies her knee but no longer is afraid of it failing her. Her friends no longer tease her about her "trick knee." And she's even thinking about getting back into soccer.

Chapter 20

HIP AND GROIN PAIN

Pains in the hip and groin seldom strike dramatically: They begin as a twinge or an ache that can develop into full-blown pain or just continue to ache. Runners are frequently tempted to ignore such pains—which isn't a good idea.

When runners arrive at my office complaining of a "hip joint" pain, usually their injury is actually to the outside of the hip. The hip joint itself lies deep within the groin and, unless you suffer a stress fracture or have an arthritic hip, the pain you feel will normally be on the outside of the pelvic bone.

Frequently the injury will feel like a bone bruise or a "hip pointer" and is most often due to a leg-length problem, with one leg significantly longer than the other. The longer leg is subjected to more force and the area outside the pelvis becomes irritated. With enough force, a bursa (a sac filled with fluid that's there to provide cushioning) may become painfully inflamed. Frequently the lateral portion of the hip will hurt to touch. This injury will normally warm up during running, then will be extremely tight a few hours afterward.

Problems in the hip and groin area can range from arthritis to stress fractures, from inflamed bursae to tendinitis. It's also possible

HIP AND GROIN PAIN

Statistically, injuries to the hip and groin area of runners occur relatively infrequently, accounting for less than 3 percent of the injury total. But women are three times more likely to be hurt in this area than men.

This big discrepancy has to do with the anatomical differences between the sexes. Women generally have wider hips than men. This genetic trait, designed to make childbirth easier, can lead to injuries in the hip area as well as groin pulls in the surrounding soft tissue. Having wider hips increases the angle of your leg when you strike the ground. Your foot then has to roll inward (pronate) more to flatten on the ground during heel strike. This adds to the already substantial forces of running, and even a minor abnormality can touch off an injury.

While this type of pain *can* be minor—caused by something as simple as a difference in the length of your legs—it could also indicate a stress fracture or a more serious problem. Doctors usually assume that runners suffer from musculoskeletal problems, so it's easy to overlook possibilities such as appendicitis or a hernia.

to aggravate an existing hip injury—say from a hard fall—by continuing to run on it. In worst cases, the blood supply to the hip can fail and the bone dies, requiring surgery or even hip replacement.

For these reasons, it's best to have your hip injury checked out by your doctor.

Sometimes You Have to Take Time Off

I first met Ann Marie at a 10-K race in San Diego. After the first mile or so, when the pack had thinned out, we found we were running stride for stride, so we ran the rest of the race together.

Ann Marie, a clerk in a local grocery store, had been running

Because women have broader pelvises than men, not only are the leg bones at different angles to start with, but the angle of the leg when it hits the ground is greater and the foot has to roll inward more. This extra force translates to more hip and groin injuries in women.

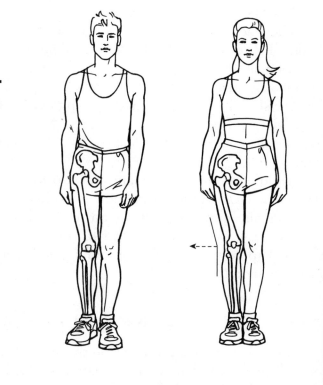

for more than five years. She found that her training runs greatly relieved the stress of dealing with customers, but it was racing she really loved. She entered as many 10-K races as she could—sometimes four a month.

But the reason she was taking time to chat during this particular race—instead of pushing to the max—was that she had a nagging groin pain she couldn't shake.

The pain had started after a race more than two months ago. She found that she could still train, although her groin was pretty sore by the end of her runs. Eventually, standing at work caused so much pain that she took some vacation time to get off her feet.

But Ann Marie just couldn't stand to give up her racing. Even though she was nearly limping from the pain by the end of the race, she still managed to run a 6:00 pace.

I strongly recommended that she seek medical treatment and, possibly because I was a runner, too, she listened. X-rays confirmed that she had suffered a stress fracture of the neck of her femur. Continuing to run had kept it from healing.

Ultimately Ann Marie had to lay off running for almost four months. By that time enough bone callus had built up around the fracture site to let her start mild running every other day. She wasn't allowed to run any races for another six months after that, and it took a full year before Ann Marie was able to run and work without pain.

I did "run" into Ann Marie not too long ago at another 10-K, where she crossed the finish line a good five minutes before I did.

"I really appreciated your advice," she told me, "and I want you to know that it doesn't hurt to run anymore. But what makes me the happiest is that I'm not running with you slow guys in these races anymore!"

Fitting Together All the Clues

Kelly came to my office complaining of a sore hip. She had been running for four or five years and had never been injured. She'd even escaped the normal aches and pains that most runners suffer.

Kelly usually ran a three-mile loop near her house, five days a week. She felt that since she ran rather slowly (about nine minutes per mile) she didn't need to warm up, but she did perform a 10-minute stretching routine after running.

As a travel agent, Kelly had opportunities to take exciting trips. One was a two-week vacation on a small sailboat, which meant no running. When she returned and started her three-mile runs again, she felt slight discomfort in her right hip. It wasn't a sharp or severe pain, so she figured she'd just "stiffened up" on her vacation.

Following the advice of running friends, Kelly tried to "run through" the problem. It grew worse, and she finally made an appointment to see me. She was in pain on the first visit, despite not having run for several days. When she pointed out the location of her pain, it was nowhere near her hip joint, which is fairly deep in the groin area.

Kelly's source of pain was actually on the outside portion of her femur—called the greater trochanter—which sits below the pelvis. When I probed that area, she really jumped. Her hips and pelvis, however, were completely pain-free.

Kelly's gait analysis showed an unusual gait: She overpronated on her painful right foot and underpronated on her left foot. And her running shoes showed a revealing pattern. The right shoe showed a relatively normal pattern, with wear concentrated on the outside of her outsole. But the outsole of the left shoe was worn about twice as much as the right one, and even more to the outside.

These clues told me that most likely Kelly's right leg was shorter than the left. She overpronated on her right foot, and overpronation actually shortens the leg, since the foot flexes up during pronation. Her left foot underpronated, which conversely lengthens the leg as the foot flexes downward.

Also, generally the shoe with the increased outsole wear belongs to the longer leg. About three-fourths of the time, when pain results from a leg-length discrepancy it's in the *shorter* leg.

Finally, when I studied Kelly's posture, I saw that her pelvis was uneven and that her right leg looked shorter than her left. Her shoulders showed the opposite pattern, with the right higher than the left. This, too, is characteristic of a limb-length difference.

Your upper body tries to compensate for any functional or anatomical differences in your lower body. If your right leg is shorter than your left, your right shoulder will lean to that side to help keep the body aligned as much as possible. This keeps your muscles from working too hard to keep you standing straight up.

Having one leg longer than the other isn't uncommon, but problems seldom evolve unless the difference is greater than a quarter inch. Treatment isn't advised unless a problem develops, because of the chance that a change will throw a system that has already compensated for the problem out of kilter.

Kelly's painful leg was ⅜ inch shorter than the other. I fitted her with a heel lift in her right shoe, using a cork and rubber compound that was exactly half (³⁄₁₆ inch) the leg-length difference. My goal was to use as small a lift as possible to ease the pain, not to completely remedy the leg length difference.

Using a too-large lift to compensate for an imbalance can make the pain worse. In many runners their bodies have compensated for a difference in the leg length, for instance, by developing a curvature of the spine. Their bodies may react to a correction in the shoes as if there is an imbalance toward the other side—and they get more pain than they started with.

As I knew that Kelly's body had likely already made its own "compensations" to deal with the discrepancy, I wanted to minimize the risk of creating other problems.

Her response to the heel lift was amazing. Within an hour, the pain completely disappeared and Kelly was able to run her normal three-mile loop the next day. Kelly gets a new lift in every new pair of running shoes, and the problem has not reappeared.

HIP ANATOMY

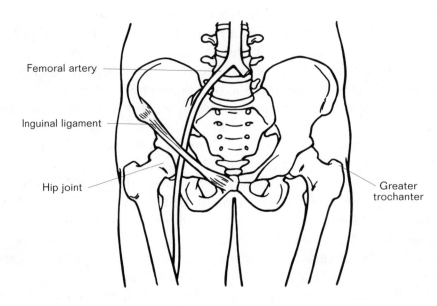

Femoral artery

Inguinal ligament

Hip joint

Greater
trochanter

A Running Pain Can Reveal Something More

Maureen, a flight attendant, had arch pain when she worked as well as when she ran. I treated her for plantar fasciitis and fitted her for orthotics.

Despite my instructions to get used to the orthotics slowly and *not* to run in them until she could walk without discomfort for a week, Maureen ran a half-marathon race in them the next day.

That was on a Saturday. Maureen was in my office Monday complaining of severe hip pain. She admitted, "I know I goofed up by wearing the orthotics for the race. But I felt so good wearing them I thought it would be all right."

The pain she now felt around her hip told her that she'd made a serious mistake. Her story reminded me of renowned physical therapist Gary Gray's three rules of rehabilitation:

1. Create an environment for optimal healing.

2. Above all else, do no harm.

3. Be as aggressive as you can without breaking rule two.

Maureen had managed to break all three of these rules. I assumed her injury was a muscle strain and put her on ice, rest and anti-inflammatory medications. But when the problem didn't clear up after two weeks, I sent her to a radiologist for an X-ray of her hip and pelvic area. The X-ray came back showing no break, but the pain persisted. So we ran a nuclear medicine bone scan.

The results were confusing and rather alarming. The radiologist who read the scan reported, "She either has a stress fracture of the head of her femur . . . or a tumor."

The traditional location for fractures in this area would have been in the neck of the femur. But her pain was much closer to the hip joint than I would have expected for a fracture. And the X-ray definitely showed no break. So I referred Maureen to her internist, who found that she did have a small soft-tissue growth in the area of her pain.

The orthotics apparently had changed her pelvic position just enough that the bone and muscles were rubbing on the growth. It had been there for several months, but the change in gait combined with the stress of the half-marathon had prompted the symptoms.

Maureen underwent surgery to remove the growth—which to everyone's relief was benign. She quickly returned to running, wiser and more cautious for her experience.

Not all cases are so cleanly resolved. One problem in treating injuries around the hip is that it's a very difficult area to rest. Your foot or knee can be easily splinted or braced to allow the injured part to mend. But only bed rest or a body cast can provide relief to the hip area—too drastic a measure for anything less than a fracture or major surgery.

For that reason, hip and groin injuries tend to last longer than other injuries. Many runners try to rush the healing process and this can have disastrous effects.

A Worst Case Scenario

Darlene, a 38-year-old advertising account executive, was an impatient person. Whether in her office or at home, she displayed the intense nature of a Type-A personality, and running provided the outlet she desperately needed.

She pushed herself to the limit in running as in everything else she did, but her schedule was quite irregular. She might run 50 miles one week and nothing at all the next two weeks due to work commitments.

She entered races ranging from 5-K to marathons and somehow usually placed in the top three in her age division. She never took time to warm up and only stretched two or three times a week.

One day after a particularly hard eight-mile run, Darlene felt pain in her groin area. She planned to race a half-marathon the following weekend, and viewed the pain as an annoying inconvenience.

Darlene grudgingly eased off her training for a few days, then ran the hilly 13.1-mile race. Her pains seemed to ease along the way, but on the final hill she felt a sharp pain in her groin.

She finished the race, then hobbled to her car and drove home. She figured the problem was her shoes, so she threw the two-week-old pair in the trash. Darlene bought new, softer shoes—and immediately ran five miles in them. Even though her hip still hurt, the pain wasn't as sharp as before so she continued pushing herself each day while trying to ignore the pain.

She kept this up for more than two months. Finally, when she realized that her condition was getting worse—and the constant pain was affecting her work—she went to see her family doctor.

He told her that she probably just strained a muscle or tendon and prescribed rest—probably the worst thing he could have told Darlene, considering her obsessive personality.

Figuring that she wouldn't let just a strain stop her, Darlene continued training. The pain got even worse. Then she saw an orthopedic surgeon. Following X-rays and a bone scan, he gave her the bad news: a stress fracture near her hip joint, at the head of her femur. She was told not to run for three months.

But Darlene had heard that fractures healed sooner than that, and she thought her doctor was being too conservative. After six weeks, she tried to put in a few miles but the pain returned. Each week, she would again test her injury—and come back limping.

When she saw her doctor three months later, her fracture was just as painful as it had been the day she first saw him. And now she was also getting muscle spasms along with pain radiating down her thigh to her knee.

The doctor ran another bone scan to find out why her hip was still painful. Now he had to break even worse news to Darlene. She had a condition called avascular necrosis at the head of her femur. This means that the blood supply to her hip had failed and her bone was not getting enough nourishment. The bone, of course, had been unable to heal.

Sometimes this condition happens for no apparent reason. It can happen after a hard hit, which is probably what happened to famed football and baseball player Bo Jackson, who suffered the same problem. In Darlene's case, it was probably due to the repeated trauma and continued aggravation of her injury.

When this happens, the prognosis is not good. The head of the femur usually dies slowly, resulting in severe pain and limited motion in the hip joint. Eventually, surgery is almost always necessary—and sometimes an artificial joint replacement is needed.

HIP AND GROIN PAIN

If you have pain or aching in the hip or groin, your doctor may prescribe:

- A shoe lift

- Ice

- Rest

- Flexibility exercises

- Strength exercises

- Physical therapy

- Injected anti-inflammatory

- Surgery

How you can help prevent this problem:

- Don't "run through" these pains

- Seek medical care for pains

Darlene is not in an enviable position, looking forward to a lifetime of hip pain and surgeries. If she had listened to her body initially, she might still be running instead of relying on crutches and canes. The lesson to be learned here is this: Give your body the time and the opportunity to heal. And don't ignore cries for help, especially when the hip and groin sound the alarm.

Chapter 21

SCIATICA: LOW BACK PAIN

A number of biomechanical faults can trigger some sort of back pain in runners—running stance or a pronation problem, for instance. What's more, runners are susceptible to some of the same contributing influences as other folks—sedentary jobs that leave back muscles weak, or lifting and bending habits that stress spinal disks.

Traditional Western medicine has a poor reputation for dealing with lower-back pains. Most running problems can be diagnosed and treated rather easily, but many health professionals have a difficult time figuring out what to do about back injuries.

Treatments by various doctors may range from heat to ice, medication and rest to taking up another sport. There's just no agreement among doctors when it comes to back complaints. And all too often, little relief is provided by the treatments they prescribe.

These failures send runners looking for answers outside traditional medicine. This is where chiropractors and acupuncturists often enter the picture. Back clinics have popped up in every large

SCIATICA

The most common running-related back problem involves the sciatic nerve, which forms a network in your buttock. If this nerve is irritated, you have an unforgettable condition known as sciatica.

Sciatica has a number of causes, from abnormal mechanics to compressed or herniated disks in your lower back, and running can exacerbate or bring on the problem. You can't clearly see the nerve or what causes its injury, but the sensations it sends to your body are unmistakable. Pain radiates down the back, though the buttocks, to the back of the thigh and around to the outside of the knee. It may even extend down the lower leg to the outside of the foot.

SOURCE OF SCIATICA

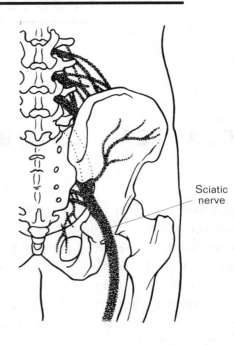

Sciatic nerve

city. Their staff often includes a psychologist or a psychiatrist to help people deal with everyday stresses that can contribute to back pain, as well as to help them deal emotionally with the possibility of a lifetime of back pain.

There are no cure-alls for back pain, but finding the right treatment can make an enormous difference, as these examples show.

The problem originates in the soft-tissue disks called fibrocartilage that separate the vertebrae of your spinal column. The disks keep the bones from rubbing against each other and allow you to bend your spine. This is especially important in the lower back, where most of the forces of bending occur. You might remember being told, "Bend with your knees, not your back." That's because while you bend your back the force at each disk can be as high as 400 pounds—*before* you pick up any weight.

Most runners' back injuries are caused by uneven pressure on these disks, which can result from bending forward too much, leaning into hills or even from biomechanical problems such as having one leg shorter than the other. Factors like these can put a great deal of pressure on your lower back—as much as three times your body weight—and injure the fibrocartilage disks. And a disk can become compressed from years of too much shock and pounding.

In addition, many runners have rather sedentary occupations. All that sitting tends to cause the joints in the back to become stiff, with limited ability to extend. Then when you go out to run you're not only calling on those stiff joints to extend, but you're putting a lot of stress on the disks. All the pressure on the disks can cause them to bulge out, which can in turn irritate the nerves that run down the sides of the spinal column—leading to chronic and frustrating pain.

Nancy's Lesson: Never Give Up

Nancy is a 20-mile-a-week runner who's also quite active in other sports, notably tennis. Midway through a four-mile run, she stopped to tie a shoe. When she bent over, she felt a sharp twinge radiate down her back and all the way into her lower leg.

For a moment, she thought she was stuck in that position, and she had a hard time straightening up again. Once upright, the pain in her back diminished immediately. The radiating pain in her leg went away within 15 minutes.

But she would recall later, "By the time I walked home, my back was on fire. It was all I could do to get into the house and just lie on the floor. In fact, lying on my back was the only thing that made me feel better."

She called a friend, who recommended that she go straight to her doctor. Among other tests, he had her lie on her back and flex her leg upward, keeping it straight. This duplicated her pain—much to her distress. Even though Nancy wasn't happy to re-experience that agony, it helped her doctor make the diagnosis: sciatic-nerve irritation.

The sciatic nerve travels from the lower back through the buttocks, down the back of the thighs, then along the back and lateral (outside) portion of the lower legs, finishing up along the outside of the feet at the toes. Nancy's pain encompassed about two-thirds of that pathway on her right leg.

Her doctor prescribed complete bedrest, a therapy that's considered obsolete for all except acute cases. He also prescribed warm packs on her back, a muscle relaxant and a painkiller. At this point, Nancy says, she wasn't even thinking about running again. "I just wanted to stand and walk without pain."

After about a week in bed—in a semistupor from the pain medication—she went back to her doctor. Her symptoms had eased somewhat, but she was nowhere near cured. The doctor told Nancy that there wasn't much she could do except continue resting and taking the medication.

Nancy, who hadn't been able to work for two weeks, was growing concerned. Another friend recommended that she see a chiropractor, and Nancy was in his office before the day was out.

The chiropractor confirmed the diagnosis of sciatica and performed adjustments on Nancy's back. These manual-manipulation techniques move the bones of the back into optimal alignment, improving the function of the joints and relieving pressure on the nerves.

The adjustment helped Nancy's problems significantly and she stopped taking the pills. Within a couple of days, however, the pain started coming back. She returned to the chiropractor's office, had more adjustments and felt good again. But the pain returned again in a few days.

Nancy became a frequent visitor to her chiropractor. Certainly she preferred the adjustments to the pills she'd been taking. But after several months, she still wasn't able to run and wanted a more permanent solution.

Her chiropractor referred her to a physical therapist. The therapist discovered that Nancy's lower back was too tight and that the postural muscles in her back were extremely weak. Those muscles are designed to help support your upper body and keep you from being hunched over. They weren't doing their job for Nancy and this increased the pressure on her bad disk. Although this muscle weakness might not have been the major cause of her sciatica, it was certainly a contributor to her pain.

The physical therapist treated Nancy for three weeks. The key exercise for Nancy's problems was press-ups. (See illustration below.) The strengthening program, along with anti-inflammatory medicine, gave Nancy her most significant relief to date.

She was able to decrease her chiropractic adjustments to once

PRESS-UPS

Lie on your stomach with your hands on the floor close to your shoulders. Look toward the ceiling as you press your chest and abdomen upward. Keep your pelvis flat and let your back sag as you stretch. Push only with your arms, relaxing your back muscles. Hold, then relax. Repeat 10 times.

a month. She still checks in with her chiropractor and continues her strengthening and postural program. Much of the therapist's work consisted of educating her on the proper techniques for bending, lifting, and even improving her running style by running more erect, not leaning into hills and smoothing out her stride.

Nancy reports, "I'm back to running, with only occasional discomfort in my back. I never really understood how debilitating back pain was until it happened to me."

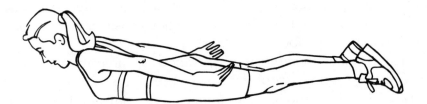

REVERSE SIT-UPS

Lie on your stomach with your arms at your sides, palms up. Lift your head and shoulders off the floor. Hold for 10 seconds, then bring your chin slowly to the floor. Repeat 10 times.

MODIFIED SIT-UPS

Lie on your back with your knees bent and your hands crossed on your stomach. With the small of your back on the floor, slowly lift your head and shoulders, keeping your face toward the ceiling, then lower them back down. You should feel this in your abdominal muscles, *not* your back muscles.

SCIATICA

You may have this problem if you experience:

- Pain in the lower back

- Pain in the buttocks

- Pain that radiates down the thigh to the knee or even foot

Warning: If you feel pain that radiates below the buttock level, seek immediate medical attention.

Your doctor may prescribe:

- Ice

- Cross-training

- Orthotics

- Physical therapy

- Strengthening exercises

- Injected or oral anti-inflammatories

How you can help prevent this problem:

- Do hamstring flexibility exercises, pages 239 and 240

- Do press-ups for flexibility, page 219

- Do modified sit-ups to strengthen your abdomen, page 220

- Do reverse sit-ups to strengthen your back, page 220

- Take care not to strain your back during daily activities

Pain Can Hit Where You Sit

Another target for sciatic-nerve pain is in the gluteal area—otherwise known as the buttock. The nerve is close to the surface in that region and can be injured with trauma or by pinching against the piriformis muscle.

This type of pain brought a runner named Mike to see me. He was referred by his chiropractor after adjustments hadn't given much relief. "Perhaps orthotics would help," the chiropractor suggested.

Whenever a runner moves, joints are flexing and extending, bones are rotating and muscles are contracting. With all this happening, a nerve can become trapped between a muscle and a bone. This was Mike's problem.

The results of my biomechanical evaluation were astonishing. Mike had a tremendous amount of overpronation, especially on the painful right side. Normal pronation is in the 4- to 6-degree range, but Mike's right foot pronated *22* degrees and his left *15* degrees. His shoes were almost completely run down to the inside—he was virtually running on his ankles.

The overpronation caused his entire leg to twist inward, the right more than the left. His legs rotated so much that his kneecaps almost faced each other. This severe torque pushed a part of his pelvic bone against the sciatic nerve. That's what was causing his pain.

Although the chiropractic treatment helped his mobility, he kept "re-injuring" his nerve due to faulty biomechanics. Periodic adjustments helped Mike somewhat, but the tremendous forces from running caused continued irritation of the sciatic nerve in his gluteal area. As long as he kept running, the nerve never had a chance to heal.

We made orthotics for Mike to control much of the motion. I fitted him for two different types of orthotics—one for running and the other for his everyday activities.

We weren't able to control all the motion—his abnormality was just too great—but we were able to bring enough of that motion under control so his gluteal pain vanished.

Occasionally Mike forgets to wear his orthotics, or tries not to use them for a particular race or training run. When he does, the pain comes right back to remind him that running can sometimes literally be a pain in the butt.

Chapter **22**

TRAINING WHILE YOU HEAL

After any injury, you must slowly return to running. How slowly? Much slower than you might think.

For instance, say you'd been doing track workouts before your injury at 80 seconds per quarter-mile interval. What pace and distance do you run your first few weeks back?

That's a trick question—the correct answer is that you don't even *think* about doing track workouts at this point.

So how *do* you start back to running? Actually, you don't—at least not right away. First you just walk. Later, you move on to alternate walking and jogging, then slow jogging, then up to running, and only *then* return—cautiously—to speed workouts.

After a layoff or an injury, your feet and legs, bones and joints are just not ready for any type of pounding. They have become somewhat lazy and vulnerable. Muscles and bones weaken during disuse. It took time to build them up before your injury, and after you've recovered it will take time to build them back up so they can take the tremendous forces of running without getting strained or injured.

In addition, chances are pretty good that your initial injury has not completely healed. Even though you may not feel any symptoms, the area that you hurt will almost always be weaker than before the injury and much more susceptible to re-injury. If you start stressing it too early, the same symptoms will likely reappear.

Too Far, Too Fast, Too Soon

Many runners, like a runner named Jim who came to see me, think that if they just slow down their pre-injury pace a bit they'll be fine. Jim strained his knee during a 5-K race, and after five weeks, his knee was well enough that he could start training again.

Since Jim normally ran an eight-minute-mile pace, he thought the sensible thing to do would be to back off to an 8:15 pace. Jim was back in my office two weeks later with—you guessed it—another swollen knee.

Donna, another runner, was coming back after eight weeks off from running because of an Achilles tendon injury. As soon as I gave her the okay to begin *easy* running, she went into full training for a half-marathon. Before long, she developed hip pain. But because her Achilles no longer hurt, Donna assumed the pains were probably just muscle soreness from her increased distance. So she kept increasing the distance—until the hip became so painful she had to seek medical attention.

The diagnosis: stress fracture of the hip, requiring a three-month layoff. The cause: Because of the injury to the Achilles tendon, Donna had been favoring her left foot. She'd transferred most of her force to her right leg and, of course, the right hip.

That explained the pain she'd been feeling in her hip for several weeks. It was a crucial warning sign that went unheeded.

I also see many runners who insist on "testing" their original injuries. They may have been training 50 miles a week before the injury and figured they would start back with an 8-mile run, just to see if everything was okay. The result: I usually have to treat them all over again. A condition that might have disappeared in a few weeks now can drag on for several months.

Walk before You Run

Many runners would rather eat dirt than consider taking up a walking program. They think walking is a stage you pass through on the way to becoming a fit runner.

Amy Tardio, a fitness magazine editor, meets my definition of a devoted fitness enthusiast. Between running, hiking and playing tennis, she has always maintained an extremely high level of fitness.

After she gave birth to her first child, she took up walking with friends a few days a week while running the other days—and discovered that she *liked* walking. It provided the exercise she needed and it was easier to talk with her friends while working out. Amy's story illustrates a growing trend toward less-strenuous but longer-duration exercise. Even some diehard runners now add walking breaks to their training.

Walking is less traumatic to your body than running. When you walk, one foot is always in contact with the ground, while on a run your entire body leaves the ground and then crashes down again with great force.

Walking *does* require more time to achieve the desired benefits. For instance, you burn approximately 100 calories per mile whether you're running or walking. But a mile walk takes about twice as long as a run of the same distance.

You may be worried that walking isn't strenuous enough to get your endurance back up to par. But you really don't need to fret about your endurance during a forced layoff: After three months of non-activity, as I've mentioned previously, you only lose approximately 10 percent of your aerobic capabilities.

The reason walking is so valuable after an injury is that while you've been recovering the soft tissues surrounding the injured area have tried to mitigate the damage by functioning differently than normal. The muscles surrounding your injury work harder to keep the injured part from going through too much motion. Thus, other muscles are doing their jobs *and* assisting their injured comrade. Also, when a muscle has been injured your brain doesn't want to move that muscle. So it recruits other muscles to do the work.

It takes time to reprogram the tissues for their normal functions in running. Walking helps this adaptation occur because it uses most of the same muscles as running, while keeping injury-causing forces at a minimum.

Select Another Sport

If you're looking for more strenuous activity than walking, cross-train instead. Runners once took an all-or-nothing approach to their sport, and many still do. When healthy, they *only* ran—when felled by an injury they were completely inactive.

The wise runner now explores other options, both to supplement running during periods of good health and as a substitute for running during injuries. It's a rare (and foolish) runner today who doesn't cross-train.

Overuse symptoms or actual injuries that are caused by too much shock or jarring, such as muscle pain, tendinitis, fractures and shin splints, can be "rested" during swimming or cycling. Likewise, a stair-climber, rowing machine or cross-country ski machine may take the stress off an injured area while still providing excellent cardiovascular workouts.

Cross-training gives your feet and legs a welcome respite from the constant pounding of running, and further protects against injury by strengthening more muscle groups than running alone.

The time to start cross-training is when you're still healthy, so you won't be trying to learn an unfamiliar sport when injured. Work the new sport into your usual training program. Then, if you need to switch completely to that activity because of an injury, you'll be able to get maximum benefits immediately.

Replace an easy run with a cross-training workout, for example, or cross-train instead of resting. Often your body doesn't need total rest, just a break from the overspecialized and specific action of running.

The more muscles you can involve in your training program, the less likely you are to suffer an overuse injury. In addition, by working more of your major muscle groups, your overall state of fitness will improve.

Let's take a quick tour through several alternative activities. These are the most accessible, effective and popular. (If you're being treated for a problem, you may want to clear these activities with your doctor. A simple rule is: If it doesn't hurt, it's okay.)

Bicycling. Riding a bike combines an excellent cardiovascular and muscular workout with virtually no impact stress to the feet and legs. I often recommend that injured runners start a bicycling program before they are able to resume running.

Many patients with stress fractures, for example, are allowed to cycle three weeks following the injury—but must wait at least six weeks before resuming running. Patients recovering from knee surgeries or traumatic ankle sprains can also progress quickly into bicycling, long before other activities are allowed. (If it doesn't hurt and isn't against your doctor's advice, go ahead.)

It's best to pedal at 100 or more rotations per minute in an easy gear. This minimizes strain to the feet and legs and maximizes cardiovascular effects.

To get maximum benefits (and the most fun) from biking, you need a certain degree of expertise. You know how to ride a bike—but you may not know how to ride a bike *well*. After finally winning the Ironman Triathlon after finishing second in the grueling race in previous years, Scott Tinley was asked what had made the difference this year. "I learned how to ride a bike," he answered.

You can pick up cycling tips by riding with a club or group; check at a local bike shop. And buy and wear a helmet, which can make the difference between walking away from a crash and spending months in a hospital—or worse.

Swimming. You won't find a better overall conditioning exercise. It gently works your legs as well as your upper body with no impact.

Swimming rarely aggravates injuries such as fractures and sprains to the legs. (Check with your doctor.) Runners with severe foot and leg injuries can hold a pull-buoy between their legs to immobilize them while pulling with just their arms.

Masters swim programs or adult swim classes are available in most areas. I highly recommend them because they develop your skills instead of letting you thrash around on your own. Because runners tend to have less body fat than the average person, swimming can be difficult to do well enough to have an enjoyable workout if your technique isn't up to par.

WHEN RUNNING BECOMES
A HARMFUL ADDICTION

Running can be addictive. Since it is considered beneficial physically and mentally, it's usually considered a "positive" addiction instead of a negative one such as cigarettes, alcohol or drugs.

But I see plenty of runners who cross the line from positive to negative addiction. At this point running is tearing their bodies down—not making them healthier.

I recall one such runner, the president of a relatively large corporation. Just like clockwork, he would return home at the end of a 12-hour day and go out for at least an hour run. He was obsessed with his running and boasted of going more than five years without missing a day's run. Finally the inevitable happened—a major overuse injury, Achilles tendinitis.

After several self-treatments that failed, this runner came to see me. When I told him he had a fracture that would require several weeks of no running, he perhaps overreacted.

"There's no way I can handle the stresses of daily life without it. Give me Valium, Doc," he said dramatically. (To his credit, this runner did heed my advice about cross-training; he took up swimming and weight-lifting, and certainly never needed tranquilizers.)

Another runner I treated was sidelined with a severe ankle injury. He confessed later, "During those weeks of inactivity, I would sit in my living room during the time I normally went for my run. I'd

Aqua-running. Many runners prefer to mimic their normal activity in the water rather than swim. They usually wear a flotation device that holds them upright in deep water while they go through the running motions. This uses the same muscles and motions used in slow endurance running—but because of the buoyancy of the water, your legs don't get the pounding they would on the road.

look out the picture window and cry every time I saw a runner go past."

That's how much he missed his running. And he was sidelined for less than a month.

Like other addictions, running can involve lying and cheating: By working out when they aren't ready, patients lie to themselves about their capability to run and they cheat themselves out of a quick recovery.

My point here is that the psychological pain of an injury may hurt worse than the physical. The prospect of inactivity—even for a few days or weeks—can be devastating. It can lead to irrational decisions, like limping on through an injury, that sabotage your recovery.

An injury that decreases or stops your running can turn you into a cranky, irritable human being. But if you continue to remind yourself that the condition is only temporary and you'll be able to return to your normal activity soon, you shouldn't have much trouble coming to terms with the injury psychologically. The simplest way to cope is by adopting some form of cross-training. Its mental benefits are as important as the physical.

But if you deny having the injury and continue to be obsessive about running, then you set yourself up for a major problem. It could end up confirming your worst fear—missing your runs for a significant period of time.

A few runners forego the vest, running in deep water with enough arm and leg motion to keep themselves afloat. This is what Olympic marathoner Julie Brown did while recovering from a stress fracture. She was phenomenal in the water, keeping herself afloat without any buoyant support for up to an hour.

You can also use the shallow end of the pool—your feet touch the bottom, so you work the same muscles as you would in normal running. (In the deep end, you're using your arms and legs to keep yourself afloat.)

In-line skating. When Rollerblade skates hit the market, standard roller skates became just about obsolete. Instead of two parallel sets of wheels, Rollerblades and other brands of in-line skates have all four wheels in a row; they are faster than roller skates and use many of the same muscle groups as cross-country skiing and running.

When I ran into Marty Liquori, a world-class runner turned TV commentator, he said, "You are the person I credit for getting me on Rollerblades." A few years earlier he was thinking of having some pretty radical surgery on his Achilles tendon and the back of his heel. This injury only hurt him when he ran speed workouts, and he wasn't planning to compete again. I advised him to avoid the surgery because he didn't need to run that fast anymore and could take up another sport.

Instead of having the surgery, Marty began in-line skating and found it a tremendous aerobic activity. He can now skate as fast as he wants without any Achilles or heel pain.

The advantages of in-line skating: It is an outdoor sport like running and can be done on many of the same courses that you run. While the actions are somewhat similar to running, the speeds are faster and there is little impact.

The disadvantages: Learning to balance on a line of wheels can prove difficult for someone who has never ice-skated. Also, skating in traffic is more risky than running there because you can skate at a higher speed and can't stop as quickly.

Exercise machines. There are a whole host of exercise machines—from stair-climbers to rowing machines to cross-country ski simulators. All are relatively easy to master and provide great strength and cardiovascular workouts. When learning to use one of these machines, ask an instructor to demonstrate its safe and effective use.

Exercise machines are also easy on your feet and legs because there is no shock or jarring. So injuries have a chance to heal while you maintain your aerobic fitness and actually increase your strength. We even use some of these machines for runners following knee surgery to help condition them and speed their return to running.

Be careful when you start out on these machines. I've known runners who jumped into one- or two-hour training sessions on a stair-climber only to suffer such severe muscle soreness and tightness that they couldn't train for a week. Start with 15 to 20 minutes of activity on exercise equipment, including stair-climbers, ski and rowing machines and stationary bikes.

Don't try to make up in one day for all the training you think you've lost while injured. As with your running program, slow but steady wins the race.

Watch What You Eat

The biggest complaint I hear from injured patients is "I've gained 10 pounds while I couldn't run." Chances are, they're exaggerating. Runners tend to have phobias about gaining weight.

You should remember that weight gain or loss is not necessarily associated with fitness gained or lost. Dieting to lose weight is a terrible thing to do to your body, especially following an injury.

Eating is your body's means of getting the nutrition you need for everyday living. When you return to training, you need even more nutrients than normal to help your body mend the injured area and to fuel your training.

If you decrease your intake of food, you lessen your body's natural ability to repair itself and to improve your conditioning. As a result, while you may see a weight loss on your bathroom scale, your body is probably starving for certain nutrients. This can easily result in a further breakdown—at the injury area or elsewhere. You should always eat sensibly, but it's especially important now.

Don't even *think* about dieting while recovering from an injury. And don't worry too much about any weight gained during your layoff. It will melt away naturally as you get back into regular training. (This doesn't mean, however, that you should gulp down a pint of ice cream every evening.)

While I'm on the topic of diet: Even when you're training at full speed, just because you're a lean runner don't assume that you can eat whatever you please without ill effect. You may *look* lean, but cholesterol could be clogging your arteries. Look at Jim Fixx, the noted running author. He was light in weight, but his diet was heavy in fats and other junk foods and his cholesterol level far exceeded healthy limits. When Fixx died of a heart attack while running at age 54, his arteries were seriously clogged.

It is often said that dieting to lose weight doesn't work—it must be combined with exercise to shed pounds. The reverse is also true. Exercising without a proper diet isn't conducive to a healthy, long life.

Start Like a Beginner

When your doctor says you're ready to run again, start as if it's the first time. Begin by adding short periods of slow running into your walking program, and gradually increase the length of the runs while decreasing the walks.

Before long, you'll be running steadily again. Then you face the temptation of increasing your mileage and pace too quickly. You have to listen carefully to your body. If running hurts, if pain increases while you're running, or you are limping, the workout is doing more damage. It's time to stop or back off.

Again, remember that an area of your body hasn't worked correctly for quite awhile. The injury that was weeks or months in the making will be a similar time in the unmaking. If you try to take shortcuts or cheat your body's natural timetable, you're asking for trouble. There are no miracle pills or magic wands to speed recovery times.

A general rule of thumb is to increase your weekly distance by only 10 percent. This limit applies to your training when you're healthy, and particularly must be observed when you're recovering from an injury. Your body may have built up scar tissue, its way of healing injuries. Scar tissue is more vulnerable to injury. It is less elastic and more prone to inflammation than the tissue it replaced— and it lasts forever. So running hard with a part of your body weakened is asking for trouble.

Don't run or run/walk more than four days a week for the first two weeks back. You need the extra time to rebound from the previous workout and continue to mend your injury. Running every day leaves you no time to recover.

Don't enter a race in the near future. I recommend waiting three months after the injury before attempting a 10-K and six months before trying a half-marathon.

In fact, don't even tempt yourself by reading race results or ads. The competition that counts at this point is you against your injury symptoms. This race back to health should be your only focus.

Chapter 23

A 7−STEP PLAN
FOR RUNNING INJURY−FREE

Stan is living proof that those who ignore history are bound to repeat its mistakes: He gets the same basic injury, a plantar-fascia strain in the arch of one or both feet, about once a year. This usually occurs in mid-January—not coincidentally, shortly after he tries to implement his New Year's resolutions.

At least Stan is honest about his training errors. He admits, "I almost never warm up before running, rarely stretch and *always* overtrain. The harder the workout, the better I like it."

Unlike many of the runners I see, the reasons for Stan's injuries seem simple. He just doesn't care too much about his body and isn't overly concerned about the harm he does to it. He assumes that I can just fix whatever problems arise. After all, hasn't this worked in the past?

I used to discuss Stan's poor running habits with him. He would sheepishly look at me and say, "Yes, maybe I did make a few small mistakes."

Then would come the excuses: "I had a race coming up that I

just had to train for"—and he had tried to cram six months' training into two months. Or, "My training partners would be too disappointed if I didn't join them for a long run"—and he couldn't warm up because everyone was waiting.

Nowadays, he doesn't even bother with excuses. He just says, "Don't lecture me, Doc. I know I goofed up again. Just fix me."

Sure, I can repair a lot of the damage that runners do to themselves. But I'm discouraged to see the same runners come back repeatedly with the same problems.

These runners haven't learned much from their mistakes and they haven't taken to heart the injury-prevention lessons that are common knowledge among runners and sports-medicine specialists. As a result, they subject themselves to a great deal of needless suffering, expense and downtime. Here, then, is a seven-step plan that I've developed over the years to help runners minimize the chances of injury.

1. Find a Friendly Surface

The best surfaces for running are firm (not mushy or slippery), relatively flat (without camber), smooth (without ruts or holes), and provide some degree of shock absorption. The more angled the surface, the steeper the incline, the harder the surface, the greater are the chances of an injury.

Grassy areas such as golf courses make relatively poor running surfaces. This may surprise some people who choose grass because it's soft. But grassy surfaces are also uneven. And many of us— more than half the population—have some biomechanical abnormality. So running on grass makes the muscles and tendons in your feet and legs work harder and leaves you more susceptible to injury.

Most ankle sprains occur on grassy turf because holes, ruts and rough terrain can be hidden, waiting to trip up an unsuspecting runner. Dirt trails are preferable to grass because you can see holes and ruts and avoid missteps, yet still receive good cushioning.

Roads are also notoriously poor surfaces, not only because of traffic hazards but because they are canted so that water will run off the center of the road. This slant causes the "upward" foot to pronate more and the "downward" foot to supinate more.

Any biomechanical abnormality will be amplified in one foot or the other when you're running on the road. This is why an out-and-back course is preferable to running one way. When you change directions, the uneven forces on your feet and legs are reversed and balance out.

Provided you wear good shock-absorbing shoes, sidewalks tend to make better training surfaces than roads because they are flat. The problem, of course, is that cement surfaces are significantly harder than asphalt or other man-made surfaces.

Outdoor tracks (440 yards or 400 meters) are almost always better than indoor tracks because they are larger and are unbanked. Indoor tracks often have a steep camber on the turns and require more laps per mile. That severe incline is murder on the knees. On any type of track, change direction frequently to minimize mechanical problems.

The beach has a soft surface, but shares one disadvantage with the road. The beach also tends to be slanted, so the biomechanical problems that plague people running on one side of the street can happen here.

The beach's surface can also be hazardous, as I learned a few years ago while taking part in an annual Christmas Eve run in Cardiff, California. The tide was high and we were forced to run on the small, loose, slippery rocks. I can't imagine a worse running surface. My ankle became so inflamed and swollen that I needed crutches to get around for the next week.

Here, ranked in order from most desirable to least desirable, are various running surfaces:

1. Soft, smooth cinder track, unbanked

2. Artificially surfaced track, unbanked

3. Soft, smooth dirt trail

4. Flat, smooth grass

5. Asphalt street or path

6. Hard dirt track or trail

7. Concrete sidewalk or road

8. Banked or cambered surface

9. Hard-sand beach

10. Rough, pot-holed dirt trail or grass

2. Warm Up and Cool Down

Before a race, you see the elite runners in the front of the pack running back and forth, warming up their various muscle groups. You also see the people toward the back of the pack standing, huddled, waiting for the gun to go off.

The elite runners know that the chances of having an injury are greater when their muscles are cold. There is a simple physiological reason for this.

When you first get up in the morning, your muscles and soft tissues are tight. In fact, your muscles are generally about 10 percent shorter then than their normal resting length.

As you start moving around, your muscles stretch to their normal resting length. When you start to exercise the muscles, they stretch to about 10 percent *more* than normal resting length. This means that from the time you get out of bed until the muscle is warmed up the muscle stretches as much as 20 percent.

A longer muscle is much less likely to become injured than a short, tight muscle. Further, muscles are designed to move bones on either side of a joint. Through basic laws of physics, a muscle is more efficient and much less likely to become injured when it is longer, since it can exert more force with less effort.

Warming up also helps prevent tendinitis. Muscles are attached to tendons, so by preparing the muscle for activity you help protect the tendon.

Worried that you'll wear yourself out warming up? The small amount of energy you expend warming up your muscles before a training run or race is more than offset by your improved efficiency and increased safety. Likewise, it is disastrous to finish a training run and just stop.

Many runners try to get the most out of their runs by sprinting the last couple hundred yards or so. Then they stand and try to catch their breath. This is *asking* for injury. It is also the time when susceptible individuals are most at risk of having a heart attack. Almost all exercise-related heart attacks occur just after runners stop running, not while they're actually running. This is because when you exercise, your body relies on your muscles to help pump or push the blood from your legs to your heart and brain. When you stop running, that muscle action stops and your heart and brain suddenly get less blood and oxygen. (This is an excellent reason for a cooldown period of slow jogging or walking.)

You will see elite runners cross the finish line, then slow down but continue running afterward to prevent these types of problems. The cooldown helps keep the blood flowing to the muscles and allows your body to work its way down from a state of high exertion to the eventual resting condition. Keep walking for a few minutes, at the very least, after every run until you have cooled down.

3. Stretch Firmly but Gently

The muscles along the front of your legs (the quadriceps and the shin muscles) tend to be the workhorses, while the muscles in the back of your legs are the ones that help you slow down or stop. These back-of-leg muscles tighten up when you run and should not be forgotten: You need to keep them flexible.

Lack of flexibility is probably the biggest cause of Achilles tendinitis and is a major factor in plantar fasciitis and shin splints. Without flexibility, your legs are an injury waiting to happen. That's because the muscles can't go through their normal ranges of motion when they are too tight.

The best time to stretch your muscles is not before you exercise but after a run when your muscles are already warmed-up and elongated. Flexibility exercises always stretch the muscles slowly and gradually.

Stretching movements should never be jerky, stiff or hard. The proper way to stretch is to stretch the muscle gradually for 30 seconds at a time to allow it to lengthen. Do this three or four times per area, daily.

Never stretch a muscle to the point of pain. If you feel pain when you are stretching, you are either stretching too hard or some injury needs attention.

If you stretch or pull hard on a muscle, it sets up a reflex where the muscle pulls back, shortening and tightening. This is not what you want. It will give you a stronger muscle, but not a looser, longer, more forgiving muscle.

Here are some specific stretches for particular body parts. (The self-test in chapter 1 will give you a good idea which areas may need particular attention.)

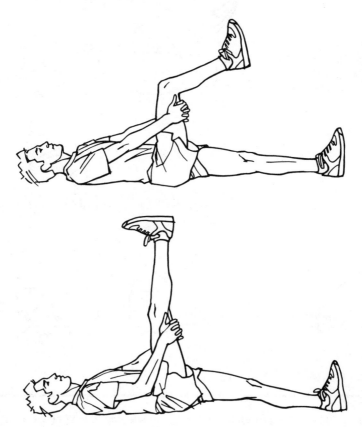

HAMSTRING STRETCH I

Lie on your back with your legs straight. Bring one knee toward your chest so the hip is at a 90-degree angle, clasp both hands behind the knee to keep the thigh stable, and straighten the knee as far as possible. Keep the ankle flexed toward the knee. Keep the opposite leg straight unless you experience back pain. Hold. You'll feel the stretch in the calf, behind the knee, and in the lower part of the thigh. Repeat with the other leg.

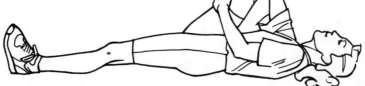

HAMSTRING STRETCH II

Repeat as in Hamstring Stretch I, but bring the knee up to your chest. Clasp both hands behind your knee, keeping the thigh stabilized. Grasping your leg behind the ankle as shown, straighten the knee as far as possible. Hold. Feel the stretch in the upper part of the thigh as well as the calf. Repeat with the other leg.

QUADRICEPS STRETCH I

Lying on your stomach, bend one knee and grasp the ankle with your hand or a towel looped around the ankle. (If you're not flexible, the towel helps a lot.) Keep your thighs together and your body straight. Squeeze your buttocks and press your hips down into the floor. Gently pull your ankle toward the buttocks. Hold. Feel the stretch across the front of the thigh. Repeat with the other leg.

QUADRICEPS STRETCH II

Stand straight with your legs together, supporting yourself with one hand on a sturdy table, chair or wall. Bend one knee and grasp the ankle with the opposite hand or a towel looped around the ankle. Keep your thighs together and your body straight. Gently pull the ankle toward your buttocks. Hold. You will feel the stretch across the front of the thigh. Repeat with the other leg.

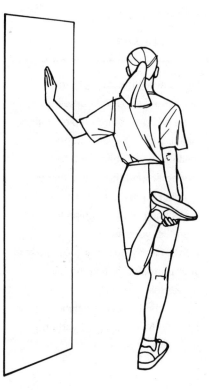

HIP FLEXOR I

Lying on your stomach, bend one knee and grasp the ankle with your hand or a towel looped around the ankle. Keeping your body straight, squeeze your buttocks and press your hips down against the floor. Gently pull your ankle toward the buttocks, lifting the knee up off the ground. Hold. Feel the stretch across the front of the thigh and the front of the hip. Repeat with the other leg.

HIP FLEXOR II

Stand straight with your legs together and support yourself with one hand on a sturdy table, chair or wall. Bend one knee and grasp the ankle with your hand or a towel looped around the ankle. Without bending forward, squeeze your buttocks and press your hips forward (don't let your stomach sag forward). Gently pull your ankle toward your buttocks, pulling the knee back. Hold. You will feel the stretch across the front of the thigh and the front of the hip. Repeat with the other leg.

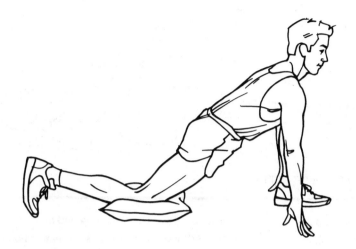

HIP FLEXOR III

Kneel on a cushion and support yourself with both hands. Place one foot in front of you, keeping the foot flat on the floor. Keep your back straight and your hips forward (do not twist your hips). Press your hips forward. Hold. Feel the stretch across the front of the hip of the leg that's behind you. Repeat with the other leg.

BUTTOCKS STRETCH

Lie on your back with your legs straight. Bend one knee and bring it toward the opposite shoulder, keeping your chest, shoulders and head down. Clasp your hands around the knee and gently press it toward the opposite shoulder. Hold. Feel the stretch in the buttocks and the outside of the hip. Repeat with the other leg.

LATERAL HIP STRETCH

Lie on your back with your legs straight. Then lift one leg up and bend the knee so that the hip and knee are both at 90-degree angles. Place one hand on the knee and the other hand on the lower leg. Gently pull your foot and knee toward the shoulder, rotating at the hip, as shown. Hold. Feel the stretch at the outside of the hip. Repeat with other leg.

ILIOTIBIAL BAND STRETCH

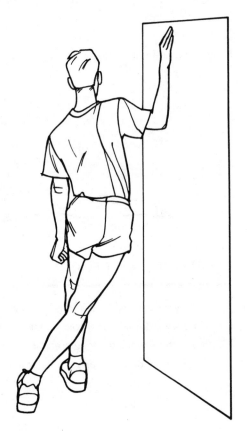

Stand with the right side of your body facing the wall, supporting yourself against the wall, as shown. Cross the right leg behind the left leg. Lean your right hip toward the wall while bending the left knee and keeping the right knee straight. Hold. Feel the stretch at the outside of the right hip and the right upper thigh. Repeat on the left side. For a variation of this stretch, cross the right leg in *front* of the left leg and repeat the exercise.

GROIN STRETCH I

In a sitting position with your back erect, bend your knees and place the soles of your feet together. Place your elbows or hands on the inner knees and gently press your knees apart. Hold. Feel the stretch in your inner thighs.

GROIN STRETCH II

Lie on your back with your knees bent, the soles of your feet close together and your feet off the floor. Put your hands on the inside of your knees and press your knees apart, as shown. Do not arch your back. Hold. Feel the stretch at your inner thighs.

CALF STRETCH (USING WALL)

Stand, leaning against the wall with both hands. Put one foot in front of the other as shown. Keep the back foot pointing straight ahead, with the heel down and your knee straight. Shift your weight forward by bending the front knee. Hold. Feel the stretch behind the knee and down the back of the lower rear leg. Repeat, but this time with the back knee bent as well, with your heel still on the floor. Hold. You'll feel the stretch lower down the back of the rear leg. Switch and repeat with the other leg.

CALF STRETCH (WITH WEDGE)

Put one foot on a wedge (a slant board at about 30 degrees) with your heel resting on the floor. Keep your toes straight and support yourself with your hands on the wall. With your leg straight, press your entire body forward and hold. Feel the stretch behind the knee and in the back of the lower leg. Repeat the stretch with the knee bent, as shown. You'll feel the stretch in the back of the lower leg, closer to the heel. Switch and repeat with the other leg.

ANTERIOR LOWER LEG STRETCHES

Stand, leaning against the wall with both hands. Bend your front leg, and point your toes under on your back leg. With the back knee facing forward and your toes in line with your knee, gently press the front of the back foot and ankle down toward the floor. Hold. Feel the stretch on the front of the lower leg and ankle. Repeat the exercise first with your rear knee turned outward, and then with it turned inward. Switch to the other leg and repeat.

ANKLE STRETCH

Sit with your feet flat on the floor with the heels and knees in a vertical line, and the knees in a horizontal line with the hips. Raise your arches, keeping the outside borders of the feet and toes on the floor. Press the outside of your feet down against the floor. Hold. Feel the stretch on the outside of the feet and lower legs. Then repeat the exercise, raising the *outside* borders of the feet and toes, keeping the inside borders on the floor.

4. Keep Your Training Schedule Flexible

The easiest way to avoid injuries is never to train hard on a day when you feel any pain when you roll out of bed. As easy and simple as this advice sounds, you'd be amazed how many people ignore it.

Let's say that you are training for a certain race and your training schedule calls for a 10 percent increase in mileage this week. Yet you're feeling a little twinge in your hamstring.

Do you go ahead and follow the schedule? Or do you alter it based on listening to your body?

You know the right answer. Yet many runners insist on adhering to the printed training schedule as if it were gospel. They refuse to deviate by a single mile from that written program, believing any modification of it would ruin their chances of running a good race. In fact, the reverse is true. They're far more likely to miss the race by slavishly following a predetermined schedule than by adapting it to current needs.

All good training schedules assume that you aren't experiencing any unusual pains before, during or after the run. If any of these pains occur, don't hesitate to modify the scheduled workouts.

If the pain is slight, you don't necessarily need to stop running, but merely cut back. Decreasing the mileage by, say, 30 percent will let you continue training while easing the strain.

That's only seven fewer miles per week for a 25-mile-a-week runner. But this reduction can work wonders in terms of restoring you to full health and vitality. Better to lose those few miles now than to miss the upcoming race because of an injury.

5. Alternate "Hard" and "Easy" Training

If you try to improve to your maximum potential, some pains are inevitable. These can occur several hours after a hard workout or race—or one or two days later.

All this really means is that you need some recovery time. Then you will be off and running again.

This is why most experts recommend never performing hard workouts two days in a row. Give yourself *at least* one day of easy running or rest between hard workouts. This is known as the "hard-easy" method of training. If you run fast one day, train slowly the next. If you run long one day, go short the following day.

Never run long two days in a row or fast two days in a row, and don't run long one day and fast the next. You'll simply cancel out the gains of the long or fast workout, because your body is desperately trying to recover. You're stressing weakened tissues that the body is trying to repair.

Some people need more recovery than others, just as some require more sleep. It might be that your body performs best if you run hard one day, then easily the next two days or even more. Experiment with your reactions to various combinations of hard versus easy, as well as comparing the merits of easy running versus rest or cross-training.

6. Pace and Space Your Races

You can and must push your limits sometimes in order to progress. But you can't do this too often or by too much.

In other words, you must pace yourself. This is true both for individual runs and over periods of weeks, months and years.

The most important time to pay attention to proper pacing is while racing. At races, you can easily get caught up in the emotion of the crowd and be drawn into starting too fast.

I remember standing at the starting line for the Boston Marathon a few years ago, having trained to average a seven-minute mile pace for the race. This would have brought me in at about three hours.

You can imagine my shock when I passed the first mile in 5:53. I thought that the timekeeper or possibly the mile marker were in error.

But when I passed the two-mile marker at 12 minutes even, I knew I was in trouble. I would pay dearly later on for starting so fast, and I learned later in the race why a relatively small elevation in that race is called "Heartbreak Hill."

Pacing also has longer-term applications. Racing is very hard and potentially damaging work and you put your future at risk if you race too often. So you must "pace" your races in terms of frequency. Give yourself plenty of time to recover after any race.

The general rule: Take one easy day or rest day for each mile of the race. And certainly don't race again until that period has passed. For example, allow an entire easy week following a 10-K race and an easy month after completing a marathon. Top marathoners believe they can only run two or three good marathons a year; this grueling event takes that great a toll.

Yet I occasionally read about runners who enter a marathon *every week* for a year. I'm not sure how they do it without getting injured, but there are always some people who can beat the odds. You can be sure, of course, that frequent marathoners aren't putting maximum effort into each race.

A few people can also smoke three packs of cigarettes a day and live to be 100. But that doesn't mean you, too, can break the rules without being penalized.

7. Keep Records of Your Running

Runners have long been teased about being compulsive. After all, you don't normally see tennis players and basketball players logging their playing time, courts played on, weight and pulse, feelings and injuries.

But it makes perfect sense for runners to keep logs. Charting your distance, pace, type of course, running weather, choice of shoes and other key factors gives you a much-needed perspective. With a running log, you can objectively trace your progress and detect errors.

I know one runner who couldn't figure out why he would intermittently develop plantar fasciitis and arch injuries. For months he attempted to "run it out" without success. He tried changing shoes, terrain, surfaces, speed and distance—but no luck.

Fortunately, when he came to see me he brought his log. There in black and white was the history of his injury.

Whenever he ran speed workouts in the morning, his plantar fascia would hurt two days later. If he ran those same workouts at noon or in the evening, the pain wouldn't occur. Similarly, he could take his slow distance runs in the morning with no pain.

The key was the pain after fast workouts in the morning—a

time when runners tend to feel tighter, move slower and are more susceptible to injury.

All this runner had to do was increase his warmup time on his morning speed runs and all was well. His intermittent pains never returned.

As to why his plantar fascia hurt two days later instead of the next day, well, running often has this delayed-reaction effect. Soreness—whether from injury or simply overwork—typically peaks the *second* day after the triggering incident, not the first day.

Your log can also help you determine if you're training too little or too much. Review it weekly with an objective eye. Pretend it is someone else's training program you're reviewing and you're checking its effectiveness and safety.

Ultimately, the most important "book" you'll ever read is your own personal training diary. It can tell how you were injured, how you recovered and how you can keep this part of your history from repeating itself.

ABOUT THE AUTHORS

JOE ELLIS, a podiatrist, specializes in the treatment of sports-related injuries. He has long been interested in the topic, and presented several papers on research methods in biomechanics before he received his doctor of podiatric medicine degree from the California College of Podiatric Medicine in San Francisco.

A longtime runner, Dr. Ellis was one of the initial panelists for the annual *Runner's World* shoe survey and currently is on that magazine's science advisory board. He has written hundreds of articles on running injuries, in addition to lecturing internationally and serving as a consultant to the Asics/Tiger shoe company.

Dr. Ellis is the medical director for his sports-medicine clinic in La Jolla, California. He lives in nearby Cardiff-by-the-Sea with his wife, Deborah, and their children, Tiffany and Nicholas.

JOE HENDERSON has run and written about the sport since he was a teenager in the 1950s. He has run more than 700 races since then and has published at least an equal number of articles and more than a dozen books. Most recently, he wrote *Think Fast: Mental Toughness Training for Runners* (Plume, 1991) and co-authored *Bill Rodgers and Priscilla Welch on Masters Running and Racing* (Rodale Press, 1991).

Henderson was the first editor of *Runner's World* and his column has appeared in the magazine since 1968. He lives in Eugene, Oregon, with his wife, Barbara Shaw, who is also a writer.

INDEX

Underscored page references indicate boxed text.
Boldface page references indicate illustrations.

Biomechanics, 35–42
  irregularities in, 42–44
  running surface and,
    236
Blisters, **108**, <u>109</u>, 112–15
  frequency of, <u>3</u>
  shoe fit and, 56
Blown rubber, in shoes, <u>49</u>,
    52–53
Board-lasted shoe, <u>49</u>, 57,
  58, 66
Body-fat percentage, injuries
  and, 4–5
Bone(s)
  bruise, 119–22
    metatarsal pad for, 88
  covering, <u>171</u>, 172–73
  femur, **180**
    tumor on, 211–12
  fibula, 33, **170**, **180**, <u>190</u>,
    191
  foot, 33–34, **33**, **149**
  tibia, 33, 34, **170**, **180**,
    191
Bone spur, 36, 137
  under heel, 70, <u>139</u>,
    140
  tarsal tunnel syndrome
    and, 136, <u>136</u>
Bowleggedness, 9
Boyer, Charles, 107, 110
Braces, 85–87, **87**
  chondromalacia patella
    and, 186
Bronson, Jeff, <u>40</u>, 91, 129–32,
  133
Brown, Julie, 229

Bruise. *See* Bone(s), bruise
Bursae, **202**, 205
Bursitis, 205
Buttocks
  pain, 221–22 (*see also*
    Sciatica)
  stretch, **243**

C

Calcaneus, **33**, 34, **149**
Calf muscle(s), <u>149</u>
  flexibility, 9–10
    test for, 10, **10**
  gastrocnemius, 9, <u>149</u>
  injuries, frequency of,
    <u>3</u>
  soleus, 9, <u>149</u>
  stretches, **246–47**
Calf tendon, rupture of, <u>24</u>
Calluses, **108**, <u>109</u>
  shoe fit and, 56
Cantilever, in shoes, <u>49</u>
Carbon rubber, in shoes, <u>49</u>,
    52–53
Cardiovascular endurance,
  rest and, 76, 225
Cartilage, <u>180</u>, **180**, <u>198</u>. *See
  also* Chondromalacia
  patella; Meniscus injuries
Casting, 104–5
Chiropractor, 94–95
Chondromalacia patella,
  179–88, <u>180</u>, **180**, <u>187</u>
Combination-lasted shoe, <u>49</u>,
  57, **58**

K

Knee, **202**
 cartilage, <u>180</u>, **180**, <u>198</u> (*see also* Chondromalacia patella; Meniscus injuries)
 function of, 197
 injuries
  frequency of, <u>3</u>
  high-arched feet and, 45–46
  iliotibial band flexibility and, 11–12, **11**
  neoprene sleeves for, **86**
  overpronation and, 43
  Q-angle and, 9
  treatment for, 76
 pain
  corrective shoes for, 67
  ignoring, consequences of, 202–3
 problems
  chondromalacia patella, 179–88, <u>180</u>, **180**, <u>187</u>
  iliotibial band syndrome, 189–96, <u>190–91</u>, <u>195</u>
  meniscus injuries, 197–204, <u>198–99</u>, <u>203</u>
  plica injuries, 197–204, <u>198–99</u>, <u>203</u>
  strain, overpronation and, 44
  tarsal tunnel syndrome and, 135

runner's (*see* Chondromalacia patella)
 surgery, cross-training after, 227
 trick (*see* Meniscus injuries)
Kneecap, **180**, **199**. *See also* Knee
Kostrubala, Thaddeus, 76

L

Lacing shoes, 111, **111**
 overpronation and, 66
Last (shape of shoe), <u>50–51</u>, 57, 59, **58**, **59**
 anatomical, <u>49</u>
Last (shoe construction technique), 57–61
 board, <u>49</u>, 57–58, **58**, 66
 combination, <u>49</u>, 57–58, **58**
 slip, <u>51</u>, 57–58, **58**
Lateral, in shoes, <u>51</u>
Lateral compartment of leg, **170**
Lateral foot, **27**
Lateral hip stretch, **244**
Lateral meniscus, <u>199</u>
Leather uppers, 56–57
Leg. *See also specific parts of leg*
 anatomy, **170**
 bones
  femur, **180**, 211–12
  fibula, 33, **170**, **180**, <u>190</u>, **191**

tests for, 135–37
tibial nerve irritation,
171
plantar, **127**
protective reaction of,
134–37
tibial, 35, **130**, 171
Nike running shoes, 55
Nutrition, 123, 231–32
Nylon uppers, 57

O

Ober test for iliotibial band
flexibility, 11–12, **11**, 192
Orthopedic surgeon, 93
Orthotics, 61, 87–88, 101–4,
103, **104**
plantar fasciitis and,
142–43, 146–47
tarsal tunnel syndrome
and, 134
Os trigonum, 137. *See also*
Bone spur
Outersole/outsole, 51, 52–53,
52
overpronation and, 64, 66
worn, 53, 60, **60**
Overpronation, 7–8, 43
body-fat percentage and,
5
bowleggedness and, 9
chondromalacia patella
and, 183
flat feet and, 45
gender differences and, 4

iliotibial band and, 11,
189–93, 190
leg-length discrepancy
and, 209
plantar fasciitis and, 44
Q-angle and, 9
sciatica and, 222
shoes and, **7**, 55–56,
64–66, 68–69
stress fractures and, 43
tendinitis and, 44
Oversupination, 38–39
Overuse injury, 22, 226
Overuse problems, 2, 12
Overweight runners, injuries
and, 5

P

Pacing races, 250–51
Pain. *See also specific injuries*
attending to, 22–24
before and after running,
25–26
blocks, 20–22
checklist for, 28–29
defined, 28
ignoring, consequences of,
202–3
meaning of, 20–31, 29
psychological, 229
running with, 27–31
sharp, 23–24
Pain-relief products, 80–88,
99–101, 183
Patella, **180**, **199**. *See also* Knee

plica injuries, <u>203</u>
sciatica, <u>221</u>
shin pain, <u>176</u>
skin damage, <u>116</u>
tarsal tunnel syndrome,
    <u>136</u>
toenail damage, <u>116</u>
Progressive Sports Therapy,
    165–66
Pronation, 7–8, 38, 39–42,
    39. *See also* Overpronation;
    Underpronation
    foot bones and, 34
Proprioception, wraps and,
    84–85
Propulsion, 37, **37,** 42
Psychological effects of in-
    jury, <u>229</u>
PT, 93–94
PU, for shoes, <u>51</u>, 54–55

Q

Q-angle, 8–9, **8**
    chondromalacia patella
    and, 183
Quadriceps, **27**, 30, **210**
    injuries, frequency of, <u>3</u>
    soreness in, 30
    stretches, **241**
Quarter squats exercise,
    185
Quiz
    injury predictor, 4–14,
    <u>15–19</u>
    pain, <u>28–29</u>

R

Racing
    injuries and, 14
    pacing of, 250–51
Recovery periods, 27–28,
    249–50
    injuries and, 13
Re-injuries, 13, 224
Rest
    cardiovascular endurance
    and, 76, 225
    as injury treatment, 75–76
Resupination, 42
Reverse sit-up exercise, **220**
RICE (Rest, Ice, Compression,
    Elevation), 74–79, **74**
Roads, as running surface,
    235–36
Rubber, in shoes, <u>49</u>, 52–53
Rubs, 82–83
Runner's knee. *See* Chondro-
    malacia patella
Running
    as addiction, <u>228–29</u>
    gait, 37–42, **37**
        changes in, <u>40–41</u>
    injury-free, plan for, 234–52
    log for, 24, 27, 98, 251–52
    with pain, 27–31
    returning to, after injury,
    232–33
    stance, overweight and, 5
    style, changes in, <u>40–41</u>
    surfaces for, 31, 235–37
    in water, 228–30
Running shoes. *See* Shoe(s)

S

V

Viscoelastic innersole/insole, 169, 196

W

Walking, 223, 225–26
Warming rubs, 82–83
Warming up, 237–38
Washing shoes, 65
Water, running in, 228–30
Weight-related injuries, 4–5
Weil, Lowell, 38
Wet test for arches, 6–7, **6**

Women
  body-fat percentage, 5
  injuries common to, 4, 206,
    207
  Q-angle, 8, **8**
Workout logs, 24, 27, 98,
  251–52
Workout machines, 94,
  230–31
Wraps, 84–85, **85**

Z

Z-plasty, 156